The Monogamy Gap

Series in Sexuality, Identity, and Society

Series Editors
Phillip L. Hammack and Bertram J. Cohler

The purpose of this series is to foster creative scholarship on sexuality, identity, and society that integrates an appreciation for the historical grounding of sexuality research, seeks to transcend or integrate the boundaries constructed by disciplinary approaches, and takes theoretical and methodological risks to move the field forward. As such, the books presented here identify with a new kind of inquiry in sexuality research—one that moves us beyond questions of "origins" and "categories" toward the *meaning* of desire, experience, and identity in particular contexts. They are designed to be useful in both teaching and research.

BOOKS IN THE SERIES

The Monogamy Gap

Men, Love, and the Reality of Cheating

ERIC ANDERSON

OXFORD
UNIVERSITY PRESS

OXFORD
UNIVERSITY PRESS

Oxford University Press, Inc., publishes works that further
Oxford University's objective of excellence
in research, scholarship, and education.

Oxford New York
Auckland   Cape Town   Dar es Salaam   Hong Kong   Karachi
Kuala Lumpur   Madrid   Melbourne   Mexico City   Nairobi
New Delhi   Shanghai   Taipei   Toronto

With offices in
Argentina   Austria   Brazil   Chile   Czech Republic   France   Greece
Guatemala   Hungary   Italy   Japan   Poland   Portugal   Singapore
South Korea   Switzerland   Thailand   Turkey   Ukraine   Vietnam

Published by Oxford University Press, Inc.
198 Madison Avenue, New York, New York 10016

www.oup.com

Library of Congress Cataloging-in-Publication Data

Anderson, Eric, 1968-
  The monogamy gap: men, love, and the reality of cheating/Eric Anderson.
   p. cm.—(Sexuality, identity, and society)
  Includes bibliographical references and index.
  ISBN 978-0-19-977792-1 (hbk.)
1. Men—Sexual behavior. 2. Monogamous relationships. 3. Sex. 4. Love. I. Title.
HQ28.A53 2012
306.84'22081—dc22   2011005352

9 8 7 6 5 4 3 2
Printed in the United States of America on acid-free paper

Dedicated to my friend, Dr. Mark McCormack.

CONTENTS

It is with great enthusiasm that we introduce the first solo authored volume in the Oxford Series on Sexuality, Identity, and Society with *The Monogamy Gap: Men, Love, and the Reality of Cheating* by Eric Anderson. The idea for the book series emerged between 2007 and 2009 as we collaborated on an edited volume for Oxford called *The Story of Sexual Identity: Narrative Perspectives on the Gay and Lesbian Life Course*. In that volume, now considered the first in the series, we sought to create a dynamic colloquy among scholars working from diverse disciplinary perspectives, united in their commitment to a narrative approach to the study of sexual identity. It had become clear to us that formal opportunities for such colloquies were few and far between, scattered across a number of professional meetings and a wide array of scholarly journals. In our view, there was a need for mechanisms to promote scholarship that would dare to ask timely and perhaps controversial questions, transcend disciplinary borders, and advance *ideas* about human sexuality in the twenty-first century. We recognized the need for scholars in sexuality studies to have a supportive home for this kind of intellectual work, and the warm reception we received at Oxford for *The Story of Sexual Identity* suggested we had found the right place for just such a home. The stewardship of Lori Handelman and Abby Gross allowed our vision for the series to come to fruition. For their commitment to the support of this kind of scholarship, we are most grateful.

We are delighted to initiate the authored volumes of the series with Eric Anderson's bold new look at the institution of monogamy in *The Monogamy Gap*. We were in fact first introduced to his work through his exceptional memoir, *Trailblazing*, published in 2000 by Alyson Books. Having established himself as a formidable scholar of masculinity studies with volumes such as *In the Game: Gay Athletes and the Cult of Masculinity* (2005, State University of New York Press) and *Inclusive Masculinity: The Changing Nature of Masculinities* (2009, Routledge), Anderson brings his highly accessible and theoretically nuanced style to the study of monogamy. There is much to appreciate about Anderson's much-needed treatment of this subject. We will highlight three features of the work that we find particularly resonant with our intention for the series.

First, *The Monogamy Gap* embodies our vision of transdiscplinarity in sexuality studies. Anderson takes a *problem-centered*, rather than *discipline-centered*, approach to the study of monogamy. Thus he considers perspectives from sociology, psychology, biology, and gender studies as he constructs a coherent account of why men "cheat." This approach allows him to theorize and to interpret his data with sensitivity to both large scale sociocultural and political factors, such as the social and economic setting in which monogamy developed as a cultural "ideal," and to individual experiences. His integration of hegemony theory (from sociology and gender studies) and cognitive dissonance theory (from social psychology) in his analysis of data reveals the interpretive rigor that can emerge between the cracks of paradigms historically kept apart in a world of disciplinary silos and over-specialization. In other words, Anderson's approach embodies our intent for volumes in the series to challenge received paradigms within the disciplines by taking an *integrative* approach to the study of lives in context. In our view, mind and society are mutually constituted and hence are most fruitfully studied in tandem. Anderson's work achieves this transdisciplinary, integrative spirit.

If our first hope for the volumes in this series is that they take an integrative approach to the study of sexuality, our second is that this approach will result in a challenge to our received paradigms, taxonomies, or basic assumptions about sexuality and identity. *The Monogamy Gap* achieves this aim masterfully. Anderson challenges the received taxonomy of human relationality in this volume, arguing that our preconceived notions of meaningful and committed relationships are steeped more in our blind acceptance of hegemonic institutions than an authentic assessment of how individuals negotiate love, sex, and relationships. In other words, the monogamy ideal is more connected to the historic attempt to regulate and control desire than it is to some empirically known form of "success" in human relationality. The data upon which Anderson draws his claims reveals that a rejection of monogamy need not go hand in hand with a diminished capacity for love and commitment between two (or more) individuals. Rather, the practice of non-monogamy can and does lead to meaningful, fulfilling relationships. This argument is certainly familiar, having been voiced at some volume since the historic revolutions in gender and sexuality that commenced in the mid-twentieth century, but rarely has it been accompanied by the rigorous theoretical work and data analysis provided in this book. In our view, this critical stance toward received concepts is absolutely vital to the stimulation of new forms of knowledge. We expect that Anderson's work, like those of other authors we seek to promote in the series, will open up new spaces in both scholarly and popular discourse precisely because of its unwillingness to see monogamy as a form of human relationality grounded in "nature." Rather, Anderson conceives of monogamy as a social institution which has, in many ways, interfered with fulfilling and meaningful relationships by promulgating false and misleading sets of expectations among partners.

A third basic element we had hoped to promote in the works that appear in this series is a focus on science as a form of *understanding* rather than a tool for *prediction and control*. In our view, this approach challenges the historic relationship between science and sexuality. It is well known that throughout much of the history of the study of human sexuality, scientists produced knowledge that largely supported the status quo of sexism and heterosexism. Our inspiration here appropriately comes from a pioneer in challenging this relationship. The psychologist Evelyn Hooker once claimed that she was not bothered by the fact that psychologists, despite decades of attempts, could not successfully develop the ability to "detect" homosexuality from established tests. She argued that the "first goal of science is understanding" (Hooker, 1959, p. 281).

In our view, a sexual science that produces knowledge intended to promote understanding of the lived experience of gender and sexuality serves two vital functions for individuals and societies. First, it provides a voice for individual subjectivity, which we understand in Foucault's (1982) twin sense of the term: "subject to someone else by control and dependence; and tied to his own identity by a conscience or self-knowledge" (p. 781). Accessing the voice of sexual *subjects*, we come to understand the way in which individuals interpret and engage with master narratives of gender, sexual identity, or forms of relationality. The second function of producing such knowledge, then, centers on the exposure of master narratives as often constraining possibilities for new ways of being and relating. In other words, a sexual science which might serve *transformative* and *liberating* ends must be concerned with the meaning individuals make of their received world of concepts, categories, and narratives.

The Monogamy Gap fulfills all three of these original goals we had envisioned for works in the series. It produces knowledge that is grounded in a transdisciplinary theoretical framework, carefully and closely adheres to the lived experience of relationships captured by rigorous qualitative methods, and is concerned foremost with the understanding of human relationality in the early twenty-first century. Anderson successfully documents individual processes of meaning-making as he simultaneously challenges received taxonomies of relationality. He pushes both disciplinary and cultural boundaries in his analysis and deals with cultural and institutional critique in a sophisticated and empirically honest manner. The end result is, also as we had envisioned for works in the series, the articulation of a new theoretical lens through which to view relationality, what Anderson calls *dyadic dissonance theory*.

The Monogamy Gap, like other forthcoming books in the series, presents an engaging, accessible, and sophisticated account of the institution of monogamy and the way in which men negotiate their own desires and actions within a cultural narrative of monogamy as ideal. We trust that readers, academic and non-academic alike, will appreciate the audacity and honesty with which new ideas and insights into human relationality are provoked through this work, and we are confident of its place in the canon of a new era in sexuality studies.

Phillip L. Hammack
Santa Cruz, California

Bertram J. Cohler
Chicago, Illinois
May 2011

REFERENCES

Foucault, M. (1982). The subject and power. *Critical Inquiry, 8,* 777–795.
Hooker, E. (1959). What is a criterion? *Journal of Projective Techniques, 23,* 278–281.

PART ONE

Introduction

Overview of the Research

The purpose of this book is to examine critically the pervasive, hegemonic understandings of sexual relationships that condemn cheating while holding monogamy as a moral ideal. I use 120 interviews of university men in order to examine why this demographic of men (straight and gay) cheat, and to examine critically the unreasonable expectations of monogamy that influence these behaviors.

My focus on men is a result of my expertise as a scholar of masculinities (Anderson, 2002, 2005a, 2008b, 2009; Anderson, Adams, & Rivers, 2010; Anderson & McGuire, 2010), and it does not represent the assumption that women are faithful; women also cheat (Banfield & McCabe, 2001; Treas & Giesen, 2000). The narratives of women (both who cheat and whose partners cheat) are interesting and important, but they are not included here. Some of what I say in this research might be illuminative as to the reasons why women of this age demographic also cheat, but I have yet to do specific research on that topic.

I am interested in the multiple factors in the relational and cultural context that influence how young men view monogamy, open sexual relationships, and cheating; why they cheat; and how they rectify their cheating in relation with their esteem for monogamy. I analyze the results of my research through several complementary theoretical lenses that combine to inform my theory *dyadic dissonance theory.*

I first apply Gramsci's (1971) hegemony theory to monogamy, calling the belief that monogamy rightly maintains its privileged social position, *monogamism.* I show that, as part of the operation of hegemony, a cultural reverence for monogamy prevents critical scrutiny concerning the *costs* inherent in monogamy (Drigotas & Barta, 2001). I suggest that there exists a cultural unwillingness to examine adequately the price that monogamism has on the sexual and emotional health of (ostensibly) monogamous couples. This is how hegemony operates: It prevents us from criticizing the dominant idea, and this, in turn, silences all criticism. Thus we readily critique those in open relationships; we readily chastize those who cheat; but we fail to critique those in monogamous relationships, and we do not see this as problematic—that is the power of hegemony.

Following a brief romance phase (in which emotional and somatic desires align) I show that coupled men find themselves increasingly desiring sex with others, despite monogamy's hegemonic cultural dominance. This places them into a state of contradiction—they essentially want something they do not want—and this brings me to the second theory I utilize. I examine this state of wanting and not wanting extradyadic sex (sex outside the relationship) through cognitive dissonance theory (Aronson, 1969; Bem, 1967; Festinger, 1957). Cognitive dissonance theory illuminates the cognitive processes one goes through when one desires two things that are mutually exclusive. I argue that monogamy places men into cognitive dissonance because emotionally they want to be monogamous, but their body craves sex with other people somatically (body urges).

After the romance phase wears off, men initially rectify the tension of wanting monogamy and sex with others by using pornography while masturbating, "spicing up" their sex lives, or having a break from their partners during which time they have sex with someone else. However, in time, these techniques lose their effectiveness. As a relationship progresses, men's desires for sex with others simultaneously grows. In other words, despite the love, history, and intimacy that men share with their partners after 6 months, or sometimes 2 years, of being together, they begin to strongly desire sex with someone else. These men do not desire to break up with their partner, with whom they are developing an increasingly important emotional bond, yet their sexual frustration grows. The cognitive dissonance occurs as they try to reconcile their sexual urges with the social mandates of monogamy.

I show men in this study describe the loss of their sexual freedom with sorrow. To them, it feels like a form of socially compelled sexual incarceration. I also show that these men fear telling their partners about their desire for sex with others (particularly the straight men I interview) because hegemonic perspectives on monogamy prevent them from doing so. The dominant perspective on lost sexual attraction or desire is equated with failed or lost love, even when accompanied by a strong emotional bond. Accordingly, the societal belief is that failure to maintain sexual desire for one's partner is an insult to the lover and an indictment of the relationship. As a result of this, men experience fear at the prospect of telling their partners they desire sex with someone else. These men fear that their partners will break up with them if they are honest. Thus, honesty about decreasing sexual desires for one's partner and increasing sexual desires for sex with others is viewed as a risky strategy for dealing with the sexual desires that occur with the long-term sexual monotony of monogamy. But silence is dangerous, too. Oftentimes when sex dies in a relationship, those within it are falsely led to believe that the love has also died. In monogamy, it seems that love is erroneously measured in sex.

The result of this dissonance (combined with the hegemonic stranglehold of monogamy) is that men end up cheating. I find two types of cheating, which I call *spontaneous* and *premeditated* cheating. In spontaneous cheating, men subtly manipulate situations to increase the likelihood that a one-off opportunity for cheating will occur. They do not necessarily tell themselves that they are going to cheat, but they place themselves in situations where the circumstances make it more likely. This is exciting, as it flirts with danger, but it is not necessarily premeditated.

In the spontaneous scenario, men often cheat under the influence of alcohol. This is partially because it lowers their inhibition but also because alcohol provides an extra layer of protection in the event that they are caught. Stressing the lack of planning, alcohol permits men to say, "It just happened." I suggest that while spontaneous cheating is somewhat unplanned (no hotel rooms are booked, for example), it is nevertheless a well-reasoned strategy to meet one's physical desires, losing less esteem in one's partner's (and society's) eyes if caught.

However, spontaneous cheating is usually repeated. I show that the more men cheat, the more likely they are to continue cheating. This is because men increasingly rectify or justify with themselves why they are cheating. Feeling less guilt after each cheating episode, they plan their cheating more carefully. For these men, loving their partner and wanting to remain in a relationship with them leads them to conclude that cheating is a way of meeting both of their desires: Their desire for the pretense of monogamy (and all of the social graces that provides) and their desire for extradyadic sex.

With premeditated cheating, men effectively make a cost–benefit analysis. It is based in a clear-headed decision to have sex (which I define as any form of sexual contact) with another. Cheating becomes a sensible choice out of the cognitive dissonance they feel, and men take strategic steps to prevent themselves from being caught.

Thus whether it be through spontaneous or premeditated cheating, I suggest that cheating becomes a rational response to an irrational situation. Men choose to cheat to relieve their sexual urges for others, because they are given no other opportunity to relieve them. When they go uncaught, cheating works reasonably well as a source to provide exciting energetic sex (made more exciting because it is also taboo). Thus, in this book, I argue that cheating occurs not through failed love, or even immorality, but instead I argue that cheating (not affairs) represent a rational response to their own cognitive dissonance.

It is my argument that cheating, whether it be spontaneous or premeditated, serves men fairly well. Cheating is less risky to the stability of relationships than honesty, and it permits the desired sex without the loss of their partner's emotional intimacy. Even if cheating is discovered, it is often reasoned as less offensive than admitting that one wanted extradyadic sex in the first place. Men can blame the alcohol, beg for forgiveness, and resume their relationship under the pretense that they truly want monogamy (which they partially do). Thus, cheating not only acts as a source of acquiring extradyadic sex, but it prevents men from having to confront the institution of monogamy. As one of my heterosexual British participants said, "At least with cheating there is the attempt at monogamy."

Another way of examining this statement is to suggest that cheating is not against monogamy. Instead, it is *part* of monogamy. Monogamy, for these 120 men, is more about an attitude than a mandate. The attitude is that we *should try* not to cheat, but, given that indiscretions occur, partners oftentimes employ a system of forgiveness for cheating. They do not condone cheating, but incorporate it into monogamy, nonetheless.

In this research, I also show that cheating is the norm among undergraduate (university-attending) men. Despite the fact that these men wish they did not cheat, multiple forms of covert nonmonogamies nonetheless exist. Of the men who had a long-term partner (not all of the men I interviewed had ever had a partner) around 78% have cheated in some capacity. In deriving this statistic, I only include men who have cheated on their current or most recent partner. In otherwords, this statistic does not reflect men who 'have ever' cheated; it reflects the percentage of men who have cheated on their current partner.

I define "cheating" as performing any sexual activity that would lead one's partner to feel that he had violated the implicit or explicit rules of their monogamous relationship. In other words, I don't use the participants' definitions of cheating (which they might tweak to avoid feeling guilty); I use their partners' notions of cheating. Thus, the 78% rate of cheating I show in this research is elevated over similar research of university-aged men, which sometimes only accounts for intercourse. Furthermore, half of my sample is comprised of men who play a team sport, a demographic who are likely to have elevated rates of cheating.

My research is also provocative for other reasons. First, I show that university men normally cheat because they want or "need" recreational sex, not because they seek an emotional affair. This means that cheating exists as an ironic symbol that these men *actually* love their partners. If they did not love their partners, they would leave their partners. They desire to remain with their partners, they just want sex with someone else for recreational purposes.

I argue that the dominant social belief that intimacy is proved through monogamy is too simple an understanding of the reality of men, love, and human sexuality and that it is unreasonable to equate sexual fidelity with love. Again, if the men in my study did not love their partners, they are socially and legally free to leave their partners. Cheating, therefore, is not a reflection of a lack of love.

This research also adds to our understanding of relationships and cheating by showing the *process* that men go through in order to cheat. In doing so, this book disputes dominant messages about cheating men "not loving their partners." It contests the myth that many therapists harmfully reproduce—that cheating is rarely ever about sex (Pittman, 1989). While affairs (which include dating and romance) are about something other than sex, this research shows that cheating for sex really is just about the sex. This book therefore also carries advice with it. Advice that many will find offensive: Breaking up with a partner simply because he cheated is a socially pressured decision that does not likely serve one's best interests. Relationships take a long time to build; destroying them over sex is perhaps short sighted.

But this is not to suggest that cheating is entirely harmless. It is not. In this book I also show that cheating causes a great deal of relationship trouble. I articulate the anxiety and fear that men feel about the possibility of one's partner finding out about their cheating, showing how this leads to a variety of psychological and relationship difficulties. But I do not take this as a sign that cheating is therefore problematic and that the purveyors of monogamy are correct. Matters, again, are not that simple. Cheating *does* create relationship difficulties, but this only occurs because of the strictness of monogamy. Monogamy places men into a position of wanting, often desperately wanting, some form of sexual interaction with another that their partners do not permit. This then firmly places the blame for much cheating on monogamy itself.

Some view the answer to this as simple: that men should 'suck it up,' that men should not cheat, regardless of how bad their bodies desire extradyadic sex. But this position underestimates the relationship between our sexual desires and emotional health. This is akin to asking a gay man to remain in the closet: The emotional consequences are devastating. In the case of monogamy, I show that frustration toward one's partner grows, because men (even if subconsciously) view their partners as stopping them from having the sex they desire. This leads to disharmony, and aggressions manifest in other, harmful ways toward one's partner.

This research also has implications that stretch beyond the undergraduate gay and straight men that I interviewed. Even though there may well be other reasons why other demographics of men cheat—such as a way for older men to reclaim their youth, or enact power over women or younger gay men—I nonetheless suspect that these reasons only add to dyadic dissonance theory and do not replace it. Cheating is found in high rates among men and women of all ages in multiple other studies, and I believe that cheating occurs in high frequency because monogamy simply does not work well enough for most men (and perhaps women, too). We have been sold a myth about monogamy; we have not been told the truth. Monogamy does not (and almost always cannot) provide a lifetime of rich sexual excitement for human beings.

This research therefore highlights multiple problems that monogamy brings to a couple, regardless of their sexuality. It suggests that the model of monogamy most couples aspire to is built on a faulty premise—one that disregards our biological desires for multiple sex partners. In essence, monogamy is a Catch-22 for men and women living in a monogacentric culture—a culture that only values monogamy.

I therefore suggest that our cultural penchant of using monogamy as the litmus test of a relationship places an unreasonable ultimatum on a relatively unimportant variable, and this leads to unnecessary relationship termination. We know that cheating remains the primary reason couples break up (Amato, 2003; Amato & Rogers, 1997), and adult couples with children are more likely to cheat (Burdette, Ellison, Sherkat, & Gore, 2007) than those without. We also know that parental divorce is associated with lower quality marriages for the children of divorced parents (Amato, 1996). Thus, if one is truly concerned with protecting marriage, with protecting kids from the consequences of divorce, and promoting marital bliss, it is monogamy that needs to be critically examined—not cheating.

In this book I critique monogamy, but I am not suggesting we should stigmatize monogamy the way that open sexual relationships and polyamory are currently stigmatized. Instead, I suggest that we need multiple forms of culturally acceptable sexual relationship types—including sexually open relationships—that coexist without hierarchy or hegemony. We need the flexibility of moving in and out of relationship types as best suits the needs of the couple at the time. I suggest that the first stage in developing such a culture comes through recognition that one's love for one's partner is not dependent upon sexual exclusivity. Although this is not a book about polyamory, I suggest that we need to begin to rethink and consider the value of these relationship types as well; however, I am under no illusion that this will happen at a wider cultural level anytime soon.

This is because, even though the men in this study have troubled experiences of monogamy, they also view open sexual relationships with disdain. And even when men are able to see themselves out of the trappings of monogamy, ownership issues prevent them from considering permitting their partners to also engage in extradyadic sex. In other words, a large majority of the young men in my study view open sexual relationships as potentially good for themselves, but problematic as a couple because they would grant their partner the same sexual freedom. Most men in this study wanted extra-dyadic sex for themselves, but they did not want their partner to have the same privilege.

Thus, monogamy remains a mutually reinforced system of sexual ownership because it is an institution predicated in jealousy. Accordingly, rather than contesting monogamy for its faults; rather than recognizing that other forms of relationships might better navigate the dissonance that comes with long-term relationship coupling, men continue to reproduce our cultural value of monogamy, rectifying their dissonance through cheating.

2

Developing a Critique of Monogamy

The premise of this book is that much of men's cheating is rational. Cheating emerges as a rational response to the irrational social expectations of monogamy. To explain theoretically how it is that we live in a culture in which people of all sexual orientations desire sexual fidelity and loath cheating, but nonetheless end up doing both, I develop *dyadic dissonance theory.*

This is a multidisciplinary model. In explaining this model I draw from empirical research in sociology, psychology, evolutionary psychology, biology, and neuroscience. However, to explicate my theory, I use qualitative sociological research on 120 straight and gay male undergraduate men from several universities in both the United States and the United Kingdom. With this book, I provide a comprehensive, yet easy-to-read, treatment of the academic literature from these numerous academic disciplines.

This book develops a critical, honest, scholarly argument that interrogates the cultural and personal belief that sex with only one other person promotes our social, emotional, and moral health. This is not necessarily a manifesto against monogamy as practiced in the early stages of a relationship; but it is an indictment of our culture's insistence that monogamy is the *only* proper way to be in a relationship. It is also a warning: A warning that monogamy may not provide the healthiest disposition in the later stages of a relationship. Ultimately, the data suggests that monogamy causes a great deal of damage in many relationships, and that we need other culturally viable and esteemed relationship models—models that permit us to have recreational sex outside our relationships, while retaining the emotional intimacy that we have built up over years with our partners.

I hope that readers will emerge from this book with a better understanding of the way monogamy structures harm into our relationships, and why open relationships, or even polyamorous relationships, might provide answers for some. Even if you view monogamy as the ideal relationship type, I hope that after reading this book you will recognize and respect other relationship models, as well as those who practice them.

CHALLENGING SOCIAL CONVENTIONS

I have never truly understood the reverence for monogamy. Long before I became a sociologist of gender and sexuality, it was clear to me that if one had to preach continuously about the joys and benefits of something, the reality was likely far different. It seemed to me that if monogamy were so wonderful, nobody would want to cheat. If sex with one person were so amazing, nobody *would* cheat. But because most people do cheat, and because some people cheat *a lot*, I somehow knew that the benefits of monogamy were perhaps not as authentic as the proselytizers of monogamy proclaimed.

I remember a conversation from my teenage years that helped crystallize this belief. I was a high school distance runner. My teammates and I covered a plethora of conversations on our runs down the beach in sunny Southern California. I don't remember exactly where the conversation occurred on this particular run, but I suppose we were running past the Huntington Beach pier when my best friend, Ken, asked, "When you are married, how many times a week will you have sex with your wife?" The one-upmanship of my heterosexual male teenage friends quickly began. "Three," one answered. "Four," said the next. Soon we were at five, even six, times a day. As an adolescent who questioned dogma and fundamentalism in many forms, I asked my friends on that run, "Wouldn't you get tired of sex with just one person?" My other teammate, Mike, answered, "Only if you were a fag." *Foolish me.* Of course, this was a foundation of heterosexuality at the time: If one was not up for sex, all the time, with almost any reasonable female, he was undoubtedly, unquestionably gay (Anderson, 2008a).

One of my more nerdy teammates, Matt, began to calculate just how many times one would have sex (with his wife, of course) if he were married for 50 years. Perhaps it was slightly ambitious, but Matt calculated that one would have intercourse three times a day (ah, the imagination of 16-year-olds who weren't getting any). But even with the astonishing figure he approximated, nowhere in this conversation was the recognition that, just maybe, well into one's old age, one might actually grow bored of sex with the *same* person.

I understood where my friends were coming from. We were 16 and we could hardly imagine turning 20, let alone 60. I also understood that the underlying image my teenage friends ruminated on was that of a girl steeped in teenage sexual capital. They eschewed the idea of having sex with out of shape, old women. In their minds, their future wife would remain forever young, slim, and beautiful.

Still I wondered, even if one's partner remained young and beautiful in perpetuity, wouldn't you nonetheless get bored of sex with that same person? I therefore asked my teammates, something along the lines of, "You would have sex with her three times a day, even when she's 70? Are you saying that you would rather have sex with your wrinkled, saggy wife of 70 than a goddess of 16?" The question brought to my heterosexual teammates an inescapable, indelible image of having sex with a grandmother—an image that contradicted their idealized notions of sex. It also brought a moment of sobriety to the conversation. "Of course you will," one answered. "You will grow to not want young girls anymore." Others laughed at the absurdity of not thinking 16-year-old girls attractive. "You're going to tell me I won't find *that* hot anymore?" Ken said, pointing to the girls tanning in the sun.

It was here, that Rob, the team moralist, stepped in. "You wouldn't want sex with anyone else. Not if you loved your partner. You would only want sex with your wife." He added something to the effect of, "Well, if you love your wife, you will think she's the most beautiful person in the world and you would never want sex with anyone else." The boys grew silent. Some virtue of *morality* had entered the conversation, and none dared contest it—at least not then, in the mid-1980s. The conversation changed.

Today, I suspect that at one level my teammates knew that they would someday want sex with other women, but it is also likely that they believed the common mantra that—if they truly loved their future spouses—they would not want it. *This just doesn't make sense*, I thought. *Am I the only one who sees the absurdity of this?*

Perhaps this, then, is why I found the humor of Al Bundy, from the American television show, *Married with Children*, so funny. The show (1987–1998) featured a married man who no longer desired sex with his wife. Monogamy to Al was something unwillingly thrust upon him. Although his wife was attractive, it was not her whom he wanted sex with; it was sex with multiple *other* women.

Like much good comedy, I assumed the show must be popular because it some- how ruminated in a type of truth that we did not want to seriously discuss. The actual idea, that one might not want sex with his wife, could only be expressed through Al as a comedic figure—the court jester of monogamy—because, on every other count, he was *such a loser*. Thus, we could judge Al for being a loser in not wanting sex with his wife, too. This took the sting out of the actual critique of the sexual habituation that occurs with long term monogamy.

By the time I was 18, I began challenging social conventions of all sorts. I was hardly a radical, but I at least began to unweave society's dominant messages about sex, politics, and Christianity. For example, I recall watching a smutty television show, where an 18-year-old woman was dating a 70-year-old man. The studio audience jeered, calling their love sick and perverse. I, on the other hand, had no issues with it. If he's happy, and she's happy, *so what*, I thought.

I believe one reason I rejected dominant understandings of sexuality in society was that I am gay, and I was closeted throughout my adolescence. While being closeted throughout the incredibly homophobic decade of the 1980s (Loftus, 2001) was daunting, I now attribute my sociological imagination—my critical sociological sense of analysis—to being closeted (Anderson, 2000). This is because, in the mid-1980s Orange County, California, there was nothing worse than to be a "fag." Still, I always knew that there was actually nothing wrong with me. I knew that my teammates had not come to their homophobic disposition out of a sense of immutable facts about gay men. Instead, they were homophobic because the institutions they belonged to, indeed their wider American culture, had failed them. Education, school, politics, and Christianity, all preached homophobia on an illogical, nonsensical, and historically fictional basis.

My sociological imagination grew because I always knew that I was gay and that there was nothing wrong with me. Accordingly, being gay was a gift. It equipped me not to trust adults; not to take for granted perceived widsoms. From around 7 years of age I knew that just because society's institutions thought something was wrong—just because teachers, religious leaders, and politicians preached something—didn't make it so. I was gay, and I knew there was nothing wrong with that when all the world said there was. But for the reader less concerned with my sexuality, and more concerned with monogamy, what is important to understand is that from a very early age, I knew that institutions could fail us. Being gay helped me learn to be a critical thinker of social institutions, norms, and dominant paradigms; and my critical eye spilled over into other arenas as well. This included monogamy.

Today, I spend most of my academic career analyzing cherished institutions. For example, I have spent much of my academic career critiquing the way we run and value organized competitive team sports. See my book, *Sport, Theory and Social Problems: A Critical Introduction* (Anderson, 2010a). Whether it is on "homosexuality is bad," or "sport is good," I have just never seen "the masses" as necessarily being correct. Just because everybody thinks so, doesn't make something so.

LEARNING TO CRITIQUE MONOGAMY

There was no need for me to be monogamous when I was in high school, and even throughout my undergraduate years. This was because I didn't come out until I was 25. Being celibate made *not* cheating rather easy. From this perspective, sex with *just* one guy sounded wonderful (something sociologists call relative deprivation). I was extremely horny but unable to get sex. I was so desperate I would have condemned my beloved dog, Strider, to hell in order to have sex with a guy, just once. This is the result of desperation and deprivation, and in chapter 12 this will be an important point.

But after coming out at 25, I came into a group of gay men who were equally marginalized for their homosexuality. The experience was not as liberating as one might expect. Instead of these young gay men learning from their social oppression and applying this framework to other institutions (like monogamy), the community of young gay men I socialized with instead adopted society's dominant message concerning monogamy. This was the post-AIDS effect on gay youth. Rather than celebrating the ease with which we could have sex—rejoicing in consummating what society still loathed—my peer group was steeped in monogamist baggage, a legacy that influences gay youth today.

I started a gay youth night at a Long Beach coffee shop. Every Wednesday evening, sixty young gay guys would stand around in the warm air talking about what a slut someone was for having sex with someone else. While I was certainly much happier out of the closet than in, it nonetheless seemed to me that my peers had simply replaced one form of sexual oppression with another. We were no longer heterosexist, but we were monogamists.

There was however a time when the gay male community eschewed the institution of monogamy. In the 1970s, gay men had lots of casual sex before developing relationships; and after developing a relationship, open relationships were more common. But HIV/AIDS forced a rethinking of this, and gay youth who grew up in the era of AIDS learned to adopt the monogamous perspective. This was particularly important for staying off infection, but it overlooks that there are multiple sex acts which are HIV risk-free.

But AIDS reshaped more than just how we thought about monogamy. It made us a profoundly more sex-negative culture. Promiscuous sex, even when one was single, was stigmatized. This didn't stop my friends from actually having promiscuous sex. It just meant that they pretended to be interested in a relationship with someone, thereby making sex okay. The lesson to be learned from this was that everyone was having sex with everyone; everyone was cheating on their boyfriends; and nobody was brave enough to point out the obvious—the current system of valuing one thing and doing the other was highly hypocritical, and emotionally, socially, and culturally damaging.

I recall a conversation with a friend about this. I wasn't the anti-Christ of monogamy back then; I was just speaking from what seemed to be a sense of logic, a concept informed by my noticing that nobody in our small gay community was actually *practicing* monogamy. "Clearly, monogamy doesn't work," I said to him in the hue of late 1990s IKEA lighting. He snapped back (literally) with a diatribe about love, commitment, and fidelity being wrapped into one word: *monogamy*. My friend was not just intellectually energized to contest me, his standpoint was also *emotional*.

His emphatic points followed the mantra of almost all I encountered who espoused the virtues of monogamy. The argument has not changed much since. It is the persistence of this argument by both gay and straight men that led me into taking monogamy up as one of my favorite "talking points." Here, after hundreds of conversations, I began to understand the structure of the argument and assess its weaknesses and fallacies. This led me to formal academic research, and ultimately this book, where I finally flush out my complete *dyadic dissonance theory*.

DYADIC DISSONANCE THEORY

My *dyadic dissonance theory* explains why men want monogamy but also cheat. It does so without moralizing against, or maligning men as insensitive pigs.

Instead, it suggests that young men socially accept dominant myths about monogamy before they begin their sexual lives. In other words, just as a child learns their parents religion before developing their own critical faculties, young boys hear that monogamy is the only proper way to have a relationship, and they believe that sex with just one other person is capable of producing a lifetime of highly enjoyable sex. Perhaps by the time they are teenagers, they understand, at some level, that their sex lives with just one partner will eventually be dull, but they believe that by spicing up their sex, they will keep it energetic. This perspective is easy for young teenage boys to maintain when they are 'deprived' of any sex from this perspective, being in an open sexual relationship seems rather greedy.

Whereas the "dyadic" in dyadic dissonance theory refers to a couple, the "dissonance" refers to the cognitive dissonance that grows as a relationship matures. This dissonance is between what we want emotionally and what we want somatically (sexual desires). As sexual habituation with one partner begins (normally after around 3 months of sexual activity), the young men I interview find themselves spicing up their sex life. But this strategy only lasts so long. By 2 years of monogamy most men have experienced a sharp decrease not only in the frequency of sex, but in the enjoyment that they receive from their monogamous sex.

Men now experience two contrasting emotions. At an intellectual and "moral" level of reasoning, they continue to desire monogamy. They see themselves as being moral men and believe that cheating is immoral. But at the same time, they desperately desire sex with others. It is here that my theory suggests that monogamy serves as a structural expectation of oppression.

Men are trapped in this dissonance. If they entertain with their partners the possibility that sex and love are separate and that they could maintain the love with their partner while seeking thrilling sex with outsiders (an open sexual relationship), they risk losing their partners. Even mentioning this is thought to be an affront to love. Love, they falsely believe, is enhanced through sex, and sex with outsiders is falsely believed to detract from the love of a couple. We all too often falsely believe that if our partner ceases to desire us sexually, he or she also ceases to love us.

In desiring but not wanting to cheat, men set out to rectify their dissonance through pornography, visualizing themselves having sex with someone else while having sex with their partner, and/or flirting with others online. Eventually, however, these imagined/cyber forms of extradyadic sex are not enough. Men strongly desire to have sex with someone else, and they often begin to feel anger or aggression at their partner because (at one level) it is their partner that is preventing them from having the type of sex that every cell in their body demands.

It is here that men realize that cheating can help them satisfy their sexual desires while maintaining the love they share with their partner. If, on the other hand, men stick by the rule of monogamy, they are destined to a life of frustration at not being permitted to have what they so desperately desire. Men therefore position themselves into places and situations in which they cheat. Cheating permits men to best satisfy their desires. Cheating exists as a rational choice to an irrational situation.

This is the basis of my dyadic dissonance theory. This is the basic explanation of why men cheat. But my theory also covers the value of men's cheating. Although cheating remains almost universally taboo in modern societies, my research suggests that cheating might actually help save relationships. My theory is that cheating permits men to have the sex with others they somatically desire, while simultaneously accomplishing two other goals. First, cheating helps prohibit one's partner from doing the same, and this means that the male does not have to entertain notions of jealousy. Second, cheating (as opposed to being in an open sexual relationship) maintains social graces of being considered monogamous. They do not have to deal with social shame and stigma by admitting publicly that they are not monogamous. For many men, cheating might also function better than open relationships because with cheating they do not have to deal with the threat of losing their partners by mentioning their sexual desires for others. Thus, in one capacity (and for most of the men in my study), undiscovered cheating protects long-term monogamous relationships.

While this is where my dyadic dissonance theory ends, my research also explicates what happens after cheating. It is here that I show that cheating is not a perfect solution. Men who cheat oftentimes suffer from anxiety and guilt, and the more they cheat the more they also expose themselves to relationship termination should their cheating be discovered or divulged. Ultimately, I suggest that while cheating may temporarily relieve the sexual frustration concerning the monotony of monogamy, it is only in open relationships where long-term sexual and romantic satisfaction can be found for people who somatically desire sex with others.

MORALIST ARGUMENTS AGAINST OPEN RELATIONSHIPS

The idea of *not* following the mandates of monogamy can be upsetting to many people. It therefore brings forth skeptical counterarguments. Argument based in some loose sense of "morality." For example, many people might refute that monogamy is based in a "loose sense of morality," instead suggesting that it is biblically mandated, overlooking the great many Christian and Islamic cultures/nations that permit polygamy. Those who espouse pro-monogamy from either a theistically based morality or even without theism fail to provide a well-reasoned framework of understanding sexual relationships in human nature.

Below I categorize the tenants of four common arguments against open-relationships. They are as follows:

1) If you really loved someone, you wouldn't want sex with anyone else. This is what's natural.
2) Even if you do want sex with someone else, you *should* save yourself or give yourself to just one person. That is what's right.
3) Sex is better with someone you love. That is the way it is.

4) If you are not monogamous, you will get a sexually transmitted disease. Even if you manage to avoid disease, your relationship will suffer via jealousy and there is a very high chance your partner will leave you. That is what you deserve.

The first argument, that *if you really loved someone, you wouldn't want sex with anyone else*, constitutes a denial of mammalian biology (Bagemihl, 1999), common sense, and human evolution (Ryan & Jethá, 2010). In this book, I will borrow from the work of other scholars to show that monogamy is exceptionally rare among higher order animals. I later show that humans are unique in their position to monogamy, maintaining both traits for and against it. Essentially, I will show that monogamy seems to work for a short period but that eventually our biology rejects it. Habituation is more than a condition of attitude; I will show that habituation also brings chemical changes that make us less inclined to have sex with the same person repeatedly.

Ultimately, however, I do not think that our sexual actions should be based on what is natural or not. I do not posit that promiscuity is *always* right because it comes natural to the evolutionary tree (Ryan & Jethá, 2010). In the face of AIDS, unprotected promiscuity is certainly a moral hazard. But it is also crucially important to understand that nature drives us to take certain behaviors into our lives. It is part of our evolutionary history. These drives do not have an innate morality, but they should impact on our discussions of what is and is not moral.

The second argument, *even if you do want sex with someone else, you should save yourself or give yourself to just one person*, is rooted in a religiously constructed and Disney-promulgated fantasy; it is not based on empirical evidence. It is instead an argument of emotive language; language of unsubstantiated supposed morality. But this is like saying people who kill chickens hate them. The argument overlooks the fact that an action can have multiple moral or ethical reasons behind it. In other words, love and sex are independent variables that can overlap, but do not have to.

Our social value of monogamy today—the impetus behind the statement that *even if you do want sex with someone else, you should save yourself or give yourself to just one person*, is also a form of sexual morality that historically changes. Like all notions of morality, it depends on the context of the times. I will later show the reasons we value monogamy today, suggesting that they are the product of salaried labor, modernity, and organized monotheism. All of these variables are discussed as attempts to control human nature (Rubin, 1975) for particular political or religious reasons.

The third argument, that *sex is better with someone you love*, implicitly recognizes that we are capable of loving one person but desiring sex with another. But this argument fails to consider that human beings grow desensitized to stimulus and constantly seek new stimuli. Our entertainment, food, company, and conversation are all judged better when they are varied, exciting, and new. We may choose to revisit long-standing favorites, we might find comfort in the familiar, but we do not desire them day in and day out without at least some variety from time to time.

Accordingly, I will show that statements like *if your sex isn't that good you just need to spice it up* or, *then that says something about you*, are attitudinal statements akin to victim blaming. These arguments imply that the individual who is growing bored of sex with his or her partner is doing something wrong; that normal people are, year in and year out, increasingly stimulated by passionate sex with the same partner. Of course, normal people are not year in and year out increasingly stimulated by their partners. As I show through the work of dozens of other scholars, sex with the same person grows boring. Yet by holding monogamy as an idealized, never-ending form of sexual bliss, the purveyors of monogamy blame the individual rather than the institution of monogamy for acting upon sexual desires.

The fourth argument, *if you are not monogamous, you will get a sexually transmitted disease. Even if you manage to avoid disease, your relationship will suffer via jealousy and there is a very high chance your partner will leave you*, is really what inspired me to write this book. I have seen far too many relationships torn apart, not for a lack of love, commitment, and shared history, but because the partner who was cheated on *believed* this drivel. I wrote this book because most types of cheating have nothing to do with lacking love, and everything to do with desiring sex with someone else. Affairs are the business of divided love, cheating is the business of libido.

If someone desires to break up a functioning, loving, and rewarding relationship, it should be for better reasons than the fact that their partner had an orgasm with someone else. It is my contention that, when cheating does occur in a relationship, it is necessary to resist the view of peers who, more often than not, demonize the cheater and encourage the noncheater to terminate their relationship.

MONOGAMISTS AND THOSE WHO CONTEST THEM

Still, there are some who are so emotionally invested in the romantic myths of monogamy that no reasoned argument will help them to critically evaluate their belief system. Even when I provide this type of individual with the droves of empirical evidence that I detail in this book, they will continue to deny, ignore, or moralize away my findings; they continue to stigmatize cheating and open relationships generally, not just for themselves, but for others too. These are the type of people who say that open relationships are wrong because "they just are." They are the type of people who in 1885, Hyrum called "monogamists."

There is little one can do to convince a monogamist that sex with others is generally moral or acceptable when agreed upon with their partner. Monogamists have uncritically adopted society's moral standpoint and are unlikely to yield. If you are one of them, I ask you to ponder for a moment: *why would you be against another's open relationship?* I can understand why you might prefer monogamy for yourself, *but why can you not understand why many do not?*

Perhaps by the end of this book, monogamists who have purchased it to help them understand why someone has cheated on them, will find themselves asking similar questions about their own relationships and those of others. Still, others will have bought the book because they have already begun to critique monogamy. For you, those interested in challenging others about their value of monogamy, I offer you a warning. The arguments in this book do not easily translate into "action" with one's partner or even in convincing one's friends.

Do not be misled into thinking that just because you understand why men cheat, and just because you know why open relationships might be a more emotionally and physically healthy form of loving, that all this will be understood by those with whom you discuss it. People are resistant to a message that goes against what they have been told is right, proper, and natural, especially when it is a central part of their belief system. And if you do try, be prepared to accept a *great deal* of stigma. While our society has laregely removed the stigma from homosexuality, pre-marital sex, and even oral or anal sex, monogamy maintains a stranglehold on people's ability to think critically about sexual coupling—and the way they deal with this is to attack the messenger. The lowbrow crowd will likely be content to simply label you a pervert, while those looking to dismiss you in slightly more critical manner will simply say:

"ALL HE/SHE DOES IS JUSTIFY CHEATING"

The arguments I make in this book might (particularly) upset women, including some feminists who might see it as nothing more than a well-reasoned justification for why men should be able to cheat. But one should take pause before beating that drum: Feminist academics (of which I am) have been calling for nonmonogamies in human relationships for decades now. Feminists have always been skeptical about marriage; particularly when it involves the governance by a church or state. These scholars use Marxist theory to position monogamy as inherently patriarchal and capitalist (Jackson & Scott, 2004; Robinson, 1997; Rosa, 1994), and they oppose monogamy because of the ownership system it burdens women with.

For example, drawing on the work of Engels (1884) as well as Munson and Stelboum (1999), Barker and Langdridge (2010a) argue that current forms of monogamy emerged in order for women to provide unpaid care for the workforce. Rubin (1975) referred to this as the "traffic" or "exchange" of women, highlighting that women have traditionally been taken in battle, given away in marriage, exchanged for favors, or bought and sold to settle men's affairs.

Other feminists also critique the notion of love and romance as serving the privilege of men. For example, Atkinson (1974) argues that love is part of a political institution that is a necessary part of male domination, while Mint (2010) and Robinson (1997) argue that jealousy is part of this equation: suggesting that not only is jealousy socially constructed, but that jealousy over sexual ownership maintains women's emotional and financial dependence on men. Rosa (1994) adds that monogamous relationships distance women from friendship networks, through which they might challenge these problematic discourses. And Barker and Langdridge (2010b) suggest that, collectively, these arguments relate to a wider perspective whereby self-monitoring and scrutiny of the coupled relationship keeps people from wider critical engagement with society.

Jackson and Scott (2004) add to this argument by proposing consensual non-monogamy as an alternative to monogamy, whereby people (particularly women) would be less likely to become dependent, isolated, and detached from their communities. Thus, nonmonogamies are presented by these feminists as potentially liberating, cooperative, and empowering alternatives to the ownership, possession, and even violence that are located within traditional concepts of heterosexual monogamy (Mint, 2010).

Robinson (1997) sums up many of the key arguments against monogamy in her statement, "Monogamy privileges the interests of both men and capitalism, operating as it does through the mechanisms of exclusivity, possessiveness and jealousy, all filtered through the rose-tinted lens of romance" (p. 144). Similarly, Segal (1994) concludes her book, *Straight Sex: Rethinking the Politics of Pleasure*: "Straight feminists, like gay men and lesbians, have everything to gain from asserting our non-coercive desire to fuck if, when, how and as we choose" (p. 318).

More recently, one of France's most prominent female psychologists, Maryse Vaillant (2009), suggested that wives should welcome their husbands' extramarital affairs as a sign of a healthy marriage, and that men should stop being castigated for being womanizers. Vaillant suggests that men keeping a mistress can actually improve a marriage. With similar findings to my research, Vaillant suggests that fidelity is not proof of love, and that most men don't cheat because they fail to love their partners; they do it because they need "more space." For such men, she suggests, infidelity is almost unavoidable. I echo Vaillant with my suggestion that infidelity is not proof to the psychic dysfunction of men who are still very much in love, and I argue that it can be liberating for women to understand this.

I do not, therefore, take credit with coming up with the idea that men can love their partners, despite their cheating. Even conservative family psychologist, the Rabbi M. Gary Neuman (2008), in his Oprah featured book, *The Truth about Cheating: Why Men Stray and What You Can Do to Prevent It*, suggests that cheating is not necessarily indicative of failure to love, writing: "But believe it or not, this doesn't usually mean that the cheating men didn't love their wives" (p. 9).

My dyadic dissonance theory might also deeply upset gay men who are perhaps more conscious of the high rates of cheating in their community. This is particularly true of younger gay men, who idolize the assimilative approach to acquiring equality. These are men who, compared to the generation of gay men that have gone before them, view promiscuity as incompatible with the quest for gay marriage. This argument maintains that equality will come through assimilating *every* cultural norm of heterosexuals (e.g., 2.2 kids, monogamy, and the white picket fence).

Not all sexual minorities (or all gay men) take this perspective, of course. It is not the historical perspective adopted by the gay community. As I earlier said, before the AIDS crisis gay men were much more likely to be in open sexual relationships (Blumstein & Schwartz, 1983). However, the fear of HIV combined with complicity to the fundamentalism of the "moral majority" movement in the 1980s sent gay men into a model of monogamy.

Yet the drive for sexual freedom has not died. Blake and Lowen (2010) show that the longer coupled gay men are together, the more likely they are (privately or publicly) to contest monogamy. In other words, open relationships are rare for gay men to enter from the onset, but a significantly large proportion of long-term couples evolve into them.

Thus, I hope that this book will help inspire a new generation of sexual minorities to enter into more open and sexually satisfying relationships. Gay couples can have it both ways: We can have the legal utility of civil marriage, the social graces that it provides, and still maintain sexually open, honest, and freeing relationships. Monogamy is not and never has been a necessity of marriage.

Still, many gay men will not be persuaded. They will suggest that I am simply reproducing stereotypes of gay men as promiscuous. But this is not a label I think we need to fear. Gay men *are* promiscuous. Most are *very* promiscuous. In fact, the only real difference between straight and gay men is that gay men have a much easier time getting sex—something I assure you, straight men are rather jealous of. Thus my message to gay men is that we should embrace our carnal desires. Be proud to be a slut.

Know that I am not alone. Feminists, older gay men, and academics from sociology, psychology, biology, and multiple other disciplines stand with me in their understanding that monogamy is not all things to all people. A plethora of academic research shows that love does not triumph over sexual desires; cheating is not a sign that one has failed to love one's partner; and those in open relationships are not dysfunctional. This should make us all reflect a bit more concerning the value of just being honest with our partners about our sexual desires. Hopefully out of honesty will come new systems of loving that promote emotional stability alongside sexually safe promiscuity, something sexologists sometimes call sociosexuality.

ALTERNATIVES TO MONOGAMY

If one is going to engage critically in a discussion of monogamy, it also necessitates evaluating alternatives to monogamy. By this I refer to a whole category of varying relationship types, collectively known as nonmonogamies: celibacy (choosing to abstain from sex with all people), polyamory (having more than just one romantic partner), and serial monogamy (having sex with just one person until it grows dull, breaking up with that person, and then moving to another). Alternatively, one might choose to avoid romance altogether and just enjoy relationship-free sexual encounters. Klesse (2005) defines the variety of nonmonogamies by saying,

"Non-monogamous relationships differ in terms of numbers of partners, kinds of arrangements and degrees of closeness and commitment, legal relationship status, constellations of genders, sexual or social identities, living arrangements and household forms, parenting arrangements, and so on" (p. 448). In this book, however, I choose to juxtapose monogamy with the particular form of nonmonogamy commonly known as open sexual relationships or just 'open relationships'.

Open relationships also come in many varieties, from heterosexual swingers to couples who do threesomes; or those who only permit themselves sex with another when they are out of the state. But the general consensus on open relationships is that the label implies that one maintains intimate emotional relations to just one loving partner, but that recreational sex is pursued as well—either in twosomes, threesomes, or more. In other words, open relationships have rules and procedures that couples are expected to follow; they just don't restrict sex to one's emotional partner.

Like monogamy, open relationships have a set of understandings that privilege the primary partner from those who are sought for sexual recreation. Like monogamy, there are rules to open relationships. For example, some do not cuddle or sleep with those they have sex with. Some do not have sex with someone whom is feared might develop a crush on one or both of the members of the couple. And, important to most people in this form of open relationship, sex is considered *just* sex. Most people in open sexual relationships do not confuse casual sex with what occurs within an emotionally intimate and committed relationship. There are minutiae of other possible rules, too. Some are designed to protect from emotional turmoil (and from disease) and some are rules designed to protect the emotions of those the couple has sex with. This is part of being a responsible sexual citizen.

It is easier for couples in open relationships to stick to their rules because they have the sexual escape that those in monogamous relationships do not—they are free from the sexual pressure cooker of monogamy. As you will later learn, while there are no guarantees of health and happiness with any form of coupling, a failure to explicitly establish and openly discuss the boundaries of the relationship can lead to disaster (Hoff, Beougher, Chakravarty, Darbes, & Neilands, 2010).

3

About the Study

The research and analysis that I generate for this study is primarily sociological. I am interested in what culture says about monogamy and how people deal with that. Thus, my aim is not just to describe what monogamy feels like to the 120 men I interview, or how they navigate it; but I am also interested in why monogamy is expected and desired.

I do not deny that individuals are unique, but the collective, sociological analysis of stories tells us something important about ourselves, how we think and behave, as well as about our culture. This approach allows for an examination of causal relationships—saying one thing happened because of something else. This approach also enables predictions to be made about social phenomena. Thus, while I cannot guarantee precisely who will cheat on their partner, my research enables me to predict to a high degree of accuracy that most will, and even what category of men are more likely to.

I was trained as a pure sociologist. This is to say that my PhD advisor was strongly adverse to sociobiology/evolutionary psychology (the assumption that at least some human behaviors result from human evolution), but I do not shy away from these disciplines in this book. I also draw from elements of cognitive psychology and biology. Certainly, there are differences in opinion as to what exactly evolutionary psychology and sociobiology are (Buss, 1995), but one frequent misunderstanding is that biology means we are *destined* to fulfill our genetic fate, regardless of how we think or have been socialized to think about something. This is not so. We are not mechanical soldiers who march without thinking. However, a sociobiological lens maintains that difficulties might arise when we deny our sexual impulses.

In academic terms, we often over simplify and describe this as essentialism versus social constructionism, with the first being something that is innate, and the second something that is learned. But I point out that, not only are both fundamentalist positions, but that we often use the term *social constructionism* improperly. Social constructionism does not mean that biology plays no part. If we intend to say that biology plays no part and has no effect, we should more properly describe this as social determinism. Conversely, biological determinism would mean that society plays no part. Here, it is purported that society plays no role whatsoever in how we, as humans, behave. Behaviors are instead products of our bioevolutionary background: We are mere animals. I am against this position, too. Even animals have culture. Both of these are essentialist positions, and I do not subscribe to either.

Sociobiology—and the related position of evolutionarily psychology—is a melding of these polarized positions. The position holds that at least some gender differences are strategies of sexual reproduction: that heterosexual humans have an innate impulse to pass on their genetic material, something known as reproductive fitness. Accordingly, when I say that I am a social constructionist, I mean to say that I examine how culture shapes our identities and desires, but this does not rule out our inherited traits as a factor. I find it presumptuous, even fundamentalist, to assume that any one discipline has all the answers. The best work comes from examining the weights of evidence from what multiple scholars, across multiple disciplines, have to offer.

Interestingly, in drawing from multiple disciplines concerning monogamy and cheating, I show that we are mostly saying the same thing. We have different reasons as to why matters are (and some might argue that those reasons are important), but in final analysis, all of these disciplines lead to a critical reading of monogamy in humans.

PARTICIPANTS

The men in my study are strategically selected for variables that enhance their chances of cheating. They are educated, and higher learning is associated with more liberal attitudes—including those regarding sexuality (DeMaris, 2009). They are young and athletic (both of which give them high sexual capital), and this gives them more opportunity to cheat (Atkins, Baucom, & Jacobson, 2001). As university students, they also exist within a rich sexual marketplace (Treas & Giesen, 2000), where multiple opportunities exist to hook up.

In other words, I have strategically selected various groups of men in order to enhance the chances of finding those who cheat. This permits me to delve into the question I am most concerned with: *why* they cheat. By purposefully selecting this sample, I tried to capture men who were more likely to cheat so that I could interrogate cheating. By finding men who cheat, I am better able to focus on broad theoretical understandings of how monogamy acts as hegemonic oppression, why men cheat, and the consequences of both monogamy and cheating.

In total, I interviewed 120 men, all between 18 and 22 years of age. They were selected from one of five different groups:

- Forty heterosexual men recruited from two academic classes at a British University

- Twenty heterosexual men recruited from a university soccer team in the American Northwest
- Twenty heterosexual men recruited from a university soccer team in the American Midwest
- Twenty heterosexual men recruited from a university soccer team in the American South
- Twenty gay men recruited at a British University

The progression of the groups developed organically as my research progressed. Thus, it is important to understand that I entered the research field without a strong theoretical framework in place (what sociologists call an inductive framework). I interviewed the first group of 40 heterosexual men with hegemony theory in mind, but my formulations were loose. It was, for example, only after interviewing these men that I came to find cognitive dissonance a useful tool in understanding the narratives of the men I interviewed.

My dyadic dissonance theory did not come to fruition until writing this book. For example, if one reads the article I published in the *Journal of Social and Personal Relationships* (Anderson, 2010b) titled, "'At Least with Cheating There Is an Attempt at Monogamy': Cheating and Monogamism among Undergraduate, Heterosexual Men" (which was based solely on the first group of 40 men), you will notice that I do not include rational choice theory in that article; nor had I developed my dyadic dissonance theory.

The inclusion of the 60 heterosexual soccer players from three distinct geographical settings in the United States was designed to expand my application of theory to a more diverse group of men, and to permit me time to take on board reviewers' comments about my article. I desired to understand whether the findings I deduced from the British sample of 40 men were generalizable to other groups of university men as well.

The 20 gay men were added after securing the contract to write this book. The editors of the series wanted me to expand the sample to gay men to see whether the findings I present are generalizable beyond heterosexuality (they are). While this group of men is small (just 20 interviews), the generated theory was easily compatible with their narratives. I do not think more interviews with gay men would have helped formulate further theory or significantly altered my dyadic dissonance theory. I achieved repeating data with the gay men rather quickly. Other than the increased availability (ease of acquiring) sex, the themes mirrored those of the heterosexual men.

RESEARCH DESIGN

The 40 heterosexual men in England were recruited from two separate academic classes from the same university. Each of these participants must have currently been in, or at one time been in, a heterosexual relationship that lasted for 3 months or longer. After limiting this potential sample by race, sexuality, relationship status, and religion (excluding those who strongly adhere to religious principles because this was believed to strongly influence beliefs and feelings about cheating, if not the cheating itself), there was an opportunity to interview more than 40 men from these classes. I limited my analysis to just 40 men because this was unfunded research, and I was lacking the time to collect, transcribe, and code the data. Thus, for the purposes of time management, 30 men were interviewed during the second half of the 2007–2008 academic year, and the remaining 10 men were interviewed the following summer.

For the remaining 60 heterosexual men I desired to study team-sport athletes. This is because I desired a male population that might be overrepresentative of cheating, and I knew that male athletes were reported to have more sex than non-athletes (Faurie, Pontier, & Raymond, 2004). Soccer players also represent a type of body that is currently sexualized among men (Filiault, 2007).

For these 60 men, I made no other requirements for their inclusion in my study. I did not deselect them based on race, religion (only 5 were religious, as determined by describing themselves as churchgoers), relationship status, or any other variable. Furthermore, these teams were almost exclusively comprised of white men. Accordingly, this study is mostly situated within white secular culture, with more middle-class students. I do not formally exclude students of color or working-class students from this sample of 60, but I selected students who were part of a dominant white educational culture by virtue of the locale I identified for research; accordingly, my findings are more limited to white, nonreligious, middle-class men, even if not all of the men had these characteristics.

It should also be noted that some of these soccer players had not had the opportunity to cheat. This is because they had never had a girlfriend (since the age of 17). I drew 17 as the line for inclusion of "having a partner" in order to distinguish more adult from younger adolescent relationships. While the number of men who had not had a partner since 17 was small (9 out of 60), interviews with these men gave me the opportunity to interview men about their idealized notions of monogamy without having experience of it. When I later discuss relative deprivation, I have drawn the data from these nine men.

I strategically chose universities found in a broad range of geographical locations. By interviewing men from the deep American South, men from a small conservative Catholic College in the American Midwest, and men from a large liberal East Coast institution, I was able to examine views on cheating and monogamy across varying U.S. university cultures. As it turned out, there was no difference in rates of cheating. The only discernable difference is that men from the large East Coast university seemed more familiar with and perhaps a few of them slightly more open to the concept of open relationships. But other than this, there were no discernable differences from these three groups of men.

The 20 gay men were recruited from the same university as the original 40 men. Here I used snowball sampling to collect my informants. However, for these men, as with the 60 soccer players, I made no restriction on whether they had been in a relationship (or for how long). This permitted me to interview gay men about both their idealized and their lived experiences with monogamy. Three of the 20 had not been in a relationship lasting 3 months or longer since they were 17.

Concerning the divergence of these groups of participants, it is obvious that there are methodological difficulties in creating generalizable statistics. But this research is concerned with *process*; it is concerned with developing conceptual understanding of the problems with monogamy and how cheating emerges. This is not definitive research into the percentage of men of this demographic who cheat. Additionally, because there is little difference between the findings of the American men (in the South, Midwest, or East Coast) and the British men (gay or straight), I am confident in integrating the 120 men into one cohesive group of participants and explicating data indiscriminately throughout the text. At select points of the text, I highlight the small differences in how sexuality affects the men (particularly when discussing open relationships or that gay men are more likely to be caught cheating because of the smaller social networks they inhabit), but I do not otherwise subdivide the results according to sexuality or nationality.

PROCEDURES

I informed the participants at the opening of each interview that I was not looking to judge cheating behaviors. Instead, I told them that I was interested in why men cheat. To further set the participants at ease and encourage disclosure and recip-rocation—following the methodological recommendation of Kong et al. (2002), McCormack (2010), and others (Wenger, 2002)—I disclosed to them that I was gay and my relationship history. I believe this had the desired effect of influencing further disclosure from the participants, and it raised questions for discussion. The men were also told that they would have complete and total anonymity in their discussion with me. Not only were they told that this included changing their names and institutional affiliations in the writing of the research (which I have), but that it included keeping their dating narratives anonymous among their teammates, too (which I did). Accordingly, interviews were designed to foster a nonjudgmental exchange between researcher and participant (Johnson, 2002).

Most conversations ran between 60 and 90 minutes. The order in which topics were discussed; the exact wording of questions; and the amount of time allotted to each question varied depending upon the flow of each conversation. However, questions centered on exploring the various relationships that participants maintained, how long they dated, and (if the relationship had ended) why they broke up.

Participants were also asked to describe their understanding and feelings about monogamy. The opening script allowed me to determine which participants were aware of the nature of open sexual relationships. They were then asked to describe how they felt about open sexual relationships. Discussion then centered on whether and/or how they had ever cheated on their partners (e.g., "in the whole 6 months that you dated her, how many times did you do something sexual with someone else that would upset her?") Participants were generally willing to discuss these issues, and I asked them to elaborate on the circumstances around their cheating episodes as they were comfortable.

It should be noted that I did not reify cheating as immoral by approaching it as a sensitive topic. This is because it is rather difficult to get people to admit to stigmatized acts. For example, while there may be faults with Kinsey's work on men's sexualities (Kinsey, Pomeroy, & Martin, 1948), it is also possible that one reason he got higher response rates to homosexuality than any research since is because he took a more up-front, aggressive approach. Kinsey asked, "How many times have you had sex with a man?" and not "Have you had sex with a man?" When the participant said that he had not, Kinsey refused to believe it.

I took a similar approach here. I asked, "How many times have you cheated on your girlfriend?" and then if the informant indicated that he had not, I said, "Okay, tell me about the times you've cheated on other girlfriends." If again he indicated that he had not, I said, "Cheating doesn't have to be just vaginal sex. How many times have you done anything that would upset your current partner—even just kissing?" I asked the same of other partners. I did not, however, harangue my participants the way Kinsey did. If they still maintained that they had not cheated, I responded, "Really? Are you serious? Not even once, ever?" and left the inquiry there. Finally, if they talked about cheating, we discussed it in depth. Participants were not admitting to cheating just to get me off their backs.

Questions also focused on how these young men felt about their cheating, whether they informed their girlfriends/boyfriends of it, and whether their girlfriends/boyfriends discovered the cheating in other ways. The participants were asked about how they perceived cheating affected their relationship quality. They were also asked to describe how they felt (emotionally) toward their partners (both before and after cheating), by providing me with stories or examples.

I also informed the participants that they were welcome to stay in touch with me via Facebook, to discuss the findings of my research (which I withheld from the members of each group until after I had completed all of the interviews), and to update me on their sexual lives. I received a number of messages from men, weeks, months, or even years after interviewing them. Many of these men wrote to me saying they had cheated for the first time since their interview, but these men are deemed as not having cheated with the 78% statistic I provide.

Finally, to see how the heterosexual soccer players related to women, how they navigated sexual spaces (night clubs and bars), and how they talked about cheating and monogamy in casual conversations, I conducted an ethnography for 10 days on each team. My experience as a coach gave me credit with them, and I was easily accepted into the social matrix of these teams. Here, I practiced with them, partied with them, and spent many long nights lying across couches talking about issues related to sex, sexuality, and monogamy. This is part of an emancipatory, action-research approach I take to ethnography (Adams & Anderson, forthcoming).

Concerning coding, I used a constant-comparative method of open and axial coding of my notes, until I was satisfied that my coding accounted for informants' social scripts in a logical, consistent and systematic manner. In order to establish interrater reliability, ten percent of these codes and themes were then cross-checked with another researcher who (for the soccer team ethnographies) was in the field, and the same 10 percent was cross-checked with a researcher not in the field, (Ponterotto, 2005).

However, a limitation of my methods is that I did not tape-record the conversations with the 60 men from my own university (20 gay and 40 straight). This restricts the textual analysis that can be performed on that half of my data, but it was considered necessary to remove the threat that my institutional intimacy may have posed. I feared that the presence of a dictaphone might increase participants' likelihood of strategically managing their monogamous identities through having a record of their transgressions (Spradley, 1970). Thus, I took handwritten notes during interviews (which occurred in my office), and I typed up my notes *immediately* after the conclusion of each interview with these groups of men. Although I recognize the limitations of not having precise transcripts, I maintain that my notes still permit me to capture relevant stories and accurately depict attitudes and events. However, I did record the 60 interviews conducted on heterosexual male soccer players from three other universities in the United States.

USING PARTICIPANTS' WORDS

There are debates in academic circles over how one should present data from interviews. One school of thought sees the researcher writing down the participants' words verbatim, including the use of poor sentence structure, documenting pauses, facial gestures, and even transition sounds like "um" and "like." Others remove much of the detail, simply writing the quotes down without pauses or discussion of the participant's body reactions. Still others determine that what is important is the meaning of what is said. These researchers will remove most pauses, "ums" and "likes," replace malapropisms with the intended word, and generally clean up the language of the user. This is the approach I take with this research. If I were undertaking conversation analysis, or undertaking linguistic research, this would be problematic. However, for the focus of meaning in this research, this aids flow and style with no loss to academic rigor.

MY 78% FINDING

It is impossible to conduct an accurate study to determine the rates at which men cheat. This is because it is difficult to get people to admit, even anonymously, to stigmatized behaviors and because it is impossible to obtain a random sample. Furthermore, definitions of what monogamy is vary too much. However, I show in this research that 79 of the 103 participants (excluding nine straight and three gay men) who met the qualifying standard of having a partner for 3 months since the age of 17 have cheated on their current or most recent partner. This is 78%. In other words, 78% of those who had a partner cheated, even though they said that they loved and intended to stay with that partner.

Some of the men who reported being monogamous with their current partner suggested that they have, however, cheated on previous partners. Although these data were not ascertained for each participant, it indicates that the rate of having ever cheated is obviously higher than the percentage of those who cheated on their most recent partner.

Twenty-six of the 40 heterosexual men from the British sample (65%) had done something sexual with another person that their partner of the time would feel was a violation of their monogamous terms (remembering that my definition of cheating counts anything, even a small kiss on the lips).

Of the 60 American soccer players, I used the same criteria. Accordingly, I excluded nine men from analysis because they did not have or had never had a girlfriend of 3 months or longer since the age of 17. Of the remaining 51 men, 44 (86%) reported cheating in some capacity by doing something that their current partner at the time would consider a violation of their implicitly or explicitly stated terms of monogamy.

Of the 20 gay men interviewed in England, eight had not been in a long-term relationship of 3 months or longer, since the age of 17 (probably because many had recently come out). Of the remaining 12 men, 10 had cheated on their current or most recent partner in some capacity (83%). This sample size is of course too small to draw any meaningful conclusions about the frequency of cheating among gay men of this demographic, but it does indicate that cheating is at least as likely among gay men as it is among their heterosexual counterparts.

Thus, if one wishes to analyze these statistics on an intragroup analysis, it appears that straight male undergraduate athletes cheat on partners they love at nearly the same percentage as undergraduate gay men (83% and 85%, respectively); and that heterosexual undergraduate men who are not athletes are somewhat less likely to cheat (65%). I assume that the lower rates of cheating among heterosexual nonathletes is a reflection of their lesser ability to cheat, and this is consistent with other recent research that shows that athletes cheat more than nonathletes (Vail-Smith, Whetstone, & Knox, 2010). This is because they are neither as sexualized as the athletes nor exist within quite as rich a sexual marketplace as the gay men do (because of gay hookup websites).

The final descriptive statistic I wish to contemplate considers the aggregate percentage of 78 that I use to describe this population as a whole. I do this because I do not want to continuously subdivide the total percentage of men who have cheated on their current or most recent partner by the three categories of men I interviewed; that would be tedious and repetitive. Thus, an aggregate number will help simplify the presentation of the findings as to why men cheat.

I aggregate the gay men, straight men, and straight athletes (this statistic is derived by working out the mean; adding 83, 85, and 65 and dividing by three = 78%). In doing this I bias the sample toward gay men and athletes over their heterosexual nonathlete counterparts (who actually comprise the largest population of undergraduate males in these two countries).

LIMITATIONS

This research is concerned with the social process that leads men to cheat; it is less concerned with reporting statistics of exactly what type of cheating behaviors occur among the participants, or to what frequency they cheat. This *is not* a statistically valid sample of men from whom to make generalizations about cheating rates.

I am concerned with why men value monogamy and why they are led to cheat, whatever those cheating behaviors might be. Accordingly, rather than engage in a lengthy debate about what cheating means, I simply define cheating as *any* physical sexual behavior that would be met with disapproval by one's partner—even if it is just kissing. However, I do not count "thought crimes" (fantasies of sex with others) as cheating, although I do discuss the difficulties of admitting to one's partner that one desires sex with another.

There are other limitations to my study. First, my research highlights that monogamy is (largely) a failed institution in *Western* cultures. But this is not to suggest that monogamy has failed in *all* cultures. Monogamy might be more the rule than the exception in cultures with harsh punitive measures for adultery. If one is imprisoned, whipped, branded, or killed for cheating, it will certainly reduce (but not eliminate) the chances of extradyadic sex occurring.

I also recognize that monogamism has significant intersectional properties to other categories of importance that my study does not take into account. I do not account for race (most in this study are white), class (most are middle class), age (they are all university-aged), gender (they are all male), or religion (they mostly identify as atheist or agnostic). I highlight that these intersections may combine to further subordinate those who do not follow the social expectations of monogamy (Tanenbaum, 1999; Willey, 2006); however, I do not address these intersections with this research because I did not have enough time, funding, or ability to do so. I hope other scholars will apply my dyadic dissonance theory to these groups.

THE ABSENCE OF BISEXUALS

One demographic of men that monogamy maintains extremely salient intersectional properties to cheating is bisexual men. It may stand out as odd that they are not accounted for here. Like gay men, bisexuals have faced multiple cultural challenges: Stigmatization and discrimination have been documented as characteristic of the bisexual individual's life experience (Barrios, Corbitt, Estes, & Topping, 1976; Herek, 1994; Mohr, Israel, & Sedlacek, 2001). Those identifying as bisexual have often been stigmatized as neurotic, unable to love, or "incapable of making up their minds." Bisexual individuals have also been subject to double dis-crimination, facing hostility from both heterosexuals and homosexuals (Ochs, 1996).

Furthermore, bisexuals have sometimes been described as simply being in transition into pure homosexuality or being sex crazed (Klein, 1993). Thus, the overwhelming social attitude toward bisexuality has been one of denial, erasure, and/or stigma (Anderson & Adams, 2011). This is even evident in much academic literature that favors self-identification over one's sexual predisposition (c.f. Eigenberg, 2000). In other words, men "who have sex with men" are regarded as being "on the down-low," curious, or heteroflexible, rather than simply being bisexual (c.f. Denizet-Lewis, 2003; King, 2004).

Of particular concern here, dominant discourse already constructs bisexuals as promiscuous and nonmonogamous. Given the cultural stigma attached to bisex-ual identity, where they are perceived as not being able to be satisfied by one sex (let alone one partner), it is extremely likely that narratives of monogamy and cheating will be markedly different for bisexual men and unique to their sexual identity. Klesse (2005) says:

> The assumption that bisexuals have to be nonmonogamous flows from the traditional western construction of sexuality in a dualistic scheme. If homo-sexuality and heterosexuality (thought as opposites) are perceived as the only "real" and valid forms of sexual orientation, then bisexuality can only be thought of as a "mixed" form of sexuality consisting in parts of homosexual-ity and heterosexuality . . . the "homosexual side" and the "heterosexual side" of an individual are thought to be (at least potentially) in permanent conflict . . . Consequently, authentic bisexuality is only possible in the context of a nonmonogamous life practice (p. 448).

Because I did not want to add further stigma to an already sexually stigmatized population, I chose not to interview bisexual men.

THE ABSENCE OF MEN IN OPEN RELATIONSHIPS

Although I juxtapose monogamy alongside open relationships in this research, this study is not a "how-to" book about how to open a relationship up to extrady-adic recreational sex. Nor is this a critical examination of open relationships. I draw on secondary sources to discuss open relationships, but I do not interview men in open relationships. That, again, is the stuff of another research project.

While the conclusions of this study clearly indicate that intimate relationships which permit sex with others are more consistent with our sexual desires, I do not have space within this text to teach the reader about the great variety of ways to be open, and how to deal with and learn to get over jealousy (except a short discus-sion in Chapter 12). Instead, I spend several chapters critiquing monogamy, high-lighting monogamy's weaknesses by holding it up to open relationships, but I do not critique open relationships. This is because the intention of this research is to critique the already hegemonically dominant relationship type.

For those interested in the mechanics of open relationships, I recommend Tristan Taormino's *Opening up: A Guide to Creating and Sustaining Open Relationships* (2008) or Easton and Hardy's classic, now in its second edition *The Ethical Slut* (2009). There are other readings one might find illuminating on open relationships as well (e.g., Benson, 2008; Matik, 2002; Ravenscroft, 2004). For a quicker (and free) read of how gay men navigate open relationships, I recommend www.thecouplesstudy.com. Finally, for those interested in how marriage is changing, including 4 million couples in some form of an open relationship, I recommend Pamela Haag's (2011), *Marriage Confidential: The Post-Romantic Age of Workhorse Wives, Royal Children, Undersexed Spouses, and Rebel Couples Who Are Rewriting the Rules*.

MY USE OF THEORY AND WRITING STYLE

Social theorists frequently write about their theories in academically inaccessible language. This permits various people to interpret the theory differently, and perhaps contributes to the longevity of a theory. Many use Foucault, for example, unaware of a multiplicity of debates of what Foucault *really* meant or how it might actually be applied. As a public sociologist concerned with emancipatory research, however, my aim in describing dyadic dissonance theory is the opposite of creating intellectual goulash. I desire to explicate my hypothesis in accessible language, so that the reader will understand exactly what I suggest. My aim is to present an argument, hopefully educate the reader, and participate in an academic debate— I have no interest in demonstrating my vocabulary.

Social theorists, predominantly those who study sexualities from a poststructural framework, are particularly guilty of writing their theories in academically inaccessible language. For example, Butler (1990) is so inaccessible that I accuse her of committing a shameful, violent, act of academic exclusion. This is a view echoed by Freire (1972), who argued that commitment to human liberation is incompatible with theoretical knowledge being the privilege of a small, academic minority. Most of the time I read poststructural works, I have absolutely no idea what the author is going on about. I have no desire to contribute to this culture of academic elitism. Accordingly, I mostly avoid poststructural concepts in this research. When I do borrow from poststructuralism, I avoid the language in which most poststructuralists frame their ideas.

Apart from Chapter 7 however, I do not borrow from poststructuralism much. This is because a central tenet of poststructuralist theory in sexualities research is to explicate the fluidity and multiplicity of identities and to resist categorizing them. I limit these deconstructive discussions of breaking down identity types here because I find the deconstructive school of thought only useful as philosophy. Postmodern and poststructuralist schools of thought lack political agency and real-world application. Thus, I do not engage in long philosophical debates about what it means to be a couple in the first place. I ask of the poststructuralists wedded to this framework, how exactly can one conduct an emancipatory political project if one cannot define the group one's research is intended to emancipate? How can I effectively challenge the institution of monogamy, if I can never get out of the starting block by defining what monogamy is?

PART TWO

Men, Attraction, and Love

4

The Hardening and
Softening of Men

As a scholar of men, their masculinities and their sexualities, I find it important to couch my research on monogamy among men in a sociological and historical understanding of how masculinities are socially constructed and to explicate theories of masculinity-making that some readers might think explain (or partially explain) men's cheating behaviors. This chapter therefore provides some of the historical circumstances of the era in which monogamy emerged and the conservative type of masculinity produced as a result of the industrial revolution. Most important, this chapter shows that being a man throughout the 20th century was predicated in misogyny, homophobia, violence, and domination of women. Thus, this was an era in which polygamy was replaced with monogamy; women increasingly maintained some legal rights, but men nonetheless felt a privilege to rule over them. Some therefore argue that men learned to cheat as a result of proving their heterosexuality, enacting their power over women, and reproducing patriarchy.

This perspective makes sense. If men are trained to look poorly upon women—to see them solely as objects of sexual desire—then it follows that they might be more inclined to cheat on their partners because they value them less (Korobov & Bamberg, 2004). They might also be conditioned to have more sex with multiple women—which includes cheating—in order to build their heteromasculine capital among peers. This makes heterosexual men feel powerful, distances them from the possibility of being thought gay, and grants them esteem in the eyes of their peers.

Thus, in the first section of this chapter, I explicate how modern masculinity was forged in British and American cultures. I explain the cultural mechanism that brought team-sport athletes (half of the men I interview) into a particularly valued cultural context. However, I later show that the men in this study no longer represent or valorize this type of masculinity. Instead, I pull from one of my recent books, *Inclusive Masculinity: The Changing Nature of Masculinities*

(Anderson, 2009), to show that undergraduate men today do not maintain much homophobic sentiment. I show that undergraduate men look much more favorably upon women than those of previous generations.

Despite being more emotional with their female partners, looking more favorably upon them, and respecting their sexual narratives, I nonetheless show that heterosexual men still cheat. Thus, the point of this chapter is to show that men who cheat in my study do not appear to be doing so in order to impress their peers, oppress women, or play out Freudian notions of power and masculinization at the expense of women. This chapter helps us understand that men's cheating behaviors today are not because they have been socialized into masculine deviance. My dyadic dissonance theory is not based in a socially constructed ugliness of men.

THE CONSTRUCTION OF MANLY MEN

Since Alfred Kinsey, Pomeroy, & Martin (1948) published their study of male sexualities, we have known that men cheated on their wives in "alarming" numbers. Some suggest that this is because straight men feel entitled to sexual access of women's bodies. Readers may be familiar with the concept of *droit de seigneur*, which translates into "the lord's right," a phrase used to describe the medieval legal right that allowed the lord of an estate to have sex with its virgins. Others suggest that men cheat because they don't get enough emotional attention from their wives (Neuman, 2008). Still others suggest that men are socially created to cheat as a way to prove that they are proper, virile, heterosexual men (Korobov & Bamberg, 2004).

In this section I highlight the influence that urbanization and the industrial revolution had on the gendering of men—a gendering process that might affect the way they view women and monogamy. The argument maintains that as a result of the industrial revolution, boys needed to be socialized into the hypermasculine values necessary to be successful in this new economy: to instill the qualities of discipline and obedience and to honor the hard work that was necessary in the dangerous occupations of industrial labor and mining (Cancian, 1987). These environments necessitated that men be tough and unemotional. Conversely, Cancian shows us that women were taught to be emotionally expressive and weak, as well as loyal and subservient to men. Weber argued it was the Protestant work ethic which enabled industrialization to get a foothold precisely because it emphasized discipline and hard work. From this perspective it can be suggested that the cultivated male gender characteristics associated with urbanization and industrialization have their roots in Puritan ideals.

Cancian (1987) describes these changes as a separation of gendered spheres, saying that expectations of what it meant to be a man or woman bifurcated as a result of industrialization. Men grew more instrumental (purpose driven) not only in their labor but in their personalities, too. Here, men learned that the way to demonstrate their love was through their labor, not emotional expression. Being a breadwinner, regardless of (or despite) the working conditions, was a labor of love. Conversely, because women were mostly (but not entirely) relegated to a domestic sphere, they were reliant upon their husband's ability to generate income. Mostly robbed of economic agency, women learned to show their contribution through emotional expressiveness and domestic efficiency. Accordingly, the antecedents of men's stoicism and women's expressionism, of today's gender stereotypes, were born.

An important effect on the gendering of men was also the growing understanding and awareness of homosexuality at the time. This is because large cities provided the opportunities for gay men to meet and form social networks in a way they were unable to under agrarian life. The high population density of cities meant that gay social networks, and even a gay identity, could form. Homosexuality became visible.

This coincided with scholarly work from Westphal, Ulrichs, and Krafft-Ebing, early pioneers of the gay liberationist movement. These men sought to classify homosexual acts as belonging to a *type* of person: a third sex, an invert, or homosexual (Spencer, 1995). From this, they could campaign for legal and social equality. Previously, there were less entrenched heterosexual or homosexual social identities. In other words a man performed an *act* of sodomy (or vaginal sex), without necessarily being viewed as a sodomite (or as a heterosexual). Under modern theorizing, homosexuality was no longer a collection of particular acts, but instead it was an identity. As Foucault (1980) famously wrote: "The sodomite had been a temporary aberration; the homosexual was now a species" (p. 43). And clearly, or so it seemed, the numbers of this species were growing.

Important to my analysis, the perceived increase in same-sex desire was noticed by Sigmund Freud, who argued that homosexuality was the result of a social and psychic process that occurred in childhood, largely from the absence of a father figure. In his 1905 *Three Essays on the Theory of Sexuality* (referenced in 1949), Freud suggested that childhood experiences influenced men to become heterosexual or homosexual, something he called inversion. Here, Freud linked his observation of increasing levels of same-sex sex with a change in the social ordering of the family. Freud highlighted that during the industrial era boys spent the majority of their days solely under the influence of women because fathers left for work early, often returning home once their sons had gone to bed, and because teaching young children was done exclusively by women. Boys, Freud speculated, were deprived of the masculine vapors he supposed were necessary to masculinize them. In these conditions, as Messner (1992) writes, "It was feared that men were also becoming 'soft,' that society itself was becoming feminized" (p. 14). The industrial revolution had meant that boys were structurally, and increasingly emotionally, segregated from their distant and absent fathers.

Accordingly, Freud argued that homosexuality was a process of gendered wrongdoing, that it was tied to the social organization of family life. This wrongdoing occurred because the father was absent, and he was replaced by a domineering mother. In one of his footnotes he wrote, ". . . the presence of both parents plays an important part. The absence of a strong father in childhood not infrequently favors the occurrence of inversion" (p. 146). Freud even gave child-rearing tips to help parents lead their children to heterosexual adjustment.

This created a moral panic among Victorian-thinking British and American cultures. It seemed that industrialization (because it pulled fathers away from their families for large periods of time) had structurally created a social system designed to make kids "inverts." It created what Filene (1975) called a "crisis of masculinity." In this zeitgeist, what it meant to be a man began to be predicated in not being like one of those sodomite/invert/homosexuals. This created a culture of men fearing being thought of as gay, which led men to behave in ways opposite of whatever was socially coded as gay (Anderson, 2009). Masculine (being straight) entailed being the opposite of the softness attributed to women, and ultimately, homosexual men. This included proving one's heterosexuality through hypersexualizing women and dominating their bodies.

CASTING OFF HOMOSEXUAL SUSPICION BY SEXUALIZING WOMEN

If there is one thing that a heterosexual cannot do in a homophobic culture it is prove that he is straight. Unlike a gay man, who is understood by all to be gay with one proclamation, a heterosexual must prove and reprove his heterosexuality. This, of course, is only the case if people stigmatize homosexuality. If homosexuality is not stigmatized, heterosexuals will not feel compelled to prove their heterosexuality.

Kinsey, Pomeroy, and Martin (1948) conducted the first study on human sexuality in what I call a homohysteric culture (Anderson, 2009). Here, men are under constant pressure to prove that they are not gay. It is understandable that if men desire to be thought straight, they might learn to view women as sex objects and to exploit women's bodies in order to gain heterosexual credit in the ongoing process of displacing homosexual suspicion.

For example, in her fraternity research on gang rape, Peggy Sanday Reeves (1990) builds on this Freudian notion of boys needing to separate themselves from women, discussing how male cultures (such as fraternities) construct men to view women through a sexist, objectified lens that ultimately leads to rape. Of course, if men can be trained to rape, then it also makes sense that men can be constructed to use women in order to build their own heteromasculine capital by cheating on their girlfriends. Accordingly, in her work on why men cheat, Vaughan (2003) says that the constant bombardment of the portrayal of women as sex objects in advertising "makes it very difficult for men to relate to women in any way other than sexual" (p. 34). This, Vaughan argues, leads men to cheat. Apparently she believes that if men respected women more they would not cheat.

Following from the argument then, if men are constructed to be more feminist, if they are constructed to consider women's narratives, perspectives, and feelings, they should be less likely to cheat; they should also be less likely to rape women. If men lose their homophobia, they will also have less reason to cheat. This is something I inadvertently "test" for with this research. This is because the heterosexual men I study *do not* enact this traditional style of masculinity. Men in my study do respect women, they are not homophobic—yet they still cheat.

CHEATING IN THE PRESENCE OF RESPECT FOR WOMEN AND GAY MEN

The previous section hypothesized how heterosexual men could be constructed to cheat as a product of proving their heterosexuality in a homohysteric culture. It is therefore important to highlight that undergraduate men in my multiple other studies (in both the United States and the United Kingdom) are rapidly running from the ugliness of orthodox masculinity today (Anderson, 2009). Men in multiple other studies have shown that they adopt more gay-friendly and less sexist approaches to masculinity-making (Anderson, 2005a, 2005b; McCormack, 2010).

First, the heterosexual men on the three soccer teams I studied in the United States (recall that I did 10 days of ethnography on these teams alongside the in-depth interviews) no longer maintain homophobia (Anderson & Adams, 2011). Instead, they are politically charged to change the landscape of masculinity. When one player came out as gay, this only served to bolster his standing with his teammates (Adams and Anderson, forthcoming). There was no evidence to suggest that the majority of men on these teams either intellectualized homophobia or behaved in homophobic ways. Perhaps surprisingly, only one of the 60 men expressed some reservations with homosexuality. Supporting this, on June 4, 2010, a Gallup poll of Americans found for the first time that young men were less homophobic than young women. They were found to be the least homophobic demographic of all U.S. citizens (www.gallup.com).

More to the point, as part of the ethnographic approach I took with these three teams of soccer players, I was also able to see how they related to women, the centrality of women in their social networks, and how they talked about sex with and about women. Data suggest that these teammates eschewed misogynistic attitudes, particularly regarding women as sex objects. Accordingly, data from my research clearly indicated that there exists a significant sociopositive shift regarding men's attitudes toward women (Anderson, 2008a, 2008b, 2009). The empirical evidence suggests that they *are not* misogynistic.

I spent a great deal of time watching these men interact with women in dance clubs and house parties. It was clear that many of the men were hoping to hook up, but their approach was much softer than the presentation of hard, masculine stares and scary body language. Instead, the men mostly remained within their social circles of other men, until an opportunity arose to talk to a woman. When it was clear that they had failed in their advance, they did not insult the woman who rejected them. They simply returned to their friends who normally offered emotional support.

Today's male youth are also more likely to understand women's sexual narratives. They are more likely to have conversations with women about sex—the kind of conversations they were often unable to have years ago (Anderson, 2008a). In these conversations, men hear the multiple sexual narratives of women. Coupled with a more inclusive institutional and organizational setting, today's youth are able to undo (or never formulate in the first place) much of their separatist and sexist thinking. The Internet has given men the opportunity to talk with women (even if anonymously) in chat rooms and for women to discuss with them *their* sexual narratives.

This all points to one simple fact: The White undergraduate men no longer need to act as sexist, misogynistic, or homophobic in order to win the support of their peers and be thought heterosexual. Men today are permitted much more gender and sexual freedom. Men in this study are not socialized into the sexist and homophobic culture that their fathers were, and there is therefore no reason to build one's masculine capital up by taking their aggressions out while having sex with other women by cheating on their girlfriends. Supporting this thesis, rates of rape have plummeted by three quarters since the 1980s (Pinker, 2011).

While I only interviewed half of the men in this research about their perspectives on women, my results found that men suggested that they befriend women and respect them. My observations of the three men's soccer teams studied confirm that women were well integrated into their social networks. More so, a few of the men had not yet had heterosexual sex. Yet these men were not pressured or made fun of for this. I found similar findings in research I conducted on a California fraternity (Anderson, 2008b).

Highlighting the different attitude today's youth take, McCormack (2011) and McCormack and Anderson (2010) show that when British high school boys do not present hyperheterosexual versions of themselves, they are not stigmatized or homosexualized by their lack of overt heterosexuality. For example, McCormack and Anderson (2010) report upon one student, Steve, 16, who attended a costume party in a Superman outfit. At the party a highly attractive girl offered him oral sex. Steve declined the offer, telling her that he could not be bothered to take his costume off. Steve (who was single and attractive) was not living up to orthodox notions of heteromasculinity by denying the oral sex. But this did not result in a diminution of his heterosexual capital. At school the next day, a group of boys discussed the event. But their discussion was absent of homosexualizing discourse because he turned down the oral sex. As Steve walked past the group, one of the boys called him "Mr. Lazy." While Steve was clearly being made fun of, he was not homosexualized for rejecting heterosexual sex. Furthermore, Steve did not need or attempt to recuperate his heterosexuality.

This example demonstrates that men might still want heterosexual sex, but today's youth may not use homophobia and misogyny as a way to prove they do. I do not discount that men are still constructed to be sexual creatures, and I recognize that this might have some influence on their cheating behaviors. But my dyadic dissonance theory argues that cheating results from desires for sex (whether those desires are socially and/or biologically constructed) and not out of desire to prove that one is not gay, or to play out their misogynistic attitudes by having sex with women that they view as property. To equate men's cheating with the continuation of patriarchy, or through an attempt to gain power over women through conquering their bodies in contemporary Western culture, is overly Freudian, wrongheaded, and completely unhelpful in understanding the complexity of why today's youth cheat. The answer as to why these men continue to cheat is instead explicated through my dyadic dissonance theory. And it begins with finding themselves attracted to others, in addition to their partners.

5

The Science of Sexual Attraction

Before we can begin a discussion of how relationships develop, which leads to a discussion of how men come to cheat in those relationships, I find it illuminating to examine scientifically how attraction works in the first place. This is because, whether it is in developing a long-standing relationship or a one-night stand, sex and relationships first begin with the spark of attraction.

Before moving on to the science of attraction, it is interesting to note that large-scale studies of attractiveness find a variance between what men and women desire, something particularly true in adolescence. For example, Ha, Overbeek, and Engels (2010) find that men of this age are more concerned with the attractiveness of women than vice versa. Interestingly, neither men nor women are overly concerned with status (such as work and money) at this age. And, while men might place more emphasis on looks than women, both sexes regard sexual attractiveness as the most important variable in developing sexual romantic interest.

ATTRACTION TO A FACE

It is evolutionarily illuminating to consider the ease and speed with which we visually process a face. Occurring in just milliseconds we can determine someone's gender, age, and race (Brewster, Mullin, Dobrin, & Steeves, 2010). But beyond these assessments, we also gauge personality attributes: whether the individual seems nice, intelligent, trustworthy, funny, or dangerous. Much of these determinations are derived from the degree of attractiveness, with better characters associated with better looks. Synnott (1989) calls this "the beauty mystique," its simplest form being the belief that the beautiful are good and vice versa. In this manifestation it can be traced as far back as Homer's *The Iliad*.

Aristotle suggested that facial beauty was a result of specific facial ratios, which was supplemented by Cicero's belief that the face mirrored the soul (Synnott, 1989). Thus, "facism," the judgment of an individual as a whole based on his or her facial attractiveness, has a lengthy history. Not much has changed since ancient Greece; the most important variable we gather from a face today is still whether we are attracted to it. We remember good looking faces better too. This memory imprint might be influenced by oxytocin, which makes us feel good at the sight of one we find attractive. It has been shown to help us better memorize faces (Rimmele, Hediger, Heinrichs & Klaver, 2009).

EXPLAINING FACIAL ATTRACTIVENESS

There is a great deal of research into the science of visual attraction of human faces. It shows that although we easily and instantaneously determine whether a face is attractive, it is extremely difficult to describe verbally what we find attractive. This often leads us to posit that our judgments "just are" (making for interesting arguments over friends who see matters differently). In scientific consideration of why we find certain faces attractive, many have focused on the concept of symmetry (Gangestad & Simpson, 2000; Thornhill & Gangestad, 1998). These studies find that not only are symmetrical faces more attractive, but that we have a specialized subconscious mechanism for detecting symmetry (Penton-Voak et al., 2003). In other words, a body of research suggests that symmetry preferences are driven by a mechanism that is independent of conscious detection (Perrett et al., 1999). Supporting this, when faces are manipulated by computer graphics to be more symmetrical, subjects find increased preference for the computer-manipulated faces than the original faces (Little et al., 2001; Perrett, et al., 1999; Rhodes et al., 1998, 2001).

Some might argue that this is not the innate process of humans, but instead symmetry is culturally constructed to be beautiful; thus, we learn to understand symmetry as beautiful. However, the aforementioned studies work across various cultures (Rhodes et al., 2001), not just Western societies. Furthermore, Langlois et al. (1987) showed pairs of female faces (one previously rated positive for attractiveness by adults and the other rated unattractive) to 2-month-old infants (who could not yet be socialized into attraction). The infants preferred to look at the photographs of the more attractive face of the pair (expressions of emotions were controlled for). Slater et al. (1998) later demonstrated the same preference in newborns. Here, the babies looked longer at the attractive faces, regardless of the gender, race, or age of the face they were shown. This indicates that our notions of human beauty (or at least attributes worthy of being looked at) are somewhat based on innate traits (that might then be augmented by culture). So while individual tastes may vary, the expression "beauty is in the eye of the beholder" is perhaps somewhat unfounded (Eisenthal, Dror, & Ruppin, 2005).

Other researchers add that we are even more attracted to faces that look like our own, regardless of sexuality. You may have noticed that people quite often end up with partners that resemble themselves, something known as *homogamy*. My partner, for example, is often mistaken as my brother. It is likely that this is a matter of psychological imprinting, and not a genetic fix. For example, in one study of adopted adult women, they were asked to bring a photo of their adoptive father and their husband to the researcher. When photos of the women (the test subjects) were given to an independent body of people, they picked which husband belonged to which adopted woman by examining the photos of the adopted fathers at a better average than chance would permit (Bereczkei, Gyuris, & Weisfeld, 2004). The same study found that the more emotional support the adopted daughters received from their adopted fathers, the more likely they were to select mates that resembled their adopted fathers.

When heterosexual participants of one study were asked to judge the attractiveness of photos of strangers, the participants rated the photos higher when the photos were preceded with a subliminally flashed (i.e., very fast) photo of their current lover (Fraley & Marks, 2010). Thus, the study concludes that we view strangers' faces more attractive when our lover's face is still burning in our subconscious. Even more interesting, these same participants rated the strangers more sexually attractive when their images were digitally morphed with photos of the subjects' own faces. This was controlled for by morphing the target with images of an unrelated face. In fact, the more that the image was digitally manipulated to look like the participant, the more sexually attractive the participant felt the image was. Interestingly, when these participants were told of the results, they reevaluated and downgraded the photos. This, of course, highlights the influence of sexual taboos (in this case a form of auto-arousal) on our reported attractions.

You might also be surprised that when it comes to reading emotions off of one's face, we tend to look left, focusing on the individual's right side. This is called *left gaze bias* and it is theorized that we do this because (for some reason) the right side of our face expresses emotions more accurately (Guo, Meints, Hall, Hall, & Mills, 2009). In other words, if you desire to read one's emotions more accurately, focus on the right side of the person's face. If you have a hard time believing this, ask yourself which side of the face you wink with? Humans are not the only ones who examine the right side of our faces for an indication of what we are feeling; dogs do as well.

Facial attractiveness does not, of course, come down to facial symmetry or self-representation alone. A host of other variables are also conceptualized in those milliseconds of initial judgment, and it is possible that some of these characteristics are more socially constructed. Cunningham (1986) and Cunningham, Barbee, and Pike (1990), for example, found facial categories that they describe as "neonate" to be attractive. These include a small nose and high forehead, mature (e.g., prominent cheekbones), and expressive (e.g., arched eyebrows). This might explain, for example, why traditionally masculine men were sexualized in the hypermacho 1980s, while more feminine men (e.g., Leonardo DeCaprio, David Beckham) were more sexualized in proceeding decades (Anderson, 2009). Symmetry and similarity are important to both masculine and soft-skin boys, but whether we prefer one group over the other *might* be more due to cultural determinants.

WHY WE VALUE FACIAL SYMMETRY

It is not known exactly why we evolved to find neonate, symmetrical, or similar faces more attractive. Some suggest that symmetry might indicate both pheno-typic (body type) and genotypic (genetic) quality, like the ability to resist disease (Møller & Thornhill, 1998). Thus, symmetry might reflect a "bill of good health" in that the individual was not marked by disease. Others suggest that we appreci-ate symmetry not because it conveys genetic health, but because of the way our brains more easily process images that are symmetrical.

Little and Jones (2006) suggest that a specialized mechanism for symmetry preference may be the result of specific pressures faced by human ancestors to select high-quality mates. Supporting this, women and gay men have recently been found to be better at determining facial symmetry than straight men (Brewster et al., 2010). Ostensibly, this is because women use both sides of the brain in processing a face, while straight men use just one. But the artifact might be that (unsurprisingly) gay men share some biological traits with women. However, it may also be because symmetrical faces are more easily processed by our brain's visual system. This is known as *perceptual bias theory*, because it holds that symmetry preferences arise from biases based on the properties of perceptual systems (Little & Jones, 2006), not evolutionary processes of mate selection. At first, this theory makes sense. It is supported by our appreciation of symmetry in both art (Gombrich, 1984) and architecture (Rensch, 1963).

ATTRACTION TO ONE'S SMELL

Smell also plays a role in the determination of attractiveness. Each of us has a unique odor which serves as a stimulus that some will find appealing while others will find offensive. Most of the time we cannot smell this odor because we grow desensitized to it. But sometimes we can.

Some people are more erotically aroused by body smells than others, but this is not to say they are attracted to just anyone's smell. I, for example, find the body odor of young men rather arousing, but for older or hairy men I find it offensive. This is not just association (i.e., one looks attractive, so I find myself attract to his smell), it is verifiable under lab conditions (Herz & Cahill, 1997; Thornhill & Gangstead, 1999).

Although women report a stronger effect than men, both sexes report that body scent significantly affects their sexual interest (Herz & Cahill, 1997). For heterosexual women, an attraction to smell can be even more important than facial symmetry, whereas men rate visual and olfactory cues as about equally important. Evidence even suggests that the importance of a male's scent in a wom-an's arousal varies across the menstrual cycle, as it is heightened when women are ovulating.

Thornhill and Gangstead (1999) demonstrate the power of smell in attraction in their somewhat famous T-shirt experiments. In one experiment, they had men wear T-shirts for several days, instructing them not to wash or use scented products. After a few days of wearing the shirts, women were asked to smell the shirts blindfolded, ranking the smells from most desirable to the least. The women mostly agreed on who smelled the nicest (again, without any visual clues). The women were then asked to rank the men in order of physical attractiveness (by looking at pictures). Surprisingly, those that were rated the highest for smell were also independently ranked as more attractive visually. It therefore seems that attractive people smell good. It is possible that this function might be to motivate mating with males who possess genes that increase offspring viability or other components of offspring fitness, such as sexual attractiveness (Møller & Alatalo, 1999).

Further supporting this (although I can find no academic citation for it), I once saw Professor Thornhill on a television show. Here, he asked 10 men and 10 women (all heterosexual and single) to wear a plain white T-shirt for several days. The 10 men were then asked to fold their shirts and place them on a table as to be indistinguishable from one another. He then asked each woman to independently smell and then rank each shirt without knowing whom the shirt belonged to. He did the same for the men with the women's T-shirts. He then tabulated the matching of the smells, and by the results predicted who would partner up with whom in a social setting. The 20 participants, who had no notion of their rankings nor had ever seen the others, were then instructed not to shower or wear scents before attending a party of the 20 participants. At the end of the night, the men and women broke into pairs according to the odor preference they indicated on the smell test, proving Thornhill correct.

Pheromones may also be part of a phenomenon known as genetic sexual attraction. This is an occurrence of being strongly sexually attracted to a biological relative after being raised away from them throughout the course of one's youth, and then meeting them for the first time (as an adult). A number of adopted children, for example, find that when as adults they meet the parent or sibling they never knew, they find overwhelming and sustaining sexual desire for them—always along sexual orientation lines. This has led to a number of adults falling in love with genetic relatives. There is only one academic research article on genetic sexual attraction (Greenberg & Littlewood, 1995), and it explains it through the same Freudian psycho-babble that I discussed in Chapter 4 (the same nonsense that was used to explain homosexuality). But in talking to those affected by genetic sexual attraction, it is my sense that it is more of a process of chemical attraction through olfactory attraction and the perceptual bias that Little and Jones (2006) discuss. This is then combined with a psychological factor of longing to know one's birth relatives when you have been deprived of that privilege. It is so overwhelming and mysterious that upon meeting, the bonding process is intense; reuniting is crammed into months of what would have taken place naturally over years if they were raised in the birth family. I discuss genetic sexual attraction here because it is yet another indicator that sexual attraction is more than visual—and it reminds us that nonmonogamies are not the only sexual taboo our society desperately needs to overcome.

This also leads me to suggest that we underestimate what can be obtained from smell. Medicine now uses machines that detect odors in the detection of disease. We even have dogs to help sniff out various types of cancer. I would not be surprised if we also found a relationship between sexuality and the smell one emits. I have long suspected that, in close corridors (where other smells cannot interfere), olfactory cues help gay men pick other gay men out of a group,.

Collectively, all of this face-judging and armpit-smelling suggests that, just as when two dogs meet, a lot of biological interaction occurs when two people meet. One might be highly aroused or repelled by another's smell (not always being consciously aware of it) and stimulated or deterred by the symmetry and other features of the person's face. The point is, before we begin social and psychological interactions with another person, we are first attracted or repelled by the person's biology. We more often position ourselves into their lives because of biological cues that interest us, not their social standing. It is normally this immediate sense of attraction that gets one "in the door" to a romantic relationship, not "how nice" someone is.

ATTRACTIVENESS BIAS, THE PRIMARY EFFECT

It is perhaps a sad reflection that bias toward good looks is so built into us. This clashes with other factors that make for good long-lasting relationships (more on that later), but it also biases us toward privileging people we find good looking. I recall, for example, being a graduate student standing alongside my PhD advisor. She was approached by a stunningly good-looking undergraduate male with a sob story about why he should be permitted to add a class the rules said he could not. Despite my internal desire that she accept him (solely because he was so attractive), my advisor refused. The shockingly good-looking boy seemed rather confused. After he left, my advisor suggested that she could tell he was used to getting what he wanted because of his looks. It was an eye-opening statement to me. I realized that I was not only partial to him aesthetically, but that I let that bias enter into my judgment about how I would treat him. It is the same "cute factor" that biases us toward the eating of or saving of certain animals over others. I now realize that, on a daily basis, I privilege people for their attractiveness. I am more prone to tolerate the disagreeable personality traits of someone good looking than I am to someone who is not.

Asch (1946) was the first to discuss this type of discrimination, calling it the primary effect. He found that the first information received about a person (usually visual) was more important than information gained later. In other words, first impressions matter the most. Later studies support this, showing that good looks are positively associated with multiple types of qualities, including friendliness and intelligence. Good-looking people are thought to be more sociable, kind, sensitive, and healthy (Feingold, 1992). Good-looking people are even thought to be more likely to have better job prospects than unattractive people (Dion, Berschied, & Walster, 1972).

In addition to these characteristics, Feingold (1992) conducted a meta-analysis of 200 studies on the association between good looks and personal traits, concluding that physically attractive people were perceived to be leaders, mentally healthy, and more socially skilled than physically nonattractive people. Good-looking people were therefore found to be less lonely, less socially anxious, more popular, more socially skilled, and more sexually experienced than unattractive people. Showing that this is not always driven by sexual desire (unless we are all subconsciously attracted to children), Dion et al. (1972) even found an attractiveness bias working against young children. When given photographs and written accounts of similar behaviors of 7-year-old children, adult participants were more likely to state that unattractive children had antisocial tendencies than the attractive ones.

Popkins (1998) proposes that some of these prejudgments might become true because we believe them, because we have validated these ideas in our experiences. Certainly one reason that physical appearance is a major factor in the development of personality is that attractive individuals are treated better, so they perhaps develop more desired social qualities. Furthermore, people who are expected to be nice will be told that they are nice, and they will live up to this expectation—a self-fulfilling prophecy. Given all of this positive bias toward attractive people in most aspects of our social lives, it is unremarkable that we privilege good-looking people in choosing to pursue a romantic relationship.

6

The Development of Romantic Relationships

In the previous chapter I defined the scientific basis of what causes sexual attraction in humans. In this chapter I discuss various types of love and the stages of relationship development that a couple goes through. I analyze the variance between what we are socialized to think and feel about romantic love, and how love actually plays out over the course of a relationship. I juxtapose sex alongside this relationship development, showing that at the start of a relationship sex is new and exciting, so it occurs frequently and with high exuberance. However, sex grows dull as a relationship progresses. In other words, as a relationship grows stronger emotionally (over the months and years), it grows weaker sexually.

Ultimately, it appears that natural chemical and social processes of coupling assure we hook up and blissfully stay with a partner for about 3 months, but in time these chemical love drugs wear off. This permits/influences psychological confrontation. I show that this is why so many relationships break up around the 3-month mark. I then show that, for couples who make it through the storming stage, by about 2 years, the desire for extradyadic sex (sex with others) becomes stronger, so that even those who once adamantly supported monogamy find themselves looking for extradyadic sex. It is here that they enter the monogamy gap (Chapter 9).

The stage model of dyadic relationship development I present in this chapter is unique in that it is, to my knowledge, the first interdisciplinary attempt at analyzing how we form dyadic relationships and how they unravel. I draw from psychology, sociology, and biology, which are complimentary, in how we navigate romantic relationships and discuss how our dyadic sex patterns operate within various stages.

DEFINING LOVE

Defining what a loving relationship is, and how it does or does not differ from a friendship, is in and of itself a daunting task (Nardi, 1999). At a psychoevolutionary level it seems fairly obvious that one type of love involves two or more self-conscious beings who work together to meet each other's needs for attachment, caregiving, and perhaps (but certainly not conditionally) sex. This type of love is likely to have its antecedents in the attachment between a child and parent. This is where love is most likely learned.

The ancient Greeks had four different types of love: *philía*, *éros*, *agápe*, and *storgē*. Although precise meanings are hard to interpret because these terms are contextualized according to our current culture, the basic notion is that *philía* refers to the love of a friend; *éros* refers to sexual passion; *agápe* refers to the romantic love of one's partner; and *storgē* refers to the love of a child. Noteworthy to this classification system is that love for one's partner and sexual passion are described as two *separate* kinds of love. It is these sometimes complementary but not interrelated concepts of *éros* and *agápe* that I am most concerned with in this chapter, although I occasionally draw on the concepts of *philía* and *storgē* for comparison. I highlight these Greek forms of love to indicate that organizing love into separate types is an ancient understanding.

A 20th-century interdisciplinary perspective on emotional/romantic love comes to us through the work of John Bowlby's (1969, 1979) *attachment theory*. This theory posits that infants latch on to primary caregivers (and this is not limited to a biological parent) as an evolutionary mechanism to protect them in their vulnerable years. Proponents of attachment theory conceptualize that, while we never lose our attachments to our parents, we develop a need to transfer that primary attachment to another (a partner) as an adult. Thus, we seek romantic partners as attachment figures in adulthood. Those familiar with the Freudian theory of the Oedipus complex will find similarity in this argument.

From an evolutionary perspective, attachment theorists argue that having a partner is thought to be crucial in times of hardship or need (Hazan & Zeifman, 1999). This certainly makes sense with human infants, who are born helpless, compared to other infants in the animal world. But I maintain more skepticism about Bowlby's stated purposes of adult attachment. The reason I use restraint in applying attachment theory to adults is that it seems as adults we need a community, a tribe, to thrive. Thus, attachment in adulthood is likely to come less from the need for protection, and more for the desire of procreation. Our adult attachments are more likely an evolutionary mechanism to assure that we seek carnal pleasure. I'm not saying that the only reason people enter coupledom is for sex, but I'm saying that the biological drive for coupledom is likely to be less than the biological drive for sex.

I also find the use of attachment theory oftentimes preposterous. This is particularly true when proponents of attachment theory attempt to explain the origins of male homosexuality through the presence of an overly strong mother figure and an absent father figure (Seutter & Rovers, 2004).

Whatever the reasons for our adult attachments, it is important to note that *not everyone* a person "dates" becomes a major attachment figure. Instead, there is a social process during which time we transfer our attachment from one individual to another, and the entry into this process comes through subconscious impulses derived by millennia of evolutionary history. Thus, the transformation of a stranger into a romantic partner, and then finally an attachment figure (as a couple) is a gradual process fraught with peril. Ultimately, the type of romantic love we seek through our very modern notion of love is not the result of biological urges but our social expectations (Ryan & Jethá, 2010). This highlights that our social definition of love is historically dependent. In other words, what it means to love one's partner today varies greatly from what it meant to love one's partner a decade, a century, or a millennium ago.

Understanding the complexities of love is also made more difficult when adding sexual attraction into the mix. Most of us will know from personal experience that sexual attraction is likely to overinflate our notions of romantic love: Our sexual desires are likely to influence us to think we "love" someone, when we simply want to have sex with that person. Sex acts as a drug to induce or exaggerate emotional love, but it is not in and of itself a form of romantic love. To think that sexual desire is love is to fall into the monogamy trap that produces and reproduces the monogamy gap. Further complicating matters, romantic love (in the presence or absence of sex) need not be reserved for other human beings. Some are also capable of attaching to animals or even objects (objectum sexuality) with the same (or higher) intensity.

Finally, whatever romantic love is, its importance and centrality in our lives is evidenced not only by the intensity of joy that we feel when "falling" in love with that person but it is also evidenced by extreme emotional jealousy and pain we feel when that attachment is threatened or taken from us. We fear losing our love partners in a way that is unique compared to losing others. In fact, studies show that when one's long-term love partner dies, the chances of the surviving partner dying dramatically rise (Martikainen & Valkonen, 1996), something known as the widowhood effect. A recent study even shows that the rejection experienced when being broken up with, physically hurts. Using magnetic resonance imaging, the study found activation of the sensory component of the brain known to be used in experiencing physical pain. This demonstrates that romantic rejection and physical pain are similar not only in that they are both distressing, but that they share a common somatosensory representation as well (Kross, Berman, Mischel, Smith & Wager, 2011). Accordingly, an equally important way of measuring the worth of love is not just the joy it provides but also the anxiety, boredom, anger, jealousy, and intense sorrow and physical pain experienced when romantic relationships go poorly, are lost, or are taken from us.

Perhaps all that can be definitively said about love is that, in all their immeasurable varieties, love is a dynamic emotional state, constantly changing in type, intensity, and meaning. Love is a dynamic social process that includes a multiplicity of evolutionary, social, and historical factors that compel people to be with one another in meaningful and semi-enduring ways. So for those who will withhold poststructural critique, and for those who are somewhat willing to work with my definition of romantic love throughout the rest of this book, I will define my term: I define romantic love (for purposes of this research only) as a dyad of two consenting adolescents/adults, in which goods, services, emotions, and needs are exchanged and met. I recognize it as a form of relationship that we personally, socially, and sometimes legally privilege above other equally important types of love. It normally occurs with sexual activity, at least in the onset, but sexual activity is not required, and quite often, long-term romantic love—the type that lasts until old age—the type most people aspire to—lacks a sexual component at all.

WHY MEN DESIRE ROMANTIC LOVE

Many readers will be familiar with the work of Buss (1995), who surveys 10,047 people in 37 cultures to show that in the pursuit of a mate, heterosexual women prefer men who possess money, resources, power, and high social status. Conversely, heterosexual men tend to seek youthful and attractive women who will remain sexually faithful. Buss argues that these are ingrained psychological mechanisms rooted in each gender's adaptive responses over millennia of human evolution. But men desire romantic love for socially constructed reasons as well. And, despite all of the changing social structures to our relationships—the increased divorce rate, delayed onset to marriage, and an increase in the number of people forming unions outside of marriage—the desire to establish long-term, romantic dyads has not changed much. Thus, the desire *not to be single* results from both biological and socially constructed origins (Fisher, 2004).

Evolutionarily speaking, it is also asserted that our desire to be with other people comes from the evolutionary advantage that being in a pack offers: safety and security as we developed as a species. That being said, the development of a dyadic (pair-bonded) relationship is even more important to our social health today. This is because along with modernity came new ways of forging a living that often involve moving away from the tribe (i.e., to go to college or to take a job).

Today's families are geographically dislocated; people move rather frequently. In earlier historical eras, one who did not marry could rely on extended family support and longer term friendships to hedge against loneliness. Today, however, such social networks are limited, and this places more stress upon an individual to find a partner in order to ward off loneliness. Considering this form of familial alienation, Kontula and Haavio-Manila (2004) write:

> The implication of not having a long term romantic relationship is loneliness. The lack of alternative outlets for emotional expression and affective attachments has increased the personal stakes of not only finding a partner but also choosing one who will provide a continuing source of emotional fulfillment (p. 81).

Simon and Barrett (2010) suggest that although social scientists have long assumed that relationships are more closely associated with women's emotional health, an accumulating body of evidence reveals no gender differences in the advantages of marriage and disadvantages of unmarried statuses when males' and females' distinct expressions of emotional distress are considered. Similarly, married men are reported as being emotionally happier compared to men who are not (Waite & Gallagher, 2001). Simon and Barrett (2010) add:

> Similar findings have emerged from research on the association between the quality of marital relationships and mental health; the emotional benefits of partner support and costs of partner strain are evident for symptoms of depression among women and substance problems among men. These recent findings have led to the conclusion that there has been a convergence in the importance of intimate social relationships for men's and women's mental health (p. 169).

This is supported by the fact that despite the growing culture of hooking up and the increased availability of sex, men still desire an emotional relationship. Raley, Crissey, and Muller (2007) use the *National Longitudinal Survey of Adolescent Health* data to show that the majority of young adults reported having a special romantic relationship in the past 18 months. My fear is that readers might think that because a culture of hooking up exists for today's youth (Bogle, 2008), it means that male youth are increasingly less interested in relationships and/or that they might be happier without them. This is not the case. Men in this study were worried about being single; those who have not dated much, or who are currently single, expressed a strong desire to be coupled. For example, Tim said:

> I haven't had a girlfriend in over a year now. It sucks. I want that intimacy. I mean, I have my friends, and I love them and all, but it would be nice to have that special someone. As gay as it may sound, I miss doing date things; you know, being romantic and all. It particularly sucks if I'm invited to go out with John and his girlfriend. I just feel like a third wheel.

Part of the "happiness" that Tim imagines he will have with a relationship, and that research confirms exists for men in happy relationships, is the emotional support that one receives from a partner. Supportive relationships are associated with higher levels of well-being; conversely, strained relationships are related to a decrease in psychological functioning and increased substance abuse (Umberson et al., 1996; Williams, 2003). Research also finds no significant gendered difference in the support or strain that a relationship causes to men or women when things go wrong. Men might deal differently with their stress in breaking up than women (men drink more, women use more verbal catharsis), but relationships are still important to young men today (Umberson et al., 1996).

The central question of importance with this research is not why we continue to feel that we need to fulfill our emotional needs with dyadic relationships (as opposed to polyamorous ones), but why we feel that we need to couple exclusive *sexual* desires and behaviors to just one partner when we decide to devote emotional exclusivity to them. In other words, why don't we recognize that one can have sex without love?

CATEGORIZING ROMANTIC LOVE

In this section I borrow from the work of psychologist Robert Sternberg (1986) to describe various *types* of romantic love. Notably, Sternberg contends that romantic relationships can be understood through three main constituents: intimacy, passion, and commitment.

1) *Intimacy* refers to an emotional closeness; a connectedness and bondedness that comes as a relationship matures. Intimacy is the desire for closeness with another—a sense of oneness. However, it should be noted that intimacy does not automatically grow as a relationship progresses, as it is also possible for couples to grow apart, particularly if they remain together solely for economic or familial reasons.

2) *Passion* refers to the drives that lead to romance, physical attraction, and most important, sex. One way of describing passion is by calling it erotic love, a compulsion to be around the other person regardless of the consequences. I will later describe the influence of hormones in creating a sense of passion that might also be understood as obsession. We (rightly or wrongly) recognize passion as an inhibitor of reason, so much so that we permit humans to receive lighter punitive measures when we determine that a crime of bodily injury, or even murder, occurs out of passion compared to other emotional states (Lazarus & Lazarus, 1994). Killing a lover in a rage because one caught him or her cheating in the bedroom is a crime of "passion," but killing a stranger who has cheated us out of money is to act "in cold blood." Thus, passion is commonly understood as such an intense emotional liking and sexual attraction for another that it defies self-control.

3) *Commitment* involves decision making about the existence of potential long-term coupling—personally, socially, and legally. Johnson (1999) expands upon the commitment portion of this equation by noting that individuals can commit to relationships for three distinct reasons. The first is personal; here individuals are in the relationship because they desire to be so. The second is structural; here those who commit to a relationship do so because they feel they must for financial, social, or other socially constraining factors. The final reason people commit is moral; here strong religious or cultural compulsions force us to remain married (or partnered) regardless of whether one is happy with the relationship or not. In any given relationship these three types of love

(commitment, passion, and intimacy) appear in different combinations and quantities.

There is a romantic matriculation process in contemporary culture. It begins with high passion, the relationship then progresses through the development of intimacy, and then leads to long-term emotional, financial, and social commitment. It is this matriculation that I now turn my attention to.

EXISTING RELATIONSHIP MODELS

Psychology has invested much of its early history in creating stages of human development. Gessel, Piaget, Erickson, Freud, Vygotsky, Chodorow, Levinson, Gould, Sheehy, and many others have attempted to explain various aspects of human behaviors through models of growth and development. Sociologists also propose stage models to explore relationship development; they are particularly keen on stages that involve the interaction of groups of human beings. Whoever develops them, most models describe relationships as being progressive. These are models in which one stage is replaced with, or at least bleeds into, another. A few propose relationship models as a spiral or a scaffold to show that the progression from one stage to the next is not so easily definable, but the core concept is that a relationship is a dynamic entity, always shifting and changing.

Mark Knapp's (1984) relationship escalation model is popular in explaining the immediate formation of a couple in the early days of their relationship. Knapp's model describes the first stage of a relationship lasting just seconds (initiation), in which sexual attraction is visually established. Next comes verbal communication to access interest in other aspects of the person (known as experimenting). Self-disclosure becomes the characteristic of the third stage (intensifying), and it is here that commitment begins to be expressed. The final stage (bonding) comes through the clarification of a formal relationship.

Opposite Knapp's finite stages, McWhirter and Mattison (1984) propose six stages that encompass relationships over the course of decades. The first stage they propose *blending* basically contains most of what Knapp's total of stages express. They then describe five other stages: nesting, maintaining, building, releasing, and (after 20 years) renewing.

Finally, Bruce Tuckman (1965) describes a useful four-stage model of team development: forming, storming, norming, and performing (he added adjourning in the 1970s) that many people find useful for all types of situations (friendships, relationships, and small groups). Although this model originated for the discussion of team development (in sport), and included information on leadership styles, I find it also reflects what occurs in romantic relationships.

All of these models capture parts of the occurrences of romantic relationships, but they fail to account for how sexual attraction and/or sex develops between two people. Furthermore, few of these models incorporate biology into an explanation of how we develop relationships. Thus, to explain what occurs in the development of romantic relationships and advance our understanding of the subject, I provide an interdisciplinary approach to relationship progression. That is to say, I draw from sociological, psychological, and biological literature on dating in enhancing the three aforementioned models.

I do not attempt to privilege any one discipline in the development of my model, but I recognize that one who studies neurochemistry might feel my model does not do justice to what occurs in the early minutes of a relationship. Equally, a sociologist of ageing might find my model excludes how older couples form and relate to one another. The model I propose is a melding of the aforementioned models, and it is targeted for understanding the relationship formation of young couples.

INTERDISCIPLINARY MODEL OF DYADIC RELATIONSHIPS

Stage One: Attraction

Sexual attraction is clearly very important in the initial stages of a relationship. As I discussed in the previous chapter, we recognize attraction to another in just a fraction of a second (Knapp, 1984). And while attraction is not necessary for the formation of a romantic relationship (some people do form romance despite a lack of sexual attraction), attraction is usually the first step in a relationship.

Stage Two: Posturing

After a man sees someone he is attracted to, he then must get the person's attention. This is known as posturing, and it is about making one's mark. The first objective is to make initial social contact with the object of affection, while presenting oneself in the best possible light. This initial contact sometimes occurs through the "opener" or "pickup" line, which is crafted to represent a certain identity. Increasingly, youth also posture in befriending someone on Facebook. Here, they wait for the other to appear online for a chat—a situation that provides a slower conversation and more opportunity to choose one's words skillfully.

Whether it is a formal date or casual conversation, the next step in developing a dyadic relationship is that time is secured to "hang out" with the other person. Still, thanks to the Internet, infatuation can occur even without having ever met the other person.

Stage Three: Infatuation

Early into a relationship men describe a neurological passion that heightens their emotional attraction for the other person. This passion, which I describe as romance and attraction in absence of history, intimacy, and commitment, is per-haps best described as *infatuation*. Feeling a chemical infatuation for someone we do not know is natural; and in and of itself, it is unproblematic.

We tend to choose our romantic partners for reasons of heightened neurological/ sexual stimulus, not because they are "nice" or "caring." We let our aesthetic and pheromonal attraction influence us to make that first move, not our deeper under-standing of the qualities of character the other person possesses. Furthermore, we generally do not make decisions intellectually about who we *feel* this sexual passion for. We may let positive knowledge of a person enhance our passion, but our independent judgment of how well we might get on with a certain person is a poor indicator of whether we will feel sexual passion for him or her.

Where it becomes interesting, however, is when this initial passion is misunder-stood as "love at first sight." People do not necessarily understand their feelings as infatuation. Instead, they often believe that they are in love early into their rela-tionships. Love to them is characterized by intense passion, and this passion comes before intimacy or commitment. Unfortunately—and with heavy influence from Hollywood—it is this (fleeting) component of passionate relationships that we tend to privilege. People often mistakenly believe that when they feel passion, the other components of love are also present. Recent research even shows that men in a heterosexual relationship are more likely to mutter the words, "I love you" before women. On average, men studied said that they admitted to thinking about confessing love six weeks earlier that their female partners (Ackerman, Vladas & Norman, 2011). Of course, this doesn't mean that men and women interpret these words similarly. Men might be using the words as a method of securing sex.

Because we live in a monogacentric culture, most are easily coerced into sexu-ally committing to a monogamous relationship without even the knowledge of the general background of an individual. This early commitment is so outrageous that many of the men in my study even maintained an expectation of monogamy *before* a first date. Highlighting this, one of my participants, Caleb, recently com-mitted to being monogamous with a guy he had only met on the Internet. They exchanged photos and shared emotional intimacy before declaring themselves boyfriends. They declared their monogamy toward one another, and for 6 months Caleb went without sex, waiting to see his boyfriend after university broke for the summer. As one might predict, his boyfriend turned out to be someone other than the photos indicated. Caleb was an extreme example, but the point is that in a monogacentric culture we normally add commitment to relationships with people we hardly know.

Infatuation is also biologically based. As biologists have shown, in the initial stages of courtship we swoon because of a release of oxytocin, which provides a sense of joy and love (Carter, 1998). Because of its ability to make us swoon for another, oxytocin is sometimes known as the love drug. Those familiar with impassioned romance will undoubtedly know the feeling. But oxytocin is also released through good food and even red wine. It is released through emersion in hot water (hot tub) and even walking. It is released through touch and massage (including of a pet or holding a child). Thus, you can see why long walks, hot tubs, and dinner and drinks have grown to be standard romantic dates—not because we have socially coded them as romantic independently, but because they release a hormone that causes us to feel romantic. This has led us to socially coding them as romantic.

Finally, oxytocin is elevated in the blood stream through thrill, danger, or excitement (a scary movie, a rollercoaster, etc.) So perhaps it is no surprise that we have grown to like scary movies on dates as well. When we do these "romantic" activities, we are essentially manipulating ourselves and our dates into feeling attachment toward one another. After a romantic hand-holding walk down the beach, a good meal, glass of wine in the hot tub, and a well-oiled massage, one is now primed for sex.

Other neurochemicals are released during this stage, too: dopamine, norepinephrine, lower serotonin, and adjustments to testosterone levels may help us produce a sense of infatuation with our new partners; infatuation that often borders on obsession. These hormones help block out intellectual observations of doubt, messages that might be telling us to move on to another partner. It chemically locks us onto an individual, which makes for great sex (Robinson, 2010).

Stage Four: (Chemical) Romance

Romance is heavily influenced by a number of factors: biological, psychological, and cultural factors all play a role in creating and enhancing a sense of romance. I outline several of the contributing factors in subsections, but the overall picture of stage four remains an enhanced sense of romance—a wondrous bliss that makes us feel on top of the world.

SEX

The romance stage is characterized by *lots* of sex. This is partially because the relationship is new, but it is even more impassioned for men in my study than it would be for older adults. This is because many had only had one serious sexual relationship (some had none) and there is novelty for young men in being able to have sex at their will. In other words, the men in my study are at the onset of their sexual lives. They have coveted the other person's body and now (finally!) they have access to it. Accordingly, there is a lot of sex in this period, often occurring several times a day. Men say that they revel in doing what they had always dreamed of doing—frequent sex.

Schwartz and Young support this finding (2009):

> The length of time that people have been together has its own independent effect on sexual frequency, an outcome that shows up almost immediately. The flipside of the honeymoon period early in a relationship, when newness fuels desire and couples take the time to interact sexually three or more times a week, is a dramatic diminishment of response and behavior after about 1 year (p. 5).

Sex in this stage is about more than just the thrill of orgasm. Research on sex at this stage of a relationship suggests that it has two somewhat opposing effects. First, couples spend a great deal of time cuddling, holding, caressing, and exploring each other's bodies, which bond them together. However, it can also have the long-term effect of pushing them apart.

Neurologically, sex in this stage is highly rewarding. The neurotransmitter dopamine provides feelings of enjoyment similar (but less intense) to what one feels on heroin. This motivates a person to repeat the behavior. Highlighting this, brain scans show a rapid rise in dopamine levels during partnered orgasm but interestingly, not during masturbation (Holstege et al., 2003). But dopamine falls rapidly following orgasm in both males and females, where it is replaced with rising levels of a hormone called prolactin, which is associated with the opposite of pleasure— sensations of despair (Suleman et al., 2004). Post-sex blues is not a sexual behavior commonly discussed, but a recent study of more than 200 young women has found one in three (32.9 per cent) had experienced the phenomenon at some point (Bird, Schweitzera & Strassberg, 2011). In fact, 10 per cent experienced it most of the time. Known as postcoital dysphoria, it may express itself in immediate feelings of melancholy, tearfulness, anxiety, irritability or a feeling of restlessness.

Science has yet to determine how long prolactin remains elevated after human orgasm, and its not known if postcoital dysphoria is entirely biological, psychological or both, but the belief is that the pleasurable experience of the orgasm, combined with wanting to ward off despair, leads us to seek more sex (perhaps days later). Thus, in a relationship with lots of sex, dopamine levels can be elevated for weeks, or even months. Eventually however, in both men and women, excess levels of prolactin build up, causing a loss of libido, anxiety, headaches, mood swings, and depression (Heaton, 2003). The point is, our sex is particularly rewarding at first, but it wanes in time. I am not claiming that these varying chemicals are the root source; Robinson (2010) suggests that another source might be changes in the nerve cell receptors because of habituation to sex with the same person. Either way, the end result is that we experience a habituation which prompts us to seek novelty. It may even be that the common-held advice couples receive about creating novelty in their sex lives is facilitating a faster habituation (Robinson, 2010).

LIMERENCE

The sexual passion couples feel in the romance phase is enhanced by selectively seeking and adding desirable characteristics of their personality into their general evaluation of their romantic partner. Dorothy Tennov (1979) conceptualizes this as *limerence*. Here, men obsessively think about their partner and they strongly desire to hear their interest repeated back to them. They feel a sense of elation when they learn of the other's interest in them, and this begins a process of overemphasizing the other person's positives. This is the type of date where you run home to tell your friends just how wonderful the guy or girl was. The neurological excitement is so intense that you convince yourself that you are "in love" with the other person, even though you know very little about him or her.

This process of selectively seeking information is hampered, however, when you find out that the individual you desire falls outside of your own culture of social parameters. One of the most replicated findings of relationships is that attraction alone is not always enough to forge a relationship. Instead, attracted individuals tend to act on that attraction when they have relatively equal social status (Schoen & Weinick, 1993). This is enhanced by the fact that people tend to inhabit spaces of similar social status (Baker, 1984). Equal status contact has also been found in friendship patterns and professional relationships (Fischer, 1982; Laumann, 1973; Nardi, 1999). These studies find that couples are more likely to establish relationships with people who share gender, age, race, and religious status.

STRATEGIC SELF-PRESENTATION

The romance phase of a relationship is also characterized by a strong sense of strategic self-presentation (Goffman, 1959). There are multiple types of strategic self-presentation, but the core concept is that when you first meet someone (particularly on a first date), and even into the first several months of a relationship, you strategically select what you reveal about yourself in order to present your *best* image. You therefore selectively watch what you say, how you act, and how you hold your body. You desire the other person to only see the best in you, so you avoid controversial topics and embarrassing issues. You only discuss moments in your life that were in some way embarrassing if you simultaneously poke fun at yourself. In the early days of a relationship, people therefore try to convey what they think their desirable personal characteristics are to their potential partner through acting out a performance.

This is not to say that we do not let people into what Goffman (1959) calls our back stage. I desire to be clear here: Self-disclosure *is* fundamental to the romance stage (Giddens, 1992). Disclosure builds trust between couples at this stage of the relationship, but it is important to understand that it is selective disclosure. One might reveal secrets that endear oneself to his or her partner, but not secrets that do not. Baumeister and Bratslavsky (1999) define this type of long-term intimacy as involving the "mutual disclosure of personal information resulting in an empathic, sympathetic, mutual understanding that enables each person to feel that the other understands him or her" (p. 51).

The flip side of strategic self-presentation is that in the early days of growing to know someone we are much more tolerant toward the person's misgivings. For example, a friend of mine, Tom, once told me that he loathed a particular television show, but because his date was highly attractive he withheld his true feelings for the show, even pretending to enjoy it. Thus, the romance stage is also characterized by myopia—having tunnel vision (a skitoma). These words describe a mental blocking or selecting out of information that will prevent you from more accurately judging an individual. Of course, the more attractive we find the person, the more we block out information that discredits him or her.

In this stage we are interested in giving one's partner the benefit of the doubt. Again, this is particularly true if the person is highly attractive. This tunnel vision is, of course, complicated by the fact that the other person is also in strategic self-presentation, making it harder for one to accurately see and therefore judge the negatives of another person. In other words, you only present certain parts of yourself in romance, and you only see certain parts of the other. Each exaggerates his or her positives, and each makes concessions for weaknesses that leak out. How, with all of this deception occurring, can the new lover not be viewed as perfect?

THE MEDIA'S INFLUENCE ON OUR PERCEPTIONS OF ROMANCE

All of this means that our first dates are rather thrilling. We only see the best in our partner, we have great exploratory sex, and we feel flush with chemicals that make us feel attracted and committed to the other person (Christopher & Cate, 1985; Simpson, 1987). Accordingly, the romance phase is described by heart-pounding excitement. However, it is a mistake to think of this thrill as romantic love. The conflation of passion with love is culturally produced; it is a product of modernity. And since the latter half of the 20th century we owe much of our culturally constructed notions of passion equating with love to Hollywood and cheap romance novels (Goldmeier & Richardson, 2005).

No better example of romance being mistaken for love comes from the 1997 movie *Titanic*'s main characters, Jack and Rose. Jack, a scrappy third-class passenger, "falls in love" with a first-class girl he has never met. After a few days of impassioned sex, he risks his life to save her as the boat sinks—ultimately sacrificing his life for hers. This of course makes for an epic Hollywood romance; it connects with us emotionally, and it is enhanced by an amazing score. This after all is the purpose of entertainment. But the script of *Titanic* fails to connect with us intellectually.

Exemplifying this, there is one scene in *Titanic* that resonates with viewers on a more cerebral level of what it means to be in love. The scene lasts just 2 seconds, as the boat succumbs to water. The camera glides past a nameless elderly couple who have not previously appeared in the film. As the water rapidly floods around them, they lie still in their bed—choosing to await their fate together.

In that short scene the viewer is able to determine that, juxtaposed to Jack and Rose, this couple had spent their lives together; they would now die in each other's arms. While Jack was running around like an idiot professing his love to Rose, this couple needed no such words. This quick scene resonated with the audience because, at some level, we know that *this* is "true" love. This is the commitment and the intimacy we associate with long-term love.

Stage Five: Storming

Perhaps it is a good thing that Rose lost her "lover" in *Titanic*. It allowed her to retain an idealized sense of who Jack was. She never got to know the "real"

Jack, one who would likely have infuriated her upper-class sensibilities. This is because as humans, we maintain the ability to adapt to stress or stimuli. We quickly habituate to the thrill of romance. Our nervous system grows used to stimuli, and the high it brings begins to wane. The only way to meet the threshold of excitement and romance experience again is to do something more exciting, dangerous, or novel. Doing something bigger and larger keeps romance alive. This is consistent with social learning theory: A partner's behavior becomes less rewarding as habituation sets in (Huesmann, 1980).

To keep the emotional romance alive, couples go on bigger, better, and more expensive dates. They take their first vacations together or join another couple for an evening out. Some of these activities solidify the emotional relationship, but they also provide a new sense of romance.

The same thing happens with sex. All is thrilling for a while, but by the third or fourth month of intense sexual activity, however, a certain degree of habituation has already set in. Not only does the partner fail to visually stimulate as before, but the sex grows routine as well. When this happens, couples have sex in other locations or try new positions or toys. Depending on how often they have sex, whether they live together, and whether they are in a long-distance relationship, this sometimes works for 2 or 3 years. But for the men in my study, desensitization to sex with their partner happened (on average) much sooner.

Romance also declines. This is because despite our best efforts to keep romance alive, strategic self-presentation wears off. In Goffman's terms our "front stage" (when we perform for others) begins to fade, and we let our new partners into our "back stage," where we are not so emotionally guarded. We grow tired of the acting, the policing, and the controlling of our behaviors and manners. We grow weary of avoiding political and controversial subjects. We no longer desire to misrepresent what we really think, want, or feel.

My research shows that most men have about 2–4 months of sheer bliss in their relationship before things begin to unravel. An exception comes from men who are in long-distance relationships, as these relationships significantly extend romance. This is because the members of the relationship have limited contact and thus do not habituate as quickly. For most couples, however, by the third month they grow accustomed to the relationship, and the sex becomes routine. It is therefore not surprising to know that while some men cheat during the first few months of a relationship, most do not. Sexual exclusivity permits them to protect their emotional investment, and the quality of sex is such that they do not feel somatically compelled to have sex with someone else.

Thus, as the fatigue of identity management sets in, the tunnel vision begins to fade, the sex grows more routinized, and the chemical love lessens, the veil of romance is lifted. The relationship is now set for strife.

The storming stage is perhaps best characterized as a power struggle. As self-presentation lapses, couples begin to struggle over issues of power, identity, and desire. Sometimes arguments are centered on the notion of protecting the relationship from exogamic threats (threats from outside the relationship), like jealousy of others. For example, in the early stages of a relationship, where there is no commitment but only passion, men dare not jealously inquire as to the where-abouts of their partner—there is no attempt to control the person, as this would be understood as being overly possessive/obsessed. Thus, in the romance stage, questions about one's whereabouts are framed in an upbeat, "So what did you do today?" But as the relationship develops, partners take keen interest in whom their lovers socialize with, whom they confide in, and what they do with their spare time. Their inquiry changes to questions like, "Why did you go out with John?" Similarly, one might pay for dates and feel good about it in the romance phase. But in time, paying for yet another date loses its rewarding effect—the person we pay for soon loses gratitude and grows to expect it. This leads to hidden resentments over money and power, and eventually the frustration comes out in destructive ways.

We also grow to expect our partners to place our needs and desires over their friends, forgetting that our partners have responsibilities with their friends and family, too. It is here that we can begin to feel the desire to control our partner and his or her time.

How we resolve these conflicts heavily influences our view of the relationship. For example, based on a novel study of dating couples' diaries, Downey et al. (1998) suggest that conflict resolution and relationship quality are interdependent, meaning that a partner's feelings of neglect on one day resulted in increasing levels of conflict the next. They suggest that conflict management skills during this phase of relationship development are important determinants of relationship quality.

However, in this stage of the relationship members of the couple have not yet built the communication skills necessary to deal effectively with such power struggles. This is likely to be even truer of youth. Instead, they normally approach friends with issues of concern, hoping that they will validate their own point of view, agreeing with whatever grievance they may have against their partner—who, just 3 months ago was so wonderful they never thought an argument would occur. People desire to hear from their friends that they have acted properly. They want to hear, "You are right, and she's wrong." While almost all of our friends will do this as an unwritten rule of friendship, this is not necessarily the most helpful tool in helping one learn to deal with his partner. Furthermore, if one complains too frequently about his lover to his friends, the friends will grow tired of the counseling and begin to pressure a breakup.

While the quality of sex decreases in this stage, sex can also be used as a weapon. Here, sex is withheld as punishment for violating one's emotional needs. Fortunately, this stage also includes "make-up sex." Here, couples occasionally have more impassioned sex (after fighting and making up), probably because the sex is tainted with a bit of anger.

For all of these reasons, it is at this stage that most people's relationships terminate. I cannot say what percentage of relationships progress further, but most do not: Most people break up around 3 months. Here, it is easy for those who have not grown a sense of desire to commit to the individual to break the relationship. Oftentimes relationships that end in this stage hold that the individuals are so uncomfortable around each other that they develop animosity. In other words, without a growing sense of commitment and intimacy, it is rather easy for a couple to go from romance to disdain, and to remain in a state of hostility indefinitely.

To the extent that a couple survives this period (which generally begins 3–4 months into a relationship and lasts perhaps 5 months to 2 years), it is because the couple learns to stop accusing one's partner of causing the relationship difficulties and to recognize his or her own contribution to the problem. Partners in this stage of the relationship must learn to say, "Oh, I can see now how my saying/doing that would have hurt you." When this occurs, the couple makes strides toward moving into the next stage, norming.

Stage Six: Norming

As a couple learns to communicate—to realize the role that each plays in disagreements—they begin to shed their frequent spats and bouts of fury. This is not to say that arguments and disagreements disappear forever, but it is to suggest that with each passing argument there is more time between arguments. And with each passing argument there is less of a sense of desire to break up with one's partner because of the argument. Much of this has to do with equity.

According to equity theory (Walster, Walster, & Berscheid, 1978), people who feel that they are treated inequitably will become dissatisfied and will either restore equity or terminate the relationship. Successfully navigating arguments is therefore as much about restoring equality as they are learning how to keep arguments under control.

Bowlby (1979) suggests that every interaction in which a relationship partner is helpful in alleviating distress strengthens the affectional bonds with that partner. This is because our attachment system desires stability, which is synonymous with security. By developing a commitment to alleviating stressors in the relationship, each member of the couple gradually consolidates a relationship-specific sense of attachment security. In other words, by solving problems, we engender the belief that our partner will be there for us in times of need, emotionally, physically, and financially. The knowledge of this growing standpoint leads to further attachment, which is then crucial for de-escalating other relational tensions and emerging conflicts. Thus, the storming stage, as awful as it might seem while one is going through it, provides a positive emotionality of security and commitment, which encourages relationship stability when successfully resolved in the norming stage.

There are many reasons why couples *successfully* argue in this stage. First, couples learn not to drag past discretions into their arguments. They also learn to keep arguments to the point, rather than developing them into the type of argument that becomes about arguing for its own sake. Furthermore, when arguments occur, they are resolved much more quickly than they used to be. Part of this is because, in this stage of a relationship, one begins to look for one's own faults and contributions to the stressors/arguments in a relationship. Couples learn a communication style that is more conducive to discussing issues, setting rules and practices in place to prevent harmful incidents from occurring again.

In other words, the decrease in frequency and intensity of arguments occurs because a couple manages conflicts more constructively: through negotiation, compromising, and resolving disagreements (Laursen, 1993). For a couple, it means that systems of payment for goods and services, and variations in socialization habits and needs (with other friends) can be worked out, and that different types of power are distributed to each. In other words, this is the beginning of being a "couple" and not two individuals looking to meet independent needs.

Part of this negotiation also comes in the establishment of overt rules. But the development of rules is really a symbol of something perhaps more important: commitment. Rusbult (1980) shows us that commitment is expected to affect directly whether one stays in the relationship or leaves it. Other research shows that the perceived probability of marriage is a significant predictor of relationship stability (Hill, Rubin, & Peplau, 1976; Lloyd, Cate, & Henton, 1984). Note that I use the word *commitment* in the sense of being there for each other, of seeing emotional turmoil to a point of resolution, not sexual commitment.

This stage of a relationship also sees a growth in personal intimacy. Couples not only disclose more personal information about each other, but they begin to rely on each other to have their emotional needs met. This means that one is less likely to seek outside support in "complaining" about one's partner to friends, and it means that the couple spends greater periods of time around each other without fighting. It means that as a natural process of mutualism, each member of the couple might also slowly decrease his or her outside friendship networks, and the couple will develop mutual friends.

Accordingly, the norming phase of a relationship means that we grow more attached and secure to our partners, we feel an enhanced sense of intimacy. As the storms of the previous stage seem further and further away, we begin to make a more reasoned and real commitment to one another. However, simultaneous to the growth in intimacy and commitment (which I often just describe as history) is a decrement to one's sexual/passionate/romantic life.

Sex occurs less frequently in this stage of a relationship, and when it does occur most couples develop entrenched sexual patterns—the thrilling sexual exploration of the early relationship fades. This is also the stage in which sex increasingly becomes a tool of power. Much feminist literature discusses how sex can be a weapon used in household arguments and struggles over power (Safilios-Rothschild, 1977). Rainwater (1966) found, for example, that when there is a strong division of labor and polarized gender roles in a relationship, sexual satisfaction is lower. Accordingly, individuals who discuss their lives more openly with their partners, and share in their lives more equally, also report better sex—it becomes less of a tool of partner regulation, and more of a tool of partner celebration.

It is difficult to predict the duration of the norming phase. One can imagine that the length of this phase is probably highly dependent not only on the personalities involved but on the number of times one has made it to this point in a relationship before (and thus learned beneficial communication patterns). Finally, as with the other stages in the development of a dyadic relationship, there is no ritual that marks the end of this stage, except to say that by the end of norming, commitment is very high and couples begin to discuss formalizing their relationship.

Stage Seven: Performing

The performing stage is actuated when a couple lives their lives relatively harmoniously. Much of the performing stage is socially identified by spousal similarity in personality traits. In other words, the couple thinks and acts more alike. This type of similarity has often been thought to result from convergence (i.e., couples becoming more similar to one another over time). For example, Erik Erikson (1963) suggested that a truly mature, bonded relationship *requires* that partners become so close that the boundaries of their identities actually grow blurred (Homans, 1950). Thus, the finding that married couples are quite similar was understood as an effect of living together. However, in a more recent study of married couples (Humbad et al., 2010) researchers suggest that selection processes are better for explaining spousal similarity than psychological convergence. This does not rule out that already similar couples further blend together. For example, Humbad et al. (2010) found that if one partner maintained elevated rates of aggression over the other, the less aggressive partner was likely to increase his or her aggression as the relationship progressed. Generally, the more we interact with someone, the more we will be like him or her. And when it comes to our partner, the more we grow reliant upon him or her, the more we act as one.

As our personalities intermingle, we more fully understand how each other thinks, feels, and desires. And once a dyad has been together long enough, the relationship is viewed as a singular in their social networks, who socially bestow "couplehood" (Huston & Burgess, 1979; Parks, Stan, & Eggert, 1983). The effect of this network support on relationship stability further promotes relationship security (Lewis, 1973). In other words, a strong sense of dyadic identity, which develops in the milieu of social support from others, leads to the stability of the relationship. More practically said, one's friends and family cease to ask, "Are you still with John?" and instead ask, "How is John?" This is a social symbol that others recognize that the couple has "made it." Eventually, more formal factors further our couplehood (e.g., paying a mortgage together or raising children).

This, I argue, is long-term love. It is not the type that ends as the romance fades. This is a relationship that is extremely high in intimacy; one that is extremely high in commitment. In this stage couples develop a strong sense of history—which furthers their security and "togetherness." In this stage of a relationship couples look back to years gone by, romanticizing their former lives. They talk about the future as though it is inevitable, and being coupled promotes a better future. Studies also show that long-term couples benefit from a longer life span, lower rates of alcoholism, decreased depression (Holden 2008) and illness

(Coan, Schaefer, & Davidson, 2006). People in long-term relationships even seem to recover quicker after being physically injured (DeVries & Glasper, 2005).

One thing that this stage is not characterized by, however, is sex. In this stage of a relationship, we have a very high degree of commitment and a very high degree of intimacy, but we have a very low degree of sexual passion (Hatfield et al., 2008). We may still feel the rush of oxytocin from cuddling with our partner on the couch or taking a walk together (Carter, 1998; Holden et al., 2008), but we don't get it through sex. Even if a couple continues to have sex, the neurological excitement (the passion) that this sex provides pales in comparison to what occurred in the first few months of the relationship.

A decrease in sexual excitement—a habituation to it—might even be occurring sooner for youth today than it did for older generations. The widespread availability of sex among youth today means that they have more sexual partners than they ever did, and this might lead to the need for more variety in one's sexual life (see Chapter 12).

Highlighting this phenomenon, I recently asked my class, "For those of you who have a long-term partner of 2 years or more, how many of you were dying to give him or her a massage during the first 2 months? How many of you remember lying there just massaging them, rubbing them for an hour or more, feeling like you could do it forever?" Dozens of my students raised their arms. I then asked, "And how many of you want to do the same today?" The students laughed in recognition that within 2 years they had lost their sexual passion to voluntarily want to massage their partners.

Hollywood has falsely influenced us to perceive that love *is* infatuation: that without the strong desire to have sex with your partner—without the overwhelming swoon of erotic passion—one does not have love. This is a dangerous myth, and it leads to unnecessary relationship termination. Accordingly, I pose that we need to rethink our social definition of love. Love is not wine and roses; that's for rookies. Love is a long-standing sense of security and comfort. It is often boring, but always nice.

Stage Eight: Uncoupling

Whether it is through death, divorce, or expansion, all dyads come to an end. I do not provide a lengthy discussion about this here. This is because it is not relevant to my work on cheating while in a dyadic relationship. However, for those seeking more information on understanding our emotions when a partner dies, I recommend William Worden's *Grief Counseling and Grief Therapy* (2009, 4th ed.). For those seeking more on how long-term couples break up and why, I recommend Diane Vaughan's *Uncoupling: How and Why Relationships Come Apart* (1986). For those who find that they want to open their dyadic relationship, Tristan Taormino's *Opening Up: A Guide to Creating and Sustaining Open Relationships* (2008) is a strong place to start. Finally, for those looking for a neurobiological understanding of the stages of breaking up, I suggest reading the first chapter of *Romance and*

Sex in Adolescence and Emerging Adulthood: Risks and Opportunities (Crouter & Booth, 2006).

LIMITATIONS TO MY MODEL

There are limitations to the model I provide on the development of a dyadic relationship. For example, it may not work for younger adolescents (school-aged children). This is because relationships among younger children are inherently linked to the task of separation and individuation from the family (Gray & Steinberg, 1999). Consistent with attachment theory, the materialization of romantic activity partially exists as a more general process of the development of emotional autonomy from the authority of one's parents. Thus, parents may interfere with and control their child's dating experiences, controlling the adolescents dating life. For a staged model of how relationships operate with children, I might recommend that of Connolly and Goldberg (1999).

Brown (1999) also suggests that romantic relationships among younger adolescents might not be as "genuine" (or that they are at least different) than they are for adults. This is because these relationships are sometimes used more in an attempt to obtain or increase peer acceptance than to develop a truly intimate, inward-oriented romantic relationship.

I highlight, however, that the young men in my study have already somewhat detached from their families, something evidenced from their moving away to attend university. Brown (1999) supports this, suggesting that research on college students finds that most individuals in this age group *have* developed serious, intimate, and long-term relationships. Thus, I encourage readers not to dismiss the romantic lives of my participants—and ultimately—not to explain away their cheating behaviors by suggesting that they are not yet fully developed in their abilities to maintain meaningful romantic relationships.

My model is also more authentic for university students and young adults than older adults, because those who have been partnered for many years before breaking up and repartnering may not experience the early stages of the model the same again (Brown, Feiring, & Furman,1999). If you ride a rollercoaster once, you do not feel it the same way the second time. Older adults might even move through the stages I detail faster. I think it reasonable to suggest that two people aged 65 (who having been dating for 3 years) are probably more apt to make a decision to marry than two people aged 19 who have also been dating for 3 years. Finally, for those interested in other interdisciplinary approaches to attraction, love, and the stages of progression people go through, I might recommend Helen Fisher's *Why We Love: The Nature and Chemistry of Romantic Love* (2004).

PART THREE

Monogamy and Its Discontents

7

Categorizing Monogamy Types

My use of the term *monogamy* generally refers to an overt and/or implicit expectation that a couple is socially expected to reserve all sexual interaction (including sexual kissing) to one another. However, I understand that this social value is the outcome of a complex number of cultural, materialistic, historical, and political influences (Alexander, 1980). Some of these include religious doctrine, the notion of fraternal egalitarianism (equality among men), as well as the influence of the industrial revolution and salaried labor.

I also understand that rather than being a unitary construct, multiple categories of monogamies exist. This is because the term *monogamy* refers to a highly contestable, individualized, and socially malleable set of attitudes and behaviors (Kanazawa & Still, 1999; Remez, 2000). These meanings are currently embedded within a number of other social institutions, including religion (Willey, 2006), politics (Foucault, 1990), and the nuclear, or "standard," family (Smith, 1993).

Most of the informants in this research generally understood monogamy as a restriction of their sexual behaviors, casual conversations about "cheating" mostly bring up notions of men having vaginal (if straight) or anal (if gay) intercourse. But matters are more complex than that. Thus, this chapter is about the difficulty in defining monogamy; how monogamy means different things to different people.

THE DOUBLE MEANING OF MONOGAMY

Monogamy has two meanings—both of which are about possession. In one sense monogamy refers to a marital/partnered system of coupling, as juxtaposed to polygamy. In the other sense, monogamy is about sexual restriction to a single partner. While the two definitions of monogamy overlap, they are *defined against* two very different phenomena. In this section I explain the history behind these systems of ownership, showing that we first restricted man to just one wife, then (in only the past few centuries) we restricted him to being sexually active with just that one wife.

Monogamy as a Marriage System

The historical account of human families is more about a history of polygamy than monogamy (Duncombe, Harrison, Allan, & Marsden, 2004), particularly in the non-Western world. *The Ethnographic Atlas*, representing the largest coded database of world cultures, shows that even today 85% of cultures (not nation states) are polygamous (White, 1988). For example, polygamy continues to be legal across the Muslim world as Islam permits men to have up to four wives.

There is a rich history of polygamy in the Western world as well. The antecedents of legal restrictions to just one wife in Western cultures can be traced back to the Greek city states, Athens and Sparta, which instituted monogamy by culture and law. But this was only about monogamy through coupledom, not about monogamy as a restriction of sex. The Greek citizens were allowed to keep foreign women as concubines alongside their Greek wives (Henrich & Henrich, 2007). The spread of a formalized monogamy (i.e., the prohibition of polygamy) was then infused with Christian doctrine, which tightened the cultural mandate to just one wife of any nationality in Western nations.

The monogamization project of coupledom came to total fruition in just the previous few hundred years—in America, polygamy was, for example, legal at the signing of the Declaration of Independence. Polygamy disappeared, however, not just because of religious dogma, but it was influenced by the structural effects brought about by the industrial revolution.

Not long after the age of enlightenment (and the notion of egalitarian fraternity), we entered the "modern era," characterized by a revolution in democracy and the advancement of industry and capitalism (Cancian, 1987). Machines replaced human labor, production of goods accelerated, and wage labor replaced craftsmanship. This served to lower the prices of goods, making them available to a wider market. This new economy had a significantly powerful impact, not just on how we came to value capitalism but also on how monogamy (as coupledom) was constructed among men in Western cultures.

Although the invention of the machinery and transportation necessary for industrialization began early in the 1700s, the antecedents of the type of masculinity that I discussed in Chapter 4 as "orthodox" really did not occur until the late 1800s and early 1900s. During this period, sturdy farmers (men and women alike) exchanged (or were forced to exchange) their time-honored professions for salaried work. Families replaced their farm's rent for that of a city apartment. The allure of industry, and the better life it promised, influenced such a migration that the percentage of people living in cities rose from just 25% in 1800 to around 75% in 1900 (Cancian, 1987).

This epoch may have impacted on our value of monogamy, too. It is likely that polygamy was more advantageous in rural societies because it yielded more offspring per family unit and thus provided a higher opportunity that offspring would survive the harsh premodern infant and adult mortality rate. This was important because there was greater financial reward for larger families, particularly in farming. While children were a burden for a few years, they then provided the parents many more years of free farming labor. This may be one reason why polygamy is normal in sub-Saharan African countries today. African polygamy has helped maintain very high total fertility rates of between six and eight children in most African countries (Caldwell, Orubuloye, & Caldwell, 1991).

However, because of the industrial revolution, polygamy no longer made sense in modernized countries. As work transitioned from agrarian forms to waged labor, large numbers of children did not positively impact on the wealth of the entire family; just the opposite. Children did not work the land. Rather they became a burden on the wage of the father. In urban areas, the difficulties in forming and maintaining traditional polygamous unions were exacerbated by housing shortages, smaller houses, the high risk of unemployment, low wages, the weakened kinship network (families grew more geographically distant), and the high cost of raising and educating children (Maillu, 1988). Simply put, modernity brought an end to wanting large families because large families had to be paid for.

This means that industrialization was responsible for eliminating much of America's polygamous practices; but religion was impactful, too. Polygamy only really became a significant social and political issue in the United States in 1852, when the Mormon Church made it known that polygamy (something they call plural marriage) was part of its official church doctrine. Polygamy had been introduced by the Church in 1843 in Illinois, before most Mormons moved to Utah in 1847. It was in search of statehood in 1890 that the Mormon Church officially announced it no longer condoned polygamy.

A final reason for the death of legal polygamy came through the widespread adoption of the mostly French principles of liberty, equality, and fraternity. These are ides that provide the framework for Western nations; ideas that came with Lock, Hume, Paine, and Jefferson. America has conceptualized this through the idea that every man is "guaranteed the right to life, liberty, and the pursuit of happiness." Thus, one reason marital monogamy is esteemed over polygamy was the egalitarian/fraternal notion that all men (not women) were created equal, and therefore all men deserved a wife. If one man owned many wives, he would affectively deny other men their right to own a wife. Accordingly, monogamy, as a mandated law, seems to have come with industry, democracy, and political doctrines of equality.

Monogamy as Sexual Restriction

Because polygamy has been eliminated from most Western cultures, we don't often think about being monogamous with two or more people anymore (strictly speaking, one could be monogamous to their partners in polyamorous relationships as well). In other words, one might have two wives and reserve all sex to just these two. This would be doing monogamy within polygamy.

For the most part, monogamy today refers to the abstinence of recreational sex with others outside one's dyadic relationship (whether married or dating). This is the definition of monogamy that most of us conjure when using the term today. In other words, monogamy as a system of coupledom retains such hegemonic strength that we do not even consider that other relationship types exists. We do not consider ourselves monogamous, as opposed to polygamous or polyamorous, because these are no longer options.

Just as monogamy (as a practice of having just one wife) is not a historical norm, nor is the concept of reserving all sex for just one person. We know of a multiplicity of extradyadic sexual pleasuring methods available for men throughout history. For example, while men were prohibited from taking more than one wife in Greek and Roman times, and women were prohibited extradyadic sex, men placed themselves under no such adulterous restrictions. Men were permitted, culturally and legally, to have sex outside their marriage.

Greek men sought extramarital (or premarital) sex at the moneyed houses of the upper class. If they could not pay for the luxury of sex with a sophisticated woman, they resorted to places where women could be bought for a more modest price. In fact, it has been reported that the Greeks disdained recreational sex with their wives (Hyrum, 1885), as sex with one's wife was for procreation, while sex with others was for recreation.

In the Greek world (and still in parts of Islam today) this dictum extends to sex with postpubescent boys as well. Married men sought sex with postpubescent, but preadult boys (something known as hebephilia) by visiting public bath houses or gymnasiums, where sex with males (including other adult males) was performed without stigma (Spencer, 1995). Thus, married men (whether in monogamous or polygamous relationships) heavily guarded the chastity of their wives with vigilant jealousy and legal prohibition, while partaking in sex with unmarried women, men, boys, and girls (of a certain age).

Monogamy as a practice of sexual restriction emerged slowly in Western cultures. The hegemony of the concept of having sex with just one person in life (i.e., no sex before marriage) probably reached its height in the late 1800s, but this mantra began to fade in the 1960s. Today, it is relatively unheard of: Hooking up and premarital sex is the norm. Virginity is no longer valued as it once was.

What is important today is not lifelong monogamy; instead, it is that one is monogamous to the partner he is currently with. In other words, men are permitted to have casual sex when single; premarital sex with a partner; and casual sex with others during a breakup. Men today are not clinching to their virginity. In fact, remaining a virgin until marriage today brings bewilderment to teens. Lewis, for example, told me that he once knew a Christian guy who said he wanted to be a virgin until he was married. "I thought, *he must be gay. He's got to be just saying that as an excuse to not have sex.* Why would someone not want to have sex?" He added:

> It's not like you're judged for having sex with a girlfriend. I mean, maybe some people, I mean none of my friends, but someone, like your parents, might judge you for having a hookup. But it makes no sense to refrain from having sex with a girlfriend until your married.

Others were more understanding of the desire for restricting sex until marriage, but they found it a wholly unfathomable idea for themselves. "Look," Tommy said, "I get it. Some people are so beat down by religion that they don't want sex until marriage. But you know what they really mean is that they want it, but can't have it." Joe showed hostility toward religious doctrine of no sex until marriage, too:

> Whatever religious people wanna do, that is fine by me. I think it's weird.
> I won't judge it, but you got to realize that nobody is going to judge you for
> having sex with your girlfriend. And if they did, I think people would be like,
> "Whatever dude—keep that shit to yourself."

Thus, as unfathomable as it would have seemed to 1950s America, among the heterosexual men I interviewed today, sex is *expected* from the time they are around 16. In England, where the age of consent is 16, it is permissible even earlier. Danny said, "When I had sex for the first time, I was 14. I came home, told my dad about it, and he just asked if I used a condom."

But despite the near-total absence of a belief in lifelong monogamy (as in no premarital sex and then no divorce), serial monogamy (which is culturally just referred to as monogamy) is still strongly respected in both the straight and gay youth communities. Serial monogamy is a reflection of the vanishing taboo against hooking up. In other words, while there may be some judgment for a youth having too much casual sex (women particularly), there is no judgment if this casual sex (even for females) occurs in a relationship. There is no time frame for determining how long a couple must be together before casual sex is okay, either. It is acceptable to have sex even on the first meeting, as long as the couple intends to date.

The notion of being monogamous only when in a committed relationship is a form of serial monogamy for which there exists no (or little) cultural judgment among the men I interviewed. In other words, I'm monogamous while dating you; we break up, and I'm monogamous while dating this new person. The desire for sex, coupled with the permission to have it when one is emotionally interested in exploring being in a relationship, means that there is (for some) pressure for youth to form meaningless relationships quickly. However, this newfound social liberty brings other social burdens, too.

VARIATIONS ON MONOGAMY

In thinking about how men understand monogamy, it is evident that there are parallels to sexual orientation. For example, we commonly break down sexual orientation into three components: behavior, orientation, and identity. Behavior is "what we do," while sexual orientation is what we *desire* to do regardless of what we actually do. Thus, a closeted gay man can still have sex with women, but we generally recognize that he is nonetheless gay. Finally, identity is how we construct ourselves to align or not with social understandings of sexuality. Thus, I know men

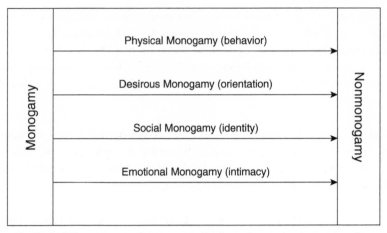

Figure 7.1 Four different types of monogamy. Each can be present in varying degrees in any given relationship.

who desire and have sex with men, but nonetheless publicly identify as heterosexual. This reflects a desire not to break from the dominant category and the power within. And, of course, this final category of identity can be broken down into personal and social. For example, I know men who are closeted, who have sex with men, desire sex with men, and personally identify as gay, but they do not identify as gay publicly.

The same analysis can be made about monogamy. Here there exists a differentiation between what we do, want, and how we identify. In each subsection that follows I discuss the basic definition and how matters are oftentimes unclear, ill-defined, and confusing (see Fig. 7-1).

PHYSICAL MONOGAMY

Of the four category types, physical monogamy is the easiest to categorize. This is because it reflects bodily, sexual behaviors. It is what one does, not what one wants to do, or how one identifies. Ant, for example, is in his second year of studies but his third year of his relationship. He says, "I'm monogamous because I don't have sex with anyone other than her. If I did I wouldn't be monogamous, now would I?" Ant thinks about other women while masturbating but maintains that this does not break his monogamous conscript because he is not acting on his desires.

However, some of the men contested what it meant to be physically monogamous, suggesting that flirting was okay, while others did not. Furthermore, many of the English men felt that they could kiss women on the cheeks, but perhaps surprisingly, others disagreed. Conversely, almost all agreed that kissing a woman on the lips would be against their monogamous rules, because this could be construed as a sexual act. Only a few men thought that they would be permitted to kiss a woman on the lips, as long as it wasn't using tongues and as long as it did not last too long. Again, few of the men discussed this with their partners.

These men also largely agreed that there was a continuum of violations to their unspoken, socially adopted rules of monogamy. A kiss on the lips was considered only a minor infraction, likely only to cause an argument with one's partner. They did not think that kissing another girl would likely result in their girlfriends breaking up with them. Furthermore, while most men thought that oral sex would be a major violation of their undiscussed understanding of monogamy, it was not thought to be *as* bad as vaginal intercourse.

Things became more difficult to define when men considered bodily pleasures that occurred in the cyber world. Some of these men considered cybersex (Webcam sex) to be cheating, whereas some did not. Frank said, "If you're just in some chat room wanking, and you are watching other people you're chatting with, that's not really cheating, is it? You're not actually doing anything with them. It's just fantasy." Others disagreed, "If you're wanking while talking to someone on the Internet, it doesn't matter whether it's just chat or camming, you're fucking cheating."

This makes even this most basic label of physical monogamy a slippery definitional category because it calls into question what "reality" is. Furthermore, almost none of the men in this study had talked about this with their partners. They mostly avoided the situation by not masturbating while on the Internet when their partners were around.

Knowing that Jarrett still has profiles posted on many gay Web sites, despite having a boyfriend, I asked him if he was allowed to look at the nude photos of the men on the profiles of the men that he was chatting to. "Yes, of course," he answered. I then asked, "And if you get horny? Are you allowed to wank while you're talking to them and looking at their pics?" Jarrett had no immediate answer. "We've not talked about that. I guess it's kinda like cheating, but it's not really cheating." I then asked Jarrett if he had ever done this. "Of course . . . but I don't do it when my boyfriend is around, that's for sure."

DESIROUS MONOGAMY

Desirous monogamy reflects participants' somatic desires, or how many sexual partners they *fantasize* about having (or would desire to have if there were no social controls on their monogamous relationships). Thus, it is similar to one's sexual orientation. It is what you want regardless of what you do, and regardless of what you tell others.

Discussions of Internet sex identify that there is a further breakdown of whether monogamy includes one's desires, or whether it only reflects a restriction on one's behaviors. For example, whereas Paul said that he would like to have sex with other women if his girlfriend would permit it (making him physically monogamous but desirously nonmonogamous), Josh (coupled for only a few months) expressed no desire to have sex with others at all. "I don't want sex with anyone else. I really don't. I'm perfectly happy having her and only her for as long as we're together." Thus, Paul does not express desirous monogamy, but Josh does.

I was surprised that a few dozen heterosexual men reported maintaining no sexual desire for other women. But then it was also evident that most of the men who advocated this position had not been in a relationship very long. Jeff, for example, was adamant that he has only ever really thought about his girlfriend. "Dude, she's hot. Why would I want to even think about anyone else?" When I asked Jeff if he thought he would feel this way in years to come, he responded, "Yeah. Why wouldn't I? She's still going to be hot." Others, however, understood that their current position of maintaining monogamous desires with their partners was only a phase. Matt said that he was very well aware that perhaps someday he would want sex with someone else. He said that because he and his girlfriend had only been together a few months, things were "all good. I see other women, but I'm happy just having sex and thinking about my girlfriend. I know it won't last, but I'm enjoying that for now."

SOCIAL MONOGAMY

Social monogamy reflects a desire to be thought monogamous by one's peers, regardless of what one does or desires. If, for example, you asked a room full of men and their wives if the men desired sex with other women, how many would say they do? Thus, social monogamy is a strategic presentation to craft the image of how people want to be perceived, regardless of what they actually do or desire.

I include anyone in this category who stick with the monogamy label, even if their behaviors did not align to it. Interestingly, with no exceptions, none of the men in this research suggested that they were not monogamous. The reason for this is clear: Men identify with monogamy, even if they are cheating. Identifying as nonmonogamous is not a reasonable social choice. Coleman (1988) suggests that even those in *open sexual relationships* normally adhere to the social definition of monogamy. This increases social capital and helps couples avoid social stigma.

Exemplifying this, I asked Jake, who admitted to several times cheating on his girlfriend, if he considered himself monogamous. "Yeah, of course," he answered. I said, "But I'm confused, you tell me that you're cheating on your girlfriend, but you still consider yourself monogamous. You're not really monogamous in that case, are you?" Jake, however, was adamant that he was. "No, I am. I am monogamous. Cheating is a violation of that rule, but it doesn't mean we're not still monogamous." Jake continued, "It's like saying you're a professor. Maybe you're sick and can't teach, but you're still a professor."

Because of the insistence of maintaining a monogamous perspective despite one's actual behaviors, I highlight that the high rate of cheating for men of this age group indicates that cheating is essentially incorporated into monogamy.

Monogamy, in its true sense, is usually just an illusion; and the illusion of monogamy is so socially desired that, just as Coleman found (1988), even those who were having extradyadic sex with their partner's permission considered themselves monogamous. For example, Collin, who considers himself very liberal, says that although he and his girlfriend of 2 years have had a few threesomes, they consider themselves nonetheless monogamous. At least that is how they present themselves to others. "Can you imagine me telling my mother that me and Amy are not monogamous? That wouldn't go over very well."

EMOTIONAL MONOGAMY

Emotional monogamy reflects that of dyadic intimacy only. Thus, having sex with a stranger would not violate this type of monogamy (unless they were also sexually monogamous), but having an emotional affair would. This category is the most complex for discussing monogamy because it includes a variety of types of affairs (work, friendship, online, and so forth) and because it might also potentially include polyamory, as well as considering definitional problems associated with the difference between friendship and a sexual and/or romantic relationship (Nardi, 1999).

Emotional monogamy is the cornerstone of open relationships, separating them from polyamorous ones. This is to say that couples in open relationships frequently have sex with strangers and some couples in open relationships make friends with some of those they have sex with. It would, however, be cheating if one member of the couple began to privilege someone else in their emotional attachment, or in providing another person with care and nurture at the expense of the partner.

It should also be pointed out that open relationships are not necessarily unstructured, or without rules. Instead, the level of discussion around the rules leads some to present open sexual relationships as superior to monogamy, not only in terms of the freedoms involved, but that the necessary levels of mutual consideration and open communication create more ethical relationships (Ho, 2006).

For example, Finn and Malson (2008) focus on "dyadic containment," which they found to be involved in the consensually nonmonogamous relationships. They argue that these relationships regulate time and emotional energy in order to muster the majority of emotional resources for the couple. In other words, they worked to maintain the safety, security, and even the specialness of their relationship from perceived dangers. Gay men and swingers, for example, commonly employ rules to distinguish the difference between sex and love. Partners in these couples are permitted sex outside their couple, but they develop strategies to prevent emotional bonds from forming with those they sexually recreate with (Adam, 2006; Bonello, 2009; de Visser & McDonald, 2007; Finn & Malson, 2008; LaSala, 2004a; Wosick-Correa, 2010).

These rules might be explicitly negotiated ahead of time or emerge as the couple navigates nonmonogamous experiences, determining which rules feel right and work for the couple and which do not. Thus, there are pluralities of ways of being sexually open in an open relationship, ways that nonetheless remain rule bound. This indicates that while open relationships contest monogamy, and are therefore political, the intention of those in the couples is not necessarily to engage in counterhegemonic activities *for* political purposes. Instead, their activities are deemed political because they are counternarratives.

At its extreme, emotional monogamy can also refer to those who prohibit friendships with others of the sex they are attracted to. For example, one of my female heterosexual students once told me that she was not permitted to have friendships with heterosexual men. This type of emotional monogamy is a power play to control one's partner out of jealousy or fear of loss. It is unacceptable to most people in modern society, and I offer a stern warning here that men who are highly jealous are much more likely to beat their partners than nonjealous men (Sharma, 1991).

Those who beat their partners are the type of men who constantly check up on them, wondering where they are; the type of men that read their partners text messages; and the type of men who say what time their partner needs to be home by. These men are more likely to commit acts of violence (Sharma, 1991). Even if these men do not end up violent, living with this type of man reduces one's social and emotional freedom. Thus, my advice is: If your partner (of any sex) is overly jealous, constantly checking up on you, and never trusting you—run! Those seeking help from domestic violence in England can visit www.england.shelter.org. Those in the United States can visit www.sheltersofamerica.com; and those in Canada can try www.shelternet.ca.

EMOTIONALLY CHEATING

Emotional monogamy helps us understand the irrationality of making physical cheating the litmus test of a relationship. Highlighting this, each year when discussing monogamy with my class, I ask the women which is more important in their relationships, the sexual connection they have with their partners or the emotional connection of honesty and communication? They always answer that it is the emotional. I then ask whether they have girlfriends (platonic) that they share emotional secrets with, things they do not tell their partners about. All do. I then remark that they are therefore emotionally cheating on their partners, and I highlight the fact that because they say they value honesty and their emotional connection to their partner more, this means that their emotional cheating is more damaging than their physical cheating.

These women are quick to defend themselves. They rationalize that we all need more than just one person in our lives; that it is healthy for them to vent issues with others and not their boyfriends. To this, I agree. But I then ask why they take this disposition on emotional sentimentality; why they take this position on having multiple friends, but they do not take this position on sex? Why can they not see that sex with others can also be healthy for a relationship? The answer, of course, is because they haven't learned this lesson yet—society doesn't let them. They have learned to be emotionally promiscuous and sexually monogamous.

LEARNING TO BE MONOGAMOUS

In interviewing men about monogamy it becomes abundantly clear that youth do not sit down and rationally discuss the variety of monogamy types and their perspectives with their partners. They do not formulate rules at the outset of a relationship. Instead, they "go with the flow." Practically speaking, what this means is that they adopt the dominant social messages about monogamy. In some senses this is clear; physical monogamy is expected from the moment a couple first dates. But when it comes to desirous or emotional monogamy, society has no clear mandates. This is why Jarrett had not negotiated his rules with his new boyfriend; they don't have as many cultural scripts to replicate. When discussing whether masturbation on the Internet is acceptable he says, "We just don't discuss it. I don't bring it up, because my fantasies always involve someone else." Some even thought that thinking of others while masturbating was an undefined area. Hayden said, "Because I don't think of her 100 percent of the time I'm getting off, somehow it means I don't love her anymore." Hayden continued, "I do love her, but when she says stuff like that; that is what makes me love her less."

These findings relate to the next chapter because they indicate that monogamy is not made through free will, or even rational choice. Monogamy exists as the only acceptable form of romantic coupling; all other forms are highly stigmatized. This is monogamism.

8

Monogamism

A key reason why men think that monogamy will provide them with a lifetime of sexual fulfilment is because our sexual freedoms have been promulgated, controlled, and sometimes even legislated by religion and government. Monogamy is currently shrouded in robust myths about being healthy, proper, moral, and natural. If it were not for the strength of the myths surrounding monogamy, young men and women would enter dyadic relationships with a greater understanding of the diminishing quality and quantity that long-term partnered sex provides. However, monogamy maintains such cultural privilege that it escapes almost all critical scrutiny.

In this chapter I first explain why social conservatives desire for us to be monogamous before using Antonio Gramsci's hegemony theory to explain monogamy's cultural esteem. This theory, originally written to explain political processes of domination and subordination, has also been applied to the concept of ruling cultural ideas and morals. I use it to explain monogamy's position as the only acceptable form of relationship before highlighting some pockets of resistance to the grip that monogamy has over romantic-sexual lives in Western cultures. It is important to understand how we are constructed to value monogamy, because key to my dyadic dissonance theory is that men are placed into cognitive dissonance (Chapter 9) because of a contrast between what they sexually desire and what society says they should desire.

THE CONSERVATIVE PROJECT OF SEXUAL CONTROL

Just why are the members of influential institutions, primarily religion and government, concerned with regulating who we have sex with, what type of sex we have, when we have it, where we do it, and the status of our relationship when doing it? The answer (much more complex than I provide here) principally concerns demonizing sexuality in order to gain social control (Rubin, 1984). Controlling sexuality is an emotional way of controlling people.

Monotheism benefits ruling religious and governmental parties partially because controlling human sexuality serves a primary mechanism of controlling a population. Human biology sways us toward acting on our sexual desires (whatever those desires may be). Understanding this as a precondition of humanity, demonizing sex assures a consistent battle between preaching to those destined to sin, and the submissive masses repenting for forgiveness. Religious leaders (at least the many who engage in this type of practice) use guilt and fear against sexual desires to keep followers in constant struggle between submission and sin, because it works. If the church can make one feel guilty about sexual desires (whatever those desires may be), the church assures it reaps the continual benefits of those paying penitence for their sexual sins. By demonizing sex, a constant clientele is guaranteed in a way that would not be if instead the church demonized those living in square houses. In this case, we would simply build homes of a different shape, and have no further need for the church. We do not maintain strong biological urges to live in square, as opposed to round or triangular homes. We are not biologically compelled to live in square houses, but we are somatically compelled into sex.

Accordingly, if churches are to make money off of the business of forgiving sin, they need people to 1) continue to sin; and 2) require the services of a religious leader in asking for forgiveness. Or at least requiring a religious leader to help motivate them into not sinning again. If, for example, Catholicism did not include the caveat of repenting; if, on the other hand, committing just one sexual sin determined one was hell-bound, regardless of all future actions or the degree of sorrow and repent, there would be no reason to continue patronizing a church—one might as well live a hedonistic life as your dye is cast. Accordingly, most (but certainly not all) forms of organized monotheistic religions (which have always been entwined with government) desire to control our sex lives as a way of brining us to our knees, of keeping us coming back in begging for forgiveness.

Modern governments also control sex (legally and/or culturally) because they think they will promote the healthy functioning of their societies or protect individuals from emotional harm. When citizens buy into this governmental control, they sacrifice their agency for the belief that the government knows what is best for the functioning of their own lives. Schwartz and Rutter (2000) say, "Most societies are not organized to help people have a good sex life. Sex drives are not extolled and encouraged by governments. But governments are certainly not disinterested parties" (p. 72). Governments view the controlling of sex as a function of government, even if this proposition goes unexamined.

Functionalists maintain that if something exists in society, it must exist because it has a function to the normal operation of everyday society. Giddens (1976) suggests that functionalism is a system that is intended to maintain equilibrium, slowly adapting to the needs of a changing environment and predicated in a value of social consensus. Functionalists have argued, and sometimes continue to argue, that permitting women to work, giving immigrants freedom, or allowing gays to marry, would fundamentally harm the family and/or social structures that keep our society working—even though granting rights to these groups never does.

Thus, functionalist views have been used to slow the progress of women, racial minorities, gays and lesbians, and those we selectively discriminate against for conservative reasons. Functionalist thinking seeks to explain all contemporary social phenomena as valid, retarding social change by adopting an inherently uncritical view of social life. A functionalist might therefore examine the state (or church) and suggest that control over sex is necessary in order to assure adequate cultural resources, to feed and educate the population, and (oftentimes) to please God. A functionalist thinker would therefore suggest that our institutions (including monogamous marriage) are like our bodies' organs, in that they work together to produce the smooth running of our society. Functionalists warn that even if you see a problem with one particular institution you should be careful in extracting or modifying it; doing so might negatively affect another institution that you did not intend to change. Thus, a functionalist might look to the entrenched existence of monogamy in our contemporary culture and assume it exists because it plays an important role in our society's healthy development. This, you have likely heard, is the "monogamy and marriage are the cornerstones of our society" arguement

As wrongheaded as I maintain functionalist thinking to be—on almost all fronts, almost all the time—the philosophical idea of cultural harmony is something that fits nicely into the monogamy framework. Functionalist mentality sees a purpose to monogamy: one they claim supersedes individual choice in relationship types. This is why they point to monogamy (and particularly heterosexual marriage) as the "foundation of the family" and/or describe monogamy as critical to the operation of modern childrearing.

Since the 1960s, functionalist thinking has, however, been increasingly challenged. But rather than functionalist examining the calls of feminism, gays and lesbians, or those less concerned with the sexualization of our culture as calls for increasing equality, these social conservatives view the existence of gay marriage, single parents, the availability of pornography, or open sexual relationships as an assault on their values—which include the ability to oppress those who do not buy into *their* values.

Functionalists often use the Bible as their framework for making their arguments—despite the hypocrisies this necessitates. I first highlight my atheistic standpoint, in that the Bible, as interpreted by anybody, should not be a source of knowledge or purpose that translates into political action for our political leaders. But, engaging in a moment of armchair theology, I point out here that no casual reader of the Bible will deny that the Old Testament promotes polygamy. Yet somehow contemporary Biblical scholars assume (without the support of scripture) that polygamy is no longer supported in the New Testament. For those who believe that the Bible is more than a collection of fables, there is something wrong here. Just as Christ said *nothing* about homosexuality, he also said *nothing* about polygamy. Considering polygamy was so widely practiced at the time, it can only be assumed that the practice was not noteworthy.

Furthermore, of all the tediously long and painful catalogues of sins chronicled in the first, second, and third chapters of Romans (many which relate to unlawful sexual indulgences), polygamy is not once mentioned. If it were to be mentioned, it would certainly appear there. Yet somehow Christianity managed to morph a belief against polygamy without the support of scripture. In the later part of the 19th century, laws against polygamy emerged throughout the Christian world.

CONTESTING FUNCTIONALISM

In contrast to functionalism, those pushing conventional sexual/gendered boundaries often do so through a Neo-Marxian liberatory perspective understood, broadly, as a set of theories based in conflict. Conflict theorists view control of sex and sexual relations as being, at best, only partially rooted in legitimate governmental concerns. Instead, they view control of sex and sexuality as being a preoccupation with the desire to assure that nations will have the people necessary to staff armies, work in factories, and/or to create a sense of power and privilege for the already powerful, by viewing certain sex acts and sexual relationships as charmed, while stigmatizing all others (Rubin, 1984).

Largely founded in Marxist thinking, conflict theorists reject notions that it is dangerous to alter social beliefs and institutions. They do so because they view the current system as being designed to promote the power and wealth of a few, at the expense of the many. Or, in the case of monogamy, I (as a conflict theorist) write this book not only because I see monogamy as oppressive for women (see Chapter 3), but because I find it also confining for men.

When it comes to cheating, functionalists might view cheating as men damaging relationship harmony, of undermining social cohesion and family values. Conversely, conflict theorists view monogamy, and the expectation that one must be heterosexually married with 2.2 kids, the problem. The "culture war" over functionalist versus liberationist values has occurred over many decades in contemporary society. The battle has been fought over reproductive rights, premarital sex, oral sex, same-sex sex, and casual sex. Despite the progress conflict theorists/activists have made, however, functionalists seem to be winning the war over monogamy.

CULTURALLY VALUING MONOGAMY

To understand our current perspective on monogamy, it is necessary to examine our most recent cultural history concerning dating and sex. This is because the nature of dating has changed over the years. 1950s style dating saw men dating multiple women (mostly without sex and certainly without socially approved sex), before choosing one to go "steady" with. This dating progress led to a promise ring, which led to a marriage proposal, and finally marriage. After the couple had dated, gone steady, been engaged, and then married, they were then given society's blessings for intercourse—as long as it was in the missionary position. This couple was then socially and religiously locked into monogamy with their spouse, for life.

Premarital sex is permissible today, but monogamy is expected almost from the first date. However, unlike the 1950s and 1960s, it is not socially acceptable for youth today to be casually dating more than one person at a time. This does not necessarily mean that the two are a couple from the moment of the first date, but monogamy exists as a precursor to dating. Thus, one commits to monogamy before one commits emotionally. The "official" beginning of the relationship is established when each member of the young couple changes their Facebook status. Exemplifying this, one of my undergraduate students is currently in the beginning phases of romancing a young woman. He tells me that they are taking it slow; their Facebook status has not changed; and they have not declared themselves a couple yet. Despite this, they are having sex. I asked him if he could, considering that they are not officially dating, still have sex with other women. He said that even though they did not talk about it, he was fairly certain the answer to that was "no."

Dating is not the only romantic institution to have made significant changes in recent decades; marriage, too, has changed. Premarital sex, divorce, and infidelity are the norm today (Cherlin, 2004). This is perhaps an effect of our gradual but increasing divorce from religiosity, our enhanced sense of self-liberty, the advancement of birth control, the achievements of feminism (women's egalitarian and increasing financial independence), and (for gay men and lesbians) the growing acceptance of homosexuality. And perhaps much of this is helped by the Internet, which provided the social networking of similar interest groups and the anonymity of desire. All of these trends have forced gay and straight men to reinvent and reunderstand our sexual lives (Popenoe, 1993), albeit in different ways.

Despite all of these changes to our sexual/relationship systems, one thing has not changed: We still value monogamy. Jackson and Scott (2004) say, "Greater tolerance of pre-marital, even casual sex and of marital break-down and serial relationships co-exists with the continuing reification of monogamy" (p. 238). They add, "It is difficult, these days, to find any area of adult sexual conduct that most people will unequivocally say is wrong—the one exception seems to be sexual infidelity, especially adultery" (p. 238). Treas and Giessen (2000) use *National Health and Social Life* survey results to show that whether married or cohabiting the expectation of monogamy has retained its stranglehold over our ability to imagine a more free system of loving and having sex:

> Respondents who had had sex with a primary partner at least 10 times over the past year were asked about expectations for sexual fidelity . . . nearly 99% of married persons expected their spouse to have sex only in marriage, and 99% assumed their partner expected sexual exclusivity of them (p. 54).

For all of the power women have gained in the domestic, legal, and labor spheres; the decreasing stigma associated with premarital intercourse; and the ability for women to take charge of their reproductive lives, they have not been able to escape the disguise of monogamy. For all the progress heterosexual men have made in opening up to a world of less polarized gendered behaviors and of less aggressive machismo, and their newfound ability to discuss feelings of fear, loss, and fraternal love (Anderson, 2009), they too remain trapped by the falsity of belief that monogamy provides the best—the only—acceptable form of loving. For all the critical evaluation that the gay community has brought to the institution of heterosexual marriage their disestablishmentarian values of heterosexual, patriarchal "Christian" ethos; for all those men who, before the AIDS crisis, once valued the freedom of sexual proclivity and more open and honest sexual lives (Blumstein & Schwartz, 1983), today's gay male youth (as opposed to an older generation of gay men) have again somewhat succumbed to the trappings of heterosexual convention. For all of these groups, monogamy has survived critical scrutiny, despite the fact that our attitudes toward all other sexual institutions are changing.

We are rapidly running out of sexual taboos, but we have remained steadfast in our belief that nonmonogamy is immoral. Extradyadic sex (in whatever form it comes) remains understood as a destructive virus to an otherwise virtuous and noble bedrock of monogamous love. It is, I argue, a poor reflection of our society's emotional intelligence that, when we no longer desire sex with our partner—or simply desire the addition of sex with others—we are less stigmatized for abandoning a marriage rich in history and love, rather than simply seeking our thrills outside of it. One reason for this concerns the false belief that monogamy is not only a Biblical imperative, but that it is also an evolutionary one.

NONMONOGAMY IN NATURE

You might recall the media hype around the 2005 movie *March of the Penguins*. The documentary followed the harrowing experience and bond between mother and father penguin as they tried to hatch a chick against the most extreme adversities of the deep cold, starvation, and predatory hunting. The movie is, without a doubt, startling. Rather than dumping their eggs and swimming for the Caribbean, they stick it out. Anthropomorphically, we can only interpret this as bravery. Unfortunately, the movie was used by conservative American Christians to advocate the very human notion of monogamous, heterosexual marriage. Some even praised the film for promoting "family values."

It didn't take long for those espousing that we ought to learn our morality from the life of penguins to end up with egg on their face. Biologists were quick to point out that while penguins do monogamy, they only do it for 1 year. Instead of nesting for life, penguins find themselves a new sex partner each year. But it is not just that penguins, like humans, are serial monogamists; they also commit a large degree of kidnapping. Seems there is a great deal of egg stealing on the ice. Perhaps penguins aren't the best species to model ourselves after.

Those desiring to support monogamy through nature are up against astounding odds. Bagemihl (1999) and Barash and Lipton (2001, 2009) emphasize that not only does there exist great diversity of sexual behaviors in the animal world (dolphins seem to enjoy rimming), but that the relationship types animals exhibit rarely represent idealized human monogamy. They suggest that of about 4,000 mammalian species, only a handful are monogamous. The tiny list includes beavers, a few types of rodents, otters, bats, a few types of foxes, some hoofed mammals, gibbons, tamarins, and marmosets. My point is that when social conservatives (functionalists) look to "nature" to define what human behaviors "should" be, they ignore *a lot* of evidence.

MONOGAMISM AMONG THOSE WHO COUNSEL US ABOUT MONOGAMY

Monogamy is so highly valued that even those who are trained to be more open-minded about sex and relationships fall into the cultural habit of valorizing it. Illustrating this, on May 31, 2010 the United Kingdom's *Daily Mail* reported that a heterosexual New York couple were suing their counselor for $8 million. The couple alleged that the counselor sabotaged their marriage by suggesting that they seek extramarital sex, because their sexual needs were not being fulfilled within their primary relationship.

The *Daily Mail* is not one of the United Kingdom's most exalted newspapers. It is extremely right wing (equivalent to Fox News in America), and there are caveats to the story that make me question its legitimacy. But as a sociologist, what I am most interested in are the reader's comments to the story. Concerning these, it might be somewhat encouraging to know that of the 29 posts I read that day, reader's unanimously sided against the couple. However, there was no critical discourse concerning monogamy among the comments. Nobody suggested that this might actually be good advice. Rather, one reader maintained that it *must* be a frivolous lawsuit because, "Psychologists/Therapists would never give them advice like this...."

The implication is that because counselors are educated they would know the value of monogamy and would therefore never suggest to a couple they do anything but remain monogamous. Sadly, this may not be far from reality. Barker and Langdridge (2010a) suggest that:

> Popular and psychological discourses tend to present monogamous coupledom as the only natural and/or morally correct form of human relating (Rubin, 1984). There is still no consideration of the possibility of consensual non-monogamy within mainstream psychology (see Barker, 2007) or relationship therapy (e.g., Crowe & Ridley, 2000). Internationally best-selling relationship self-help books such as Gray's (2002) *Women are from Venus and Men are From* Mars or Fein & Schneider's (2007) *The Rules* continue to present (almost exclusively heterosexual) lifelong monogamy as the natural mode of human relating and the "happily ever after" that everyone

inevitably aspires to[1] with, again, no exploration of any alternatives to coupledom (p. 750).

The *Daily Mail* story was picked up by various news sources, including where I found it: America on Line. Here, one of the reader's commented, "As a relationship counselor I think it is totally inappropriate to suggest couples have affairs. The goal of counseling is to find a way in which to repair the relationship, not add to the problems." In other words, this reader was not even capable of discriminating between an open relationship and "having affairs."

It appears that, for these commenters, there is no middle ground between having an affair (which involves romantically dating someone other than one's primary partner) and open sexual relationships (which vary widely in organization but generally permit recreational sex without romantic investment). This is reminiscent of the operation of stigma, which often promotes what I call a "one-time" rule (Anderson, 2008a). In other words, in highly policed social institutions, contesting the hegemonic norm on any ground is to contest it on all grounds.

For example, homosexuality used to be so stigmatized in the United States that men were not permitted to have even one same-sex interaction (even if a kiss) without being thought gay. However, as homophobia began to decline, this "one-time rule of homosexuality" withered (Anderson, Adams, & Rivers, 2010). In fact, my research shows that today's straight male undergraduates do not consider one gay simply for having gay sex (Anderson, 2008a). My point is that monogamy has been so stigmatized that any violation of it is lumped into its most egregious violation—an affair.

LaSala (2004) also suggests that our reverence for monogamy has led therapists to pathologize long-term committed nonmonogamous relationships. Charny (1992) for example, suggests that extradyadic sex is *always* a sign that the primary relationship is in trouble.

This is not to condemn all counselors. What is important about therapists and monogamy, however, is the systematic lack of consideration of open relationships in counseling clients (Barker and Langdridge, 2010a). Concerning the aforementioned media report, it is clear to me that the counselor's suggestion that extramarital sex might help the couple was founded in good principle. But this was not discussed in any media report. In fact the AOL article followed with 10 tips to "revive your relationship fast." These included the following: *(1)* tickling each other until you each laugh; *(2)* take a hot bath together; *(3)* take dance lessons together; *(4)* list for each other all the things you love about each other; *(5)* compile a photo album; *(6)* make and keep a promise; *(7)* do something to surprise your partner; *(8)* switch roles; *(9)* talk to each other; and *(10)* more talking. All of these are perhaps fine points of advice for a kid in junior high, but they neglect to

1. The self-help literature on consensual nonmonogamy mentioned previously is still a niche market and rarely available in the relationship or personal growth sections of conventional bookstores.

confront the difficulty of one's sex life failing to match his or her somatic desires for extradyadic, stimulating, sex.

HEGEMONY THEORY

In the preface to his second edition of *The History and Philosophy of Marriage; or, Polygamy and Monogamy Compared*, Joseph Hyrum (1885) discussed the criticism he received for contesting monogamy (as a marriage system). Although his critique was juxtaposed to polygamy, the argument equally applies to monogamy as a prohibition against extradyadic sex:

> But they have condemned it almost without examination or debate, rather because it is strange than because they have proved it to be at fault. No one has given the time and research necessary to its fair elucidation . . . such treatment, besides being unjust, is unphilosophical and unworthy in a liberal and enlightened age . . . To insist upon the condemnation of this system [polyamory], without bearing its defense, is oppression . . . (p. 12).

Little has changed since Hyrum's statement. Monogamy, as a marital system or form of prohibition against extradyadic sex, mostly remains unchallenged. Thus, why monogamy continues to remain unchallenged is of academic interest. How is it that despite common knowledge that cheating is more the norm than the exception (chapter 13), most people manage to assume that these statistics do not apply to ourselves, our families, or our friends? How is it we continue to assume that monogamy is a fulfilling way of loving, and that anyone who has sex outside of their dyadic relationship is unloving of their partner? To analyze these questions, it is important to understand the power of hegemony.

Hegemony theory is an insightful conflict-theorist method of understanding the operation of power in society. Hegemony theory is concerned with examining how dominance is obtained and sustained. As I earlier said, conflict theorists view society as a system of social structures and relationships, which are ultimately shaped by economic forces and social power. In this case, I examine the social dominance of monogamy as a social system guiding the creation and perpetuation of romantic relationships. I find hegemony theory the most useful heuristic tool to do this because hegemony is a particular type of hierarchical dominance in which a ruling class, or in this case a cultural belief, is not only legitimated, but it is also naturalized in order to secure acceptance and support from those subordinated by it.

The theory is largely accredited to the writings of Antonio Gramsci (1971), an Italian Marxist arrested for his philosophy and sentenced to 5 years of confinement on a remote island. He was not the first to write about hegemony; that came from another Marxist, Vladimir Ilyich Lenin. But Gramsci developed the idea into a focused analysis in order to explain why the "inevitable" socialist revolution that Marx predicted had not yet occurred. Instead, it seemed to Gramsci that capitalism was more entrenched than ever. Capitalism, Gramsci suggested, main-tained control not just through political and economic coercion and violence but ideologically, through a *hegemonic* culture in which the values of the bourgeoisie (ruling class who own the means of production) became the commonsense values of all. Thus, a culture of consensus developed in which people in the working class identified their own good with the good of the bourgeoisie.

For Gramsci, hegemony referred to a particular form of dominance in which a ruling class legitimates its position and secures the acceptance—if not outright support—of those the ruling class controls. So while a feature to Gramsci's politi-cal hegemony theory is that there is often the threat of force structuring a belief, the key element is that force cannot be the causative factor that elicits complicity from the masses. This is what separates hegemony from overt rule.

Academic debates continue about the precise nature of Gramsci's theories. One reason for this is that his writings were mainly in his prison notebook and can be difficult to decipher. However, the basic premise of hegemony theory is that people will buy into their own oppression if the social conditions are right. In other words, Gramsci suggested that in order to compel people to empathize with the ruling class (or idea), those who do not fit within the dominant ideal (monogamy) must believe that their subordinated place is both *right* and *natural*.

In the last few decades hegemony theory has found its way out of political lit-erature and into various aspects of the social sciences. In sociology, it is best rec-ognized through Connell's (1987, 1992) "hegemonic masculinity theory". This is a form of ruling masculinity (think jock) that dominated American and British high school and university settings throughout the 1980s and much of the 1990s. It was a form of masculinity predicated in homophobia, violence, sport, beer, and a keen sense of lack of fashion or grooming. Most important to hegemonic mas-culinity (and relevant to a discussion of cheating) was that it was also based in hyperheterosexuality, antifemininity, homophobia, domination, and control over women (see Chapter 4).

Connell (1992) described that the reason the "jocks" were able to stay on top of a social stratification of masculinities was that all those subordinated by this "ruling class" (the geeks, nerds, dweebs, emos, etc.) looked up to and patronized the jocks instead of coming together to overthrow them (e.g., not attending their football games, not voting for them as homecoming king, etc.). Thus, the reason the jocks stayed in power is that the subordinated masses—in a desperate attempt to be one of the cool kids—tried to associate with them instead of denouncing them. While the jocks controlled the school because they had the capacity to commit violence, their real power came in the idolization that people gave them.

Hegemony theory works very well when applied to marginalized people (whether it be by race, sexuality, ability, etc.). Here, each falls at the bottom of a continuum of power and privilege (white people, men, heterosexuals, and the able bodied). Thus, black people are praised for speaking "well" (white), gays are praised for "acting straight," and those with a disability are praised for approximating able-bodiedness (i.e., playing basketball from a wheelchair).

Together these groups share a very common plight in terms of how they are treated by society and how they respond.

Whatever is in current hegemonic favor tends to escape critical scrutiny. We don't look for alternative ways because there is stigma for doing such. Conversely, whatever is marginalized is scrutinized. Accordingly, we ask questions like "Are gay parents good enough?" without questioning how good straight parents might be. We ask whether women are capable of doing the job the same as a man, and not whether a man is capable of doing the job the same as a woman.

These are examples of a dominant cultural group maintaining their power by requiring others to assimilate to them—this is hegemony in action. And when a disabled athlete finishes a race, a gay man acts so straight to be indistinguishable from a heterosexual, or a black woman learns to speak in a posh white accent, they are praised, and sometimes economically rewarded. You can therefore see the power (and beauty) of hegemony theory, because even the oppressed desire to be associated with the group in power, even though they will never gain full and equal membership.

Undermining hegemony is difficult, because those who contest it are met with social reprisal: It is, for most, far easier to align oneself with the masses than stand against them. Because hegemony is a culture of consensus, and because whatever class of people, ruling party, social ideal, or institution is currently in favor, undermining hegemony is never easy. However, no hegemonic system is faultless; there are always cracks, fissures, and pockets of resistance to any dominating social message. Accordingly, hegemony is actually a process of struggle, a permanent striving, a ceaseless endeavor to maintain control over the hearts and minds of subordinate classes.

MONOGAMISM: THE HEGEMONY OF MONOGAMY

Monogamy currently maintains hegemony in society; something I call monogamism. Monogamism means that being in a sexually exclusive relationship is deemed the only culturally valued relationship choice available. If you stray from its boundaries, you are policed through cultural condemnation, relationship termination and, sometimes, even the threat of physical violence (your wife's older brother). If you question monogamy, you are ostracized and critiqued as having no morals. As you will later read, even people who cheat argue that monogamy is morally right.

The fact that most men who cheat nonetheless describe themselves as monogamous makes perfect sense when analyzed within a hegemonic framework. They desire to behave like the norm, which they think is right. They critique themselves for failing to adhere to it rather than critiquing monogamy's unreasonable expectations. They do so because, there is cultural capital and social privilege for aligning oneself with the hegemonic power structure.

When I lecture on nonmonogamies to my students, I hear, "What about jealousy?" "What about STIs?" "What about if you have kids?" "What about if he gets more sex than me?" When I mention celibacy to my students, I hear, "What about loneliness?" "What about getting sex?" "What about having kids?" When I mention polyamory to my students, I hear, "How can you love more than one person?" "What will the children think?" These might indeed be valid questions, but the reason I point them out here is that my students do not ask these types of critical questions about monogamy or monogamous coupledom.

When we hear that Tom and Jane are in a monogamous relationship, we don't instantly say, "But how does Tom get his desire for sexual diversity met?" Even if we do recognize the trappings of monogamy, we tend to do so through humor, the way I described Al Bundy in Chapter 2.

Accordingly, I argue that monogamy is hegemonic because we assume, without question, that couples should be monogamous: That monogamy offers the most advantages and the fewest disadvantages. Or worse, that there are *no* disadvantages to monogamy because the sex and emotional connection that it will yield is "just so amazing" that there would be no need to ever question it. Thus, we fail to interrogate monogamy critically for the problems it generates. We don't critically evaluate monogamy because monogamy is seen as a hegemonic good. Monogamy goes uncritically examined while those who speak negatively of it are scrutinized for their wrongheadedness.

Even when authors attempt to step back and critically evaluate monogamy for its faults, they often (perhaps accidentally) reify monogamy as the ideal. They do this by asking why men cheat and reporting upon this cheating as a negative, instead of asking why monogamy fails to deliver upon its promises. For example, in his book *Boy Crazy* (2008) Michael Shelton critiques monogamy when he describes men as existing within, what I call, the monogamy gap. But even in the way he constructs his discussion, it reifies monogamy as an appropriate norm. He asks, *Why do men fail in monogamy*, rather than asking, *Why does monogamy fail men?*

My term *monogamism* is not the only one to describe the relationship between hegemony and monogamy. Vaughan (2003) accomplishes this by discussing *the monogamy myth*:

> The monogamy myth is the belief that monogamy is the norm in our society as a whole. The effect of believing that most marriages or committed relationships are monogamous is that if an affair happens, it's seen strictly as a personal failure of the people involved (p. 6).

Another term similar to monogamism has recently been introduced into the academic literature on nonmonogamies. The term *mononormativity* was coined by Pieper and Bauer (2005) to refer to dominant assumptions of the normalcy and naturalness of monogamy. This is analogous to such assumptions around heterosexuality inherent in the term *heteronormativity*. However, I use monogamism because I believe it reflects a stronger cultural stigma than a word ending in normativity. In other words, whereas heteronormativity can be the covert and *unintentional* evaluation of heterosexuality over homosexuality, mononormativity similarly implies that the hierarchical stratification of monogamy above nonmonogamies is passively reproduced. Yet there exists a great deal of political oppression against polyamory, and there remains a great deal of cultural stigma against extradyadic sex. I therefore suggest that monogamism is akin to homophobia. It is an unjust and overt form of social oppression.

In some capacities our love affair with monogamy might actually help shelter us from other socially constructed "damaging" differences. For example, population studies find that many children do not come from the fathers they think they do, something known as *paternal discrepancy* (Anderson, 2006). In fact, Bellis et al. (2005) show that findings on paternal discrepancy rates vary between studies from 0.8% to 30% (median 3.7%, *n* = 17). Ironically, the very same monogamism that prevents people from openly discussing their desire for extradyadic sex with their partners helps cover up the cheating that monogamy structures them into. Kids do not widely assume that their father is anyone other than who their mother says he is.

PARTICIPANTS' VIEWS ON MONOGAMY

Although the primary finding of my research is that monogamy doesn't work—that it fails to sustain a lifetime of sexual enjoyment—this has not altered the monogamist perspectives of most of the men I interviewed. Most men strongly allied themselves with the monogamist project, including gay men. These men believed in monogamy, mostly eschewing open relationships. Many of the men adopted a pro-monogamy stance because they believe that monogamy is consistent with *true love*. For many of these men, true love means that one would not desire sex with someone else. For others it means that they believe in sacrificing their sexual desires for others in order to preserve monogamy.

Dom met his girlfriend in a class 9 months ago and said that he thinks she's "really got it going on." Dom described himself as an exceptionally devoted partner to his girlfriend. "I do everything for her," he told me. "I drive 30 minutes out of my way, almost every day, to pick her up; and then again home at night." Although Don has cheated on his girlfriend multiple times, he does not like the idea of being in an open relationship. "I think I'll find one. You know, I'll find that right person and I won't want to cheat on her. I think if you really love someone you wouldn't want sex with anyone else other than her." I asked him, "So because you have cheated on her, it means you don't really love her?" Dom seemed baffled by the question; he was almost angry. "No. I do. I just don't think I'm ready to commit to monogamy yet."

Robin has never been with a girl for more than 3 months, and he too has cheated on several girlfriends. Still, Robin is steadfast in his belief that he will someday find the one girl that he does not cheat on. "Look, true love means that you're not going to want anyone else." I asked Robin, "When you were with your previous girlfriend, the one that lasted just 3 months, did you think you were in love with her 2 months into the relationship?" Robin answered, "Of course. I was way into her." He went on to tell me that the only reason they broke up was because she failed out of university and moved back home. "So during that time," I asked, "did you think, 'Hey, maybe this one is the one I will marry someday?'" Robin answered, "I don't think I thought marriage, but yeah. I mean it could have been possible. It's possible she could have been the one for me." I asked Robin, "So why did you cheat on her then?" "I don't know," he answered.

Joe expressed the same conundrum, telling me that he is known as a ladies' man among his peers. He said that most of his relationships don't last long. Joe also cheats—a lot. "I didn't cheat on my first girlfriend," Joe said. "But then I was 12." Joe said that he has cheated on girlfriends all throughout high school and university. I interviewed him in the last few weeks of his student life. He would be starting a full-time job the following year and expressed to me that, in some sense, he felt he was growing up and entering an "adult" phase of life. "I was looking forward to doing this interview, because I wanted to talk to you about some of these things," he said:

> Look. You know I cheat a lot . . . I love the ladies. But I always thought that when I found the right one, I wouldn't cheat. You know, I like to think that I'm not going to cheat on my wife someday. You know, like if I just have lots of sex now, I'll get it out of my system, then I won't cheat because I'd love her so much, I wouldn't want to cheat.

As with Robin, I asked Joe if he was in love with his present girlfriend. "Yes, very much," he told me. "I've been with her for around 8 months, and that's a long time for me." I asked, "You think it's possible you could marry her?" He smiled, "You know. I kinda do." "So have you cheated on her?" Joe indicated that he had. Perhaps realizing that because he cheated on girlfriends early on, it will mean that he will (of course) end up cheating on his future wife, he said, "I guess I'll just have to decide not to cheat once I get married."

Other men felt that they would stop their cheating once they married—and perhaps they will. However, a number of these men said that they knew that they would cheat on their future wives, too. Some even boasted of their skills in being able to cheat without getting caught. Brenden said:

> I'm cheating now and getting away with it. I think I have a pretty good system . . . like you never put the number in your phone as a girl's name. You put it in as one of our best mate's names . . . I've not been caught yet, so why would I not cheat? I kind of wish I wouldn't, but I think I know myself well enough that I will . . . yes, even when married.

I asked other men who predicted cheating in their future why they just did not consider being in an open relationship. Most were against open relationships, and their reasons for this were multiple. "I think open relationships are horrible!" Cliff responded. "If I'm going to be exclusive with someone I don't want them to be with someone else, because I want them all to myself."

Brenden rationalized his disapproval of open relationships because they fail to live up to the idealized, nuclear family. "I don't think open relationships are good for a family setting," he said. "What would you tell your kids? 'Hey son, I'm going out to fuck some other woman tonight, I'll be back in a few hours?'" Mike agreed, "Open relationships aren't good for families. A family is built around exclusivity; you know sacrificing for each other, not shagging whoever you can." Others were convinced that open relationships just don't work. "Open relationships don't work. I knew a couple in one and they broke up." Nick said that he even tried an open relationship himself, but that it "didn't go very well." He said, "I got jealous after she slept with another guy. I regret being jealous, but I was. So no, I just don't want my girlfriend having sex with other guys."

Frank suggested that open relationships sounded "interesting" but that they also sounded very complex. "There are just too many gray areas with open relationships. With monogamy I know how to act." Frank's statement highlights that, at face value, it might appear that open sexual relationships are much more complex than monogamy. The structure of monogamy appears simple: The answer to any form of extradyadic sex is "no," and the mentioning of it is restricted. On the other hand, open relationships require the trust of good communication and a multiplicity of rules.

But Frank and DeLameter (2010) suggest that boundary negotiations occur with monogamous couples, too. Monogamous couples must navigate how they treat others; how much time they can spend with others; and other rules to maintain what they consider sexual and emotional exclusivity. Monogamous couples have increased burdens of policing friendships and social activities that could potentially lead to cheating, compared to nonmonogamous couples. For example, how many heterosexual married men are permitted to see a movie with a heterosexual female friend unless their wives are also present? For these reasons, I question which is more difficult, being sexually open or being closed to extradyadic sex. But even if open sexual relationships require more communication, more boundary making, those who exist within them generally show the benefits outweigh the discussion necessary to navigate them (Taormino, 2008).

Nick, however, highlights that not all heterosexual men are against open relationships. "I see merit to them," he said. "I understand why they might work, how they might be more flexible to satisfy your needs."

Approximately 35% of the men I interviewed thought there was some merit to open relationships. Most couched their thoughts in a notion that an open relationship would provide them the opportunity to have extradyadic sex without strings attached. The problem, however, was that these men did not want their partners doing the same. "No way," Mark said, "I'm not having some other guy all up-inside my girl. Fuck that!" Knowing that Mark had cheated (vaginally) on his girlfriend, I asked him if he thought there might be a double standard at play. "Call it what you want," he said, "but hell no! I'm not having that."

The vehemence with which Mark talked about his girlfriend having sex with another was unusual. Most of the men couched their responses in terms of dealing with their own emotions. For example, Jonathan said:

Yeah, of course, who wouldn't want to be told that they could have sex with whomever they wanted and their girlfriend wouldn't care. That would be awesome. But if you're going to be fair about it, then she's going to have the right to do it, too. And that's a lot harder to deal with than you doing it. I'm sure it would be the same for her.

A small minority of men felt that an open relationship actually would make sense. "I'd get over the jealousy," Ash said. "In fact, I think it would be kind of hot to watch my girlfriend get fucked by a friend . . . it would have to be a friend, not some random guy." When I asked Ash why he doesn't then pursue an open relationship with his current girlfriend, whom he is currently cheating on, he answered:

It could be a possibility, but I don't think I could ever ask my girlfriend about it. If I talked critically with my girlfriend about open relationships, then she'd just say, "You're just trying to justify being able to cheat on me."

Pete felt that an open relationship would work for him, too. Like many of the men who showed interest in it, Pete thought about the idea of having threesomes with another girl. "Hell yeah," he said. "Me, her and some hot girl. I could be down for that." When I explained to him that it might also be, to be equitable, a threesome with another guy, or that he and his girlfriend could swing, Pete was surprisingly open to the idea. "Depending on what I'd have to do with the other guy, I'd be okay with that."

I was somewhat surprised to find that the gay men in my sample were as monogamist as the heterosexual men. Of the 20 gay men I interviewed, only four were somewhat open to the idea of being in an open relationship, and only one said that he had actually tried it. Others were less judgmental about it when it concerned others, but opposed to it themselves. Aaron said, "If it works for someone else, that's fine, but it's not for me."

These results are somewhat surprising because if anyone is able to out-think the conscripts of monogamism, I would presume it ought to be gay men. LaSala (2004a) supports this, showing that older gay men are most likely to be able to adopt open sexual relationships without undermining their commitment to each other; he found that 40% were open in his study. This is particularly the case with gay male couples that have been together for years (Harry, 1984). Accordingly, I think that what I have is an age effect in operation. Older gay men are more likely to be in an open relationship, and the men in my study have not been partnered long enough for this to yet come into effect. This resonates with Adam's (2006) study of gay male couples. He, too, found that monogamy scripts appeared most commonly among younger and/or men new to gay relationships. For Adam

(2006), he found this lasted about 2 years, results that echo my experience with the gay community.

Interestingly, LaSala (2004a) found little difference in the quality of relationship between the monogamous and nonmonogamous couples, except that those in an open relationship did slightly better on a measure of "dyadic satisfaction" and this was a result of those who cheated. In other words, couples in open relationships were found to be slightly happier than those not. But this is not something that resonates with the gay men I interviewed.

Andy said, "No way do I want my boyfriend off fucking some other guy. If he wants to do that, he might as well not be in a relationship." When I asked Andy why, knowing that he cheats on his boyfriend, he doesn't just end his relationship? He answered, "Because I don't want to cheat. I'm monogamous; I've just made some mistakes. That's a whole lot better than being in an open relationship. That's just wrong."

Andy's statement exemplifies the standpoint individuals take when they uncritically subscribe to monogamism. A friend of mine, Dr. Mark McCormack, conceptualizes those who uncritically subscribe to monogamy as being in a bubble: When one is within the monogamy bubble, he or she is convinced that monogamy is the only way to do things; he or she can't see the outside world clearly. The monogamy bubble represents the boundaries of the emotional/relationship universe. However, once one breaks free from the bubble, you look around to others in their monogamy bubbles and see them as ridiculous.

GAY, LESBIAN, BISEXUAL, AND TRANS RESISTANCE TO MONOGAMISM

While there is no question that we live in a monogamistic culture, hegemony is never seamless. But when it comes to sexual minority resistance to monogamy, it must be divided into pre- and post-AIDS.

For a number of decades before the AIDS virus hit the gay scene, gay male and lesbian couples were highly socially stigmatized. This led them to become more critically aware of the trappings and stratifications of social conventions. Accordingly, the gay and lesbian community championed a subculture that was critical of traditional heterosexual notions of sex, gender, and relationships. Gay men, for example, were unashamed to have sexual partners numbering in the thousands (Rotello, 1997). And when it came to loving relationships, sexual minorities created various forms of open relationships and nonmonogamous and alternative ways of loving that are based less in oppressive, heterosexual norms.

In the 1980s, Blumstein and Schwartz (1983) found that 65% of American gay male couples had some kind of nonmonogamous arrangement, research that Harry (1984) and McWhirter and Mattison (1984) confirmed. However, the AIDS crisis fueled a political assimilationist movement among gays and lesbians. This was particularly germane to gay men, who were dying from AIDS in astonishing numbers. The AIDS crisis created what Bersani (2009) called "a rush to responsibility" (p. 86). Gay men began to lose pride in being sexually promiscuous, and stigma for promiscuity rose. Bersani adds:

> Foucault's hope that gays might be in the vanguard of efforts to imagine what he called, "new ways of being together" appears, for a large number of gay people today, to be considerably less inspiring than the hope that we will be allowed fully to participate in the old ways of being and coming together (p. 86).

As the specter of AIDS fades from our minds (although it should not), more recent research on gay men shows that nonmonogamies might be making a comeback. In a study of 86 gay male couples in the San Francisco area (where there is likely to be plenty of discussion about nonmonogamies), Blake and Lowen (2010) found that 42% of the couples they studied agreed to be in an open relationship within the first 3 months. This indicates that at least within the quintessential liberal gay community there is enough cultural discussion around the concept of nonmonogamies to permit almost half to agree upon this while the relationship was still forming, but it is considerably less than the 65% that existed prior to AIDS.

Blake and Lowen also found that within 5 years 76% of their participants were in an open relationship. And by the seventh year all of the gay male couples they interviewed (recall they were selected because they were in an open relationship) were open. This, of course, does not mean that these couples were not cheating before opening up the relationship. In fact, 20% of the men opened up their relationship because they were caught cheating on their partner. However, it does indicate that 7 years appeared to be enough time to satisfactorily wither at a sexual relationship until the couples agreed upon a relationship format other than monogamy.

There are mixed messages about the views of gay men on monogamy today. Heaphy, Donovan, and Weeks (2004) argue that same-sex relationships permit couples the freedom required to construct their relationships "from scratch" because scripts for same-sex couples are not as culturally entrenched as they are for heterosexual couples (p. 168). They argue that there exists a significant counter narrative that permits flexibility, particularly in urban settings, in developing one's nonmonogamous relationship. This is because gay and lesbian couples have already critiqued societal norms about sexuality through their sexual orientation. In some cases, they have been stigmatized for this. Thus, engaging in yet another stigmatized activity is not as socially downgrading as it is for heterosexual couples.

Ringer (2001) even locates gay open relationships in celebratory ideologies, finding gay men often celebrate pride in promiscuity. This culture of pride in social stigma, generally equips same-sex couples with more freedom in creatively constructing relationship types that are also perhaps more egalitarian and democratic in nature. Same-sex couples, for example, have also been found to build families of choice (Weston, 1991), in that they actively choose whom they desire to serve what role in their family structure. This is particularly true of those who are rejected from their families because of their sexuality. These men and women have little choice but to create kinship out of friendship, and this gives gay families particularly robust kinship patterns compared to those compelled to family through blood relatives (Nardi, 1999). Gay and lesbian couples are more culturally free to be able to pack around them people who value their particular relationship style.

However, these frameworks seem to reside alongside a more socially conservative gay male perspective today, particularly with gay male youth. Perhaps one reason I found very little evidence of consensual, discussed nonmonogamies among the 20 gay men interviewed for this research is that they are still quite young in their sexual gay lives. Many had just come out of the closet, and most had not maintained strong social contacts with older gay men who are more versed in the ways of open sexual relationships. Still, the gay men I interviewed are not the only ones to value monogamy over open relationships. Shelton (2008) writes that there is an overriding belief among gay men that monogamy is the ideal, and nonmonogamies only occur after falling from that ideal.

As previously mentioned, the gay men I interviewed valued monogamy above open sexual relationships, but some saw the value of open sexual relationships. In fact, there was a distinct difference between the gay and straight men I interviewed. About half of the gay men thought "maybe someday," while straight men in this group thought "maybe someday, yeah. But my girlfriend would never go for that." Plus, many of the gay men in this study knew a gay couple in a nonmonogamous relationship, and others have encountered them on various gay Web sites. This leads me to suggest that, if I was to interview these same 20 gay men 5 or 10 years from now, I might find that a significant proportion of them have at least once been in an open relationship.

Even if matters for gay men are not as liberated as gay men used to be, the higher percentage of gay men in open relationships is evidenced by multiple recent research studies (Adam, 2006; LaSala, 2001, 2004a, 2004b; Worth, Reid, & McMillan, 2002). What is less discussed—and perhaps less visible—however, is that there is also a cultural counternarrative to monogamy in lesbian culture. Gay men do engage in open sexual relationships more than lesbians (Munson & Stelboum, 1999; West, 1996) despite nonmonogamy being thought a more lesbian/feminist style of relating (Munson & Stelboum, 1999).

Compared to the 65% of gay men in open relationships, Blumstein and Schwartz (1983) show that just 29% of lesbian couples (remember this research was carried out before AIDS) were open. This is interesting, considering that open sexual relationships are reported to contest the ownership scripts that control women's lives more than men's. This may suggest that men seek extradyadic sex more out of sexual desire than political motivation, and this might also suggest that women are less inclined to act upon their sex drives for others.

Themes of pride in counternarratives can also be found in studies on bisexuals (Anderlini-D'Onofrio, 2004) and transsexual individuals (Richards, 2010). These studies also point to the potential of nonmonogamous relationships to transcend the limitations of dichotomizing both sexuality into gay and straight, and gender into male and female. In other words, bisexual and transgendered/transsexual communities might enable the same person to relate to differently gendered people in differently gendered ways (Barker & Langdridge, 2010a). Still, just because one contests the dogma of monogamy does not guarantee that all other social conventions will subside.

HETEROSEXUAL RESISTANCE TO MONOGAMISM

Gay, bisexual, and transsexual individuals are perhaps the most active in contesting monogamy, but they are not entirely alone. There is also some resistance on the part of heterosexuals. De Visser and McDonald (2007) and Phillips (2010) offer similar celebratory stories of heterosexual couples who "swing" by attending parties where they swap partners with another couple for sex. De Visser and McDonald (2007), for example, show the innovative ways in which these couples manage relationship jealousy. In fact, before the AIDS crisis of the mid 1980s, Blumstein and Schwartz (1983) estimated that between 15% and 28% of the heterosexual American couples had some form of agreement upon the permissiveness of extradyadic sex. I have no doubt that AIDS had the same effect on the straight community as the gay community, so those rates are likely lower today.

At face value, those who openly engage in nonmonogamies are sexually political. In recent years, however, other authors have questioned the feminist, Marxist, queer, and liberatory claims that have been made about those practicing nonmonogamies, often pointing out the largely apolitical motivations given by people involved in such relationships themselves (Jamieson, 2004; Wilkinson, 2010). This raises the question of whether people need to be *aware* that they are doing something radical and challenging to the dominant ideology in order to be understood as participating in radical ways of living.

9

The Monogamy Gap

The previous chapter described our cultural affinity for monogamy, despite failing to maintain it. In this chapter I interrogate that difference, explaining when and how it emerges. I identify the difference between the somatic desire for extradyadic sex and the socialized desire for monogamy—*the monogamy gap.*

I came up with the idea of calling the social process of simultaneously wanting and not wanting extradyadic sex the monogamy gap after reading a passage from Barry Adam (2006), who wrote:

> Men in another sector in this study express a view of monogamy in contention: as an ideal to which practice should aspire, as an uncomfortable presence, or an unnecessary constraint. Some men acknowledge a gap between practice and the monogamy regime, either in themselves, in their partners, or both. It is a gap that might be managed through silence (p. 13).

I explicate this gap by applying cognitive dissonance theory to monogamy, examining how humans behave when they want something they don't want. I then elucidate how men think, feel, and behave once they recognize this dissonance before I seek biological evidence that supports human beings being hardwired into this very troublesome dissonance.

Cognitive dissonance theory complements hegemony theory in analyzing this interview data. This is because hegemony theory maintains that the categories we choose for critical examination are always those of the subordinated (Anderson, 2009; Gramsci, 1971). Accordingly, monogamism carries serious implications for these participants because those inclined to resolve the tension of the monogamy gap seek to conform to the hegemonic ideal of monogamy and thus to control their biological sexual urges; this reifies, naturalizes, and shores up monogamy's dominance in the process (Robinson, 1996). When the monogamy gap gets to be too great, most participants creatively, shamefully, and secretly rectify the tension of the monogamy gap through clandestine cheating.

COGNITIVE DISSONANCE THEORY

The men in my study report being sexually fulfilled with their sexual relationships for a number of months after they begin having sex. Andrew, for example, says that although they have been dating for about 8 months, he only sees his girlfriend once a month. At the time I interviewed him, he reported having a high amount of sex. "I just can't take any more sex this week," he tells me. "That's all we have been doing the last few days." Conversely, Jordan, who has been in a relationship with his girlfriend for 2 years, reports having considerably less sex. "We used to be going at it all the time, but now I'm much more likely to just masturbate." The difference between these two men, however, is that only one is feeling cognitive dissonance.

Whereas Andrew is perfectly content to have sex only with his girlfriend, and is more interested in sex with his girlfriend than masturbating, Jordan is more interested in having sex with someone other than his girlfriend. But since he can't have this, he prefers to masturbate over images of someone on the Internet than to actually have sex with his girlfriend. This is the Al Bundy syndrome I talked about in Chapter 2. "It's getting stronger and stronger," Jordan said of his growing desire to have sex with someone other than his girlfriend. "It's like the more I try to deny that I want sex with someone else, the stronger the feeling grows." He added:

> Maybe I'll be thinking of this chick a lot, and really want her. And I can rub one out and get her off my mind for a while, but it doesn't go away. I can feel myself being drawn to fucking her. The sad thing is, I don't want to. I love my girlfriend, and don't want to upset her. But man, I really want to fuck this other girl.

Jordan is in a state of *cognitive dissonance*. On the one hand, he wants sex with someone other than his partner, but on the other hand he does not. The two feelings are incompatible, and there is no real way to reconcile them. Accordingly, the dissonance between these competing desires causes him a great deal of stress.

Cognitive dissonance theory is a valuable tool for helping us understand the process of what happens when one's logic no longer aligns with one's emotions. For example, when I was closeted, I desperately wanted gay sex, but I did not want to be gay. If I denied myself gay sex, I was unhappy; but the first time I had gay sex, I felt guilty.

Sometimes the outcome of cognitive dissonance is a justified compromise in which one acts while simultaneously denying that he is acting. One cheats without calling himself a cheater; one has sex with men without calling himself gay or bisexual; or one says "no" as "token resistance" to protect one's social and personal identity from being thought promiscuous, but still engages in the sex.

This means that sometimes when (both men and women) say "no," they actually mean yes. The "no" protects their identity from being associated with the stigma of simply saying yes. In fact, recent studies suggest that between 37% and 68% of heterosexual women and 21% and 83% of heterosexual men report using the "token no" in at least some sexual interactions (Krahe, Scheinberger-Olwig & Kolpin, 2000; Muehlenhard & Rodgers, 1998; Shotland & Hunter, 1995; Sprecher et al., 1994).

This statement is sure to raise a knee-jerk reaction from some about date rape. But this is what happens in a sex-negative culture. If there were no stigma for hooking up, if there were no cultural stigma for being in an open relationship, "no" would mean nothing other than no. But when one desires sex, while simultaneously desiring to protect one's social identity, "no" becomes much more confusing. Harry illustrates this well. "I recall a guy telling me, 'No, I can't,' as he made out with me on the dance floor. He said it as he followed me into a taxi. He said it during the taxi ride home, and he continued to say it all throughout the sex. Afterward, he asked if we could do it again." Clearly, "no" did not mean no for this individual.

Cognitive dissonance theory is useful for analyzing the contrast between two or more varying and incompatible cognitions not only because it describes what emotional conflict one feels but also because it predicts what behaviors might emerge from an individual's cognitive dissonance (Aronson, 1969; Bem, 1967; Festinger, 1957). In other words, not only does cognitive dissonance theory explain how this state of mind emerges, but it also predicts what one will do once entering a state of cognitive dissonance.

Traditionally, studies (normally under lab conditions) using cognitive dissonance theory create a gap between two disparate wants or beliefs. The result is that people normally end up aligning their beliefs to whatever *society* maintains. In other words, whatever maintains hegemonic sway in the current moment is what will normally win out if a person feels dissonance over two belief systems. Every now and then, however, the "other side" wins the battle between id and ego.

Cognitive dissonance theory helps us understand how, despite being presented with overwhelming evidence that monogamy does not work, most readers will find themselves nonetheless ruling in favor of monogamy—opting to stay within the monogamy bubble. Despite a wealth of empirical evidence that monogamy largely fails us, cognitive dissonance theory explains why we are likely to side with monogamy—because it is the hegemonic belief system.

In this research, I mostly analyze men who are already in a state of cognitive dissonance. Accordingly, I use cognitive dissonance theory to examine the conflict between the somatic desire participants express for recreational sex (Alexander, 1980) as juxtaposed to their emotional (and socialized) desire for monogamy. I call the difference between these somatic and social desires *the monogamy gap* and I suggest that, like in other studies employing cognitive dissonance theory, participants' competing and contrasting desires produce sexual and emotional tension that ultimately lead most participants to find catharsis through cheating (Park, 1929).

ENTERING THE MONOGAMY GAP

Tom helps explain what it is like to be in the monogamy gap. He says, "Yeah, I want sex with other women. Of course, I'm male. But if I love my girlfriend enough I shouldn't want it." When I pointed out that he earlier indicated that he wanted sex with other women because he was male, he reconsidered his statement. "I don't know. That's weird. I do want sex with other women, but I shouldn't [want it]." Hence, Tom navigates two contrasting and heavily naturalized beliefs: *(1)* that the desire for monogamy results from true love; and *(2)* that men naturally desire recreational sex, even when in love.

Tom is not alone in this dissonance. Despite expressing esteem for monogamy, many participants made it clear that monogamy did not come naturally, or even with ease to them. Tony said that he struggles "all the time" with not cheating. "I get mad at her," he said. "I want sex with other women, and I know she'd never let me, so sometimes I just feel like cheating because I'm not supposed to." Martin said that he desperately wants sex with other women, too. "I can't' stop thinking about other women. I'm sure I'll cheat. I mean, I don't want to. But I will." Still Martin said that he's not happy about this. "It sucks. Really it sucks. I don't want to cheat, but I really want sex [with someone else]." Most of the participants suggested that they lived with the competing and contrasting social scripts of sexual desire for extradyadic sex and the emotional desire for monogamy. This gap does not normally appear at the relationship's onset, which is generally characterized by heightened romance and elevated sexual passion (Harry, 1984). Few of the participants felt the monogamy gap within the first 3 months of dating. Instead, it was generally experienced after 6 or more months. Mike said, "No. I had no desire for sex with other women at first. All I could think about was her."

But after these elevated levels of passion and romance declined (sometimes plummeting), matters began to change. Dan said that while he used to be content to have sex only with his girlfriend, things were changing. Referring to his earlier sex life, he said:

It was hot . . . real hot. But in time, it just lost some of its appeal. We did things to spice it up, and we still have something of an active sex life, but I can't say that some other girl wouldn't be nice from time to time.

Similarly, Jon said, "When I first started dating her, I thought she was so hot I wouldn't want any other woman for the rest of my life, but not anymore."

The declining interest and frequency of monogamous sexual activity to which Dan, Jon, and Mike refer is the norm for the men partnered 2 years or more in this study. These men generally express that, in time, their emotional desire for monogamy no longer aligns with their somatic drive for recreational sex (Ringer, 2001). This 2-year variable was so common that one might call it "a 2-year itch." This changing direction of their sexual desires (between 2 months and 2 years) highlights the myth that monogamous desire is a natural product of "true love." Their love grew simultaneously with their sex dying.

The cognitive dissonance created by the competing desires for monogamy and recreational sex is likely made particularly salient for men in college. In addition to their heightened sexual energies, these men also experience contradictory sexual social scripts: one that suggests they should prove their masculinity through adventurous pursuits of sexual conquest (Adam, 2006; Jackson & Scott, 2004) and another that romanticizes the progression of dating, love, and monogamy (Rose, 1996).

Mutchler (2000) suggests that the competing desires for sex and monogamy may be elevated in gay men as well. Gay men also have contradictory sexual scripts: one that values romance, prescribing a relationship trajectory of dating, falling in love, sexual exclusivity, and lifelong commitment, versus sex as adventure, pleasure, and exploration without commitment. This dichotomy can be so distressing to men that Trussler, Perchal, and Barker (2000) found that "the [gay] men in our study talk about desire for both monogamous relationships and casual sex at the same time as if it is the central problem of their lives" (p. 300). Adam (2006) shows that only 26% of the gay couples he studied remained monogamous, but those monogamous couples had almost always been together for less than 3 years. He wrote (2006):

Monogamy, as a firmly held principle for organizing relationships, appears to be more common among men in early stages of relationship development, younger men who refer to heterosexual models, and men whose formative years were passed in cultures with no, or limited, autonomous gay worlds. These latter men, like younger men, tend to draw their blueprints for successful relationships from heterosexual models they grew up with and from the social prescriptions promoted in the larger culture . . . the participants in this study frequently communicate a sense of monogamy as something provisional, tentative, and subject to change, even among those who nevertheless seek to construct a firm and endearing monogamous relationship for themselves (p. 12).

Men who were not in long-term relationships found it harder to understand what the monogamy gap was all about. It is fair to say that among these men there was very little cognitive dissonance concerning monogamy. Consistent with the hegemonic position monogamy maintains, some men who had not previously had a long-term partner thought their sexual positions would be perpetually upgraded if they had one. Jon said:

I'm getting some now. Yes. Some months are better than others, but I'm not exactly sex-starved. But man it would be awesome to have a girlfriend. Someone who I can just text and say, "Hey, you horny?" . . . Think about all the time I'd save. Instead of being out at the club or talking to girls on Facebook or whatever, I could just come home from class, have some sex, and then be like, "Right, time to study." . . . I kind of envy those who have that, you know? It must be cool to just do it whenever you feel like.

Adrian, whose last girlfriend only lasted 2 months, said:

I had a girlfriend last year, and I totally miss it. I think I miss the idea of having a girlfriend more than I miss her. It's just nice having someone there all the time. Someone who cares about you; and to do stuff with. . . . Yeah, I totally miss the sex, too. We didn't do it as often as I wanted, I was a lot hornier than she was but still, man it was nice. I got so much more sex than I am now. . . Well, don't get me wrong, I do alright. But it would be sick to have just one bird to have sex with, you know, five times a week. Okay, maybe three or four times, but you get the idea.

The monogamy gap was equally as difficult for men in the romance stage of a relationship to understand. These men suggested that they were thoroughly enjoying sex with their partners and did not see boredom on the horizon. For example, Mitchell, who has been in a long-distance relationship for 4 months, and had just spent a week with his girlfriend, said:

. . . oh man, I just can't do anymore sex. That's all we did all last week [he smiles]. Seriously, we just fucked and fucked . . . No, I didn't get bored of it at all. I need a break for a couple of days, but hell no; I am not going to get tired of this. I wish every week was like this. Having a girlfriend is the bomb, it's just like sex, all the time.

When I asked Mitchell if he thought that it was possible that he might grow bored of sex with her, he said:

No way. She's just too hot [he pulls out his phone to show me a photograph of her]. I know you're gay but come on. Okay, maybe you wouldn't want sex with her, I get that. But there is no way I'm slowing down. I ain't getting bored of tapping that. No fucking way.

Taylor, who has been with his boyfriend for almost 2 months, saw no end in sight of his sexual fulfillment with his boyfriend either:

I'm not as horny as some. But I like sex now and then . . . Things are good . . . Yeah, we have great sex. I think it's a lot better than with a hookup, because I'm getting to know what he likes and doesn't. And it's the same with him. For example, I like having my nipples sucked as I get close to cumming, and when you hook up with a guy it just seems weird to say, "Hey, suck my nipple as I cum." But my boyfriend knows this, so when he can tell I'm gettin' close, he's on it . . . I can't see me wanting to go back to the days of finding guys to hook up with again, when I got this going on. Why would I want sex with some stranger who doesn't know my body when my boyfriend knows just what to do?

It is also fair to suggest that a large group of men in my sample felt cognitive dissonance between their somatic wanting of extradyadic sex and their moralist belief system, which forbids it. These men expressed a desire to have sex with someone else, but they maintained a moderate to severe feeling of guilt or shame for it. These men exemplify the monogamy gap.

Gregg, an American from the Midwest who has been with his girlfriend for almost a year and a half, said:

When we first hooked up, we were going at it like crazy. We had some mad sex. We were doing it everywhere: on my desk, the floor, the car, outdoors, and we were doing all kinds of crazy shit. She was just real kinky. I mean, you ever see *Avenue Q?* [I confirm I have]. "You can't put your finger there. Put your finger there!" That kind of stuff . . . But we're not that kinky anymore. We still have sex, but it's like she does this. I do that. She does this, I cum. Sometimes she cums. It's alright, but I'm missing the kinky stuff . . . not with her though. It's like we're over that . . . I just really want to get nasty with some other girl. You know, fuck her in the ass and tie her up. Anything, really. Just something that's out of the ordinary. Something if I tell my friends about they would be like "What?"

I asked Gregg, if he was missing the kinky sex that he and his girlfriend had, why he doesn't start it up again with her:

It's not the same. Not at all. It's just not there, man. Maybe now and then I'll do something, but the feeling is not the same. I just don't get like, I wanna do that! I love her, don't get me wrong. And I totally get that she's fine . . . it's not like I don't enjoy sex with her. I do, but it's not the same raw, hardcore, you know like "yes, I'm doing this" kind of sex. Now, it's more like, "Honey, you feel like having sex?" "I guess so" kind of sex . . . Don't get me wrong, I'm not blaming her. It's an "us" thing. I feel the same. I love her, but I just don't have that drive to have that kind of sex anymore.

I asked Gregg how he handles wanting the type of sex he's no longer getting. He said, "Porn. And lots of it." He added, "Normally it's when I know she's not coming back for a while. I don't know if she'd be too upset that I use it. But I'm not exactly going to be like, "Hey, honey, I'm jerking off to girls who I want more than you."

I then asked Gregg if he wished he could have sex with other girls. He answered:

I'm not going to lie to you. Yeah. I really do. Sometimes more than others. But there are times I just want someone so bad. It can be someone from class or just someone I see on campus. But that's when I get that drive back. For example, there is this one girl, shit, I don't even know her name but she works in the Starbucks . . . Well, let's just say I've been buying a lot of coffee lately. But I want her so fucking bad. Like, I really want her.

Finally, and consistent with my point about cognitive dissonance developing after the romance stage of a relationship fades, Gregg said:

I really want her. I mean, I don't want to cheat on my girlfriend. I totally love her. I'm not saying we're going to get married some day and all that; but I wouldn't doubt it either. But I'm not going to lie to you. If she offered me some sugar with my coffee, it would be hard to turn down. You know what I mean?

As with the dozens and dozens of other men I talked to who have long-term partners that have lasted past the romance stage, Sean described a very similar scenario of thinking he would be more happy having a girlfriend because he would get more sex; then actually being that happy with it once he had it; to being conflicted about his emotions now that he is into his relationships for over 2 years and wanting sex with other women:

It sucks. I used to want what I have so badly. And now that I have it, I'm not so sure I want it . . . I see so many good-looking women around here, and I can't do anything. But I feel like shit because I want to do something. It's like God's challenging my love and faith or something, because I swear to you those women look hotter today now that I have a girlfriend than they did before I had one.

Sean said that he also found some relief from his dissonance through pornography. To be clear, almost all of the men coupled, gay or straight, regardless of how long they have been in a relationship, still use pornography (see Chapter 12). Surfing porn Web sites is part of the masturbation habits for men, regardless of their relationships status. This also means that those with girlfriends still masturbate. The only men to report not masturbating were those partnered less than three months.

There is one other commonality among Gregg, Sean, and most of the other men I studied who had long-term, monogamous relationships: They found themselves positioning their bodies closer to arenas that might be considered "dangerous" to monogamy. Recall Gregg's sudden interest in coffee, just so that he could see the girl serving it. When I asked him to tell me more about this, he informed me that as he became a regular, he had been chatting with her during his purchases. "Would you say it was flirting?" I asked. "You could call it that," he said. "But it's harmless."

Adrian not only masturbates on the Internet, but he's been using forums where he talks to others as well. He told me that while chatting to girls, he flirts too and masturbates while talking to them. Adrian first passed this off as innocent, but then suggested that if his girlfriend knew she might not be happy. "It's just better than jerking alone," he told me. I asked him if he tells the girls he's chatting (typing) to that he's masturbating. "No. Well, kinda. Like, if they ask what I'm doing I'll say something like, lonely, bored, horny." These conversations that Adrian (and others) describe to me are sometimes dressed up as humor. For example, if a girl says to him, "Oh, so you're horny huh? Are you masturbating?" he will answer, "Yeah. Spanking it right now. It's totally hard for you." But then he will add "j/k" (just kidding) to negate it, although he actually is.

BIOLOGICAL EXPLANATIONS FOR THE MONOGAMY GAP

There is compelling biological evidence that the monogamy gap I document has organic roots. Highlighting a biological basis for a monogamy gap, Paul Zak (2010) discusses how the simultaneous wanting and unwanting of monogamy might be a biological construction. Zak finds neurological antecedents for the social outcomes that I show my participants maintain after progressing through the romance phase of a relationship. Zak suggests that of the hundreds of chemicals produced in our brains, there are three hormones that modulate monogamy: oxytocin, arginine vasopressin, and testosterone.

Oxytocin initiates a cascade of brain activation that leads one to feeling both pleasurable and bonded. It has been shown to sustain emotional relationships (romantic or otherwise) through its release in the brain during sex, touch, petting one's dog, or spending time with an infant.

Arginine vasopressin motivates mate and offspring-guarding in male socially monogamous mammals through jealousy and aggression. The biological reason for this is that we increase the amount of receptors designed to lead to what Zak calls "reactive aggression" after emotionally bonding to a mate. This is why my dog will growl if he senses a threat to me today, but he did not the day I met him.

Testosterone, which is associated with seeking sex, appears in both men and women but in higher concentrations of postpubescent men. It is not only associated with libido but also with musculature and drive. Its effects in men are therefore thought attractive to heterosexual females seeking high-quality male genes.

Zak suggests that vasopressin works in tandem with oxytocin to make males desire to be around and defend our mates from others. The evolutionary advantage for "pair bonding" might therefore come in that defending one's mate is not only more likely to keep one's partner alive, but it might also be more attractive to other females (i.e., they are attracted to the protector). But this is not to suggest that men don't desire sex with others while pair bonded. If other potential mates are attracted to him because of his protection instincts, it opens up more sexual opportunities to him—opportunities that we today call cheating. This is where *testosterone* comes into play.

Zak finds that the distribution of oxytocin and arginine vasopressin receptors in the brain reveals that we are a monogamous species for emotional attachment and developing a family, but that our large degree of testosterone (which fluctu-ates for various socioemotional reasons) is thought to suggest that we evolved with females maintaining multiple sex partners to maximize fertilization. Thus, Zak suggests that we have socially monogamous brains but sexually promiscuous genitals (a biologically innate monogamy gap). Ryan and Jethá (2010) support this, arguing that we evolved having sex with multiple people. They argue that before modern understandings of conception it was believed that a child was made by the deposited sperm of many, not just one man. If a child came out both tall and smart, it was because the woman had sex with a tall man and a smart man. This seems silly to modern ears, but it's not illogical. This, they argue, is one reason women moan during sex; and why men are turned on by it. The moaning beckons other men to join in. This may also be why heterosexual men are attracted to por-nography that involves one woman and many men.

Zak supports my sociological finding that a monogamy gap exists, contending that we have conflicted ideas of monogamy because these hormones interact and contest each other as well. Testosterone conflicts with the bonding effects of oxytocin—blocking the uptake of oxytocin by its receptor. This, he suggests, motivates both men and women to seek more sexual partners (and to take more risks) even if pair bonded. Because men have five to ten times more testosterone than women, it indicates that men are more likely to take the risk of cheating—something sociological research on cheating confirms. In other words, testosterone may not be the sole reason that men cheat, but it might also play a part.

Proving his point, Zak shows that administering testosterone to men changes the cost–benefit calculation in the brain, leaving men more likely to cheat. Ryan and Jethá (2010) argue that monogamy itself drains men's testosterone; that mar-ried men constantly show lower testosterone levels compared to unmarried men of the same age. Cheating raises their testosterone levels. Because athletes and other socially esteemed individuals are more likely to develop higher levels of testosterone (Booth et al., 1989), their elevated testosterone further inhibits the bonding effect of being with their partners and insinuates a desire for more extra-dyadic sex. This is one reason I chose to study team-sport athletes for a large part of my sample: They were perceived to be more promiscuous (something perhaps promoted by their biology).

Before I leave the psychoevolutionary argument, it should be pointed out that a variety of other academic works point toward human beings evolving with non-monogamies. For example, the unique shape of the penis, with a bulbous glans (the head), its long, rigid shaft, and coronal ridge act as a scraper to remove ejacu-late already in the vagina. Thus, if many men are breeding with a woman in suc-cession, the males' pumping action sucks fluids down, away from the fallopian tubes where fertilization occurs. Then after considerable pumping (more for some than others) the male injects his own semen. The animal world is full of penises with similar functions (Bagemihl, 1999): the shark, for example, squirts high pressured salt water (a douche) into the female before his ejaculation (Barash & Lipton, 2001).

Others familiar with evolutionary adoptions will, quite rightfully, highlight the relative size of human testicles. Among males of animal species that do not practice monogamy (most) testicles are larger—a result of needing to produce more sperm to one-up other males in something of an arms race (Barash & Lipton, 2001). However, among monogamous species, testicle size to body size is relatively small. So, for the great apes, in which one dominating ape maintains control over the breeding rights of all, its brawn is not matched with his testicles. Conversely, chimpanzees, which rather enjoy an orgiastic lifestyle, have enormous testicles compared to their body size (Barash & Lipton, 2001). Jane Goodall (1990) even documents a chimpanzee mating with seven different males, a total of 84 times in just 8 days.

Barash and Lipton (2001) suggest that human testicle size is at the median, suggesting that our evolutionary history posits us as sometimes monogamous and sometimes not. This is true of our longer penises than other primates as well (some longer than others), which again is theorized to help plunge another's sperm out of the vagina. This might also mean that men with longer penises have a biological advantage in reproduction, when a woman is having sex with multiple partners.

A SOCIAL MONOGAMY GAP

It is also noteworthy to discuss that the tension between wanting sex and not wanting sex is not the only tension in these men's relationships. Barker and Langdridge (2010a) suggest that there exists a great deal of mononormative pressure to find everything in "the one true love." In other words, men might not only be struggling with their competing sexual desires concerning monogamy, but they might also be struggling (particularly at this age) about whether they want a relationship at all.

This is because the moment one enters into a "committed" monogamous relationship, it enacts a social process of integration. Biologists call this *mutualism*, the way two organisms biologically interact so that each individual derives an increased survivorship capacity, or *symbiogenesis*, the merging of two separate organisms to form a single new organism. In our romantic relationships this refers to a narrowing of friendships and other social networks, and an increase in interdependence, the "togetherness" of coupled life and the social development of a singular identity.

We recognize this socially when each member of a couple takes on just one name, known as a *portmanteau*. For example, movie stars Brad Pitt and Angelina Jolie are sometimes referred to as Brangelina. While there may be multiple advantages to having one's identity merge with another (something which particularly occurs in the performing stage of a relationship), there are disadvantages, too. And, as I assume Barker and Langdridge would suggest, while we may recognize these at some conscious level, we do not widely discuss them as drawbacks to social monogamy.

The question therefore is: Why do we think that we can find all of our needs in just one person? Just because we eventually grow a sense of togetherness with our partners, it does not mean that all of our emotional needs are met by this one person. The point is, despite a growing mutualism with our partners, they cannot entirely fulfill all of the roles that we need others to fulfill in our lives—and sometimes they detract from having your needs met. If my partner needs time away with his girlfriends, having me there detracts from those needs being met. So, when sexually monogamous couples who have been together for enough time develop a sense of symbiogenesis, the constant presence of the other might be welcomed at one level, but irritating at another. Accordingly, Barker and Langdridge suggest that cheating might reflect a rational way out of this type of dissonance—it might reflect a symbolic independence from one's partner and needing simultaneously to be dependent upon him or her. Barker and Langdridge (2010a) therefore suggest that the proliferation of open nonmonogamies might be a response to great uncertainty at a societal level about how to manage relationships.

SEX WINS OUT

Years ago, Robert Park (1929) suggested that when sexual desire exists between two people, as long as circumstances permit enough time and opportunity, sex will occur. I do not make such an absolutist claim here, but I do wish to step back from a psychological, biological, or even sociological argument for a moment, and simply conclude this chapter with some observations supporting this conception.

The notion is that regardless of social convention, sex wins out. Sex always finds a way. In their book, *The Ethical Slut*, Easton and Hardy (2009) write in response to the increasingly sex-negative culture that came with the industrial revolution (see Chapter 7), "But human nature will win out. We are horny creatures, and the more sexually repressive a culture becomes, the more outrageous its covert sexual thoughts and behaviors will become, as any fan of Victorian porn can attest" (p. 10). This is likely to be particularly true of men (Blum, 1997).

I learned this when I was quite young. I grew up in an incredibly homophobic culture, and so I desired to change my sexuality and came up with the idea that if I were to avoid thinking about guys while masturbating and instead think of women, I could redirect the source of my attractions. Through this strategy I struggled against my desires for years. Not only did I fail to reach orgasm while thinking of a woman (the closer I got to orgasm the less capable I was of controlling my thoughts), but I then subjected myself to a great deal of guilt after eventually achieving orgasm. But this guilt did not stop me from being horny again, nor did it redirect my attachments. My sexual desires were stronger than I could prevent. Sex won out.

The same is illustrated with the high degree of sex crimes in the Muslim world. I have, for example, a photo of two 16-year-old gay boys who were hung in Iran for having same-sex sex. Some Islamic cultures also condemn women to death for cheating on their husbands (Betzig, 1989), yet boys still have gay sex, and heterosexuals still cheat. The point is that despite existing within the strictest of cultures, the legal and religious prohibitions maintain hegemonic power in shaping our attitudes toward sex, but they do not prevent it.

For those of you who may have watched NBC's *To Catch a Predator* a few years ago, you may have made this observation yourself. If not, I recommend you watch the show on YouTube. The show chronicled police operations where adults posed online as 13- or 14-year-olds. Adults of all ages and backgrounds (but always men) would hit on the operatives online and then chat for hours before eventually talking about sex and their desire for sex with the "kid." These men then showed up to the front doors of the young adolescents, not knowing it was a police sting. After entering the house (an actor who looked quite young answered the door) and they filmed the dialogue between the young actor and the "predator." After a period of time, the show's host (not an officer) would suddenly emerge with several television cameras. A journalist, he would then interview the men about their sexual desires and intentions, before the man left the house only to be arrested. A persistent theme was just how many of the men said that they suspected it was a police operation before coming. Despite this, like moths to a flame they were still compelled to take the chance. At the moment of realization, many of the men said, "I knew it." For these men, despite their reservations, sexual desires won out.

The same is true of the hundreds (perhaps thousands) of Catholic priests who we now know have molested youth over the last few decades. It is not likely that they did so without fighting their socialized views of its immorality. Assuming these are men who believe in God, and that these are men who view sex with anyone outside of marriage as a sin, they must have experienced extreme cognitive dissonance over their conflicted desires. Yet, as we now know, so many of them gave in to their compulsion. Sex won out.

My point is that if our human drive to seek out the type of sex we desire is so strong that people will risk losing their families, careers, being imprisoned, or put to death—yet people will still do it—the intellectual desire, our socialized sense of morality not to cheat, is unlikely to be effective in stopping it. One cannot simply wish their sexual desires away, and given enough opportunity sex will most likely win out. Thus, although not a fastidious rule, monogamy may exist as a desired norm, but it will *never* exist as the reality. Our sexual drives have more durability than our socialized prohibitions against them.

10

Costs of Monogamism

The foundation of monogamy rests upon the principle that sexual fidelity comes as the first act of a committed relationship. This occurs before emotional mutualism and certainly before economic interdependence through informal or legal nuptials. In other words, when we first begin dating (or become exclusive in some instances), we have an unspoken but irrefutable social expectation that this new person will be sexually faithful to us. Today's youth sometimes even expect this commitment before knowing even basic emotional/personal details of the person, committing after just one date. In fact, some of the men in my study sexually committed before even first meeting their love interest. Thus, while monogamy comes at first site, we do not expect our new love interest to be committed emotionally or economically. Instead, we understand that this is a social process that occurs by way of the development of a long-term relationship.

At one level, this makes sense. Compared to a joint bank account or the sharing of one's emotional history, monogamy is the easiest and perhaps most sensible thing to commit to. While I question both the need and the benefit of a commitment to monogamy, if one desires to "commit" something to his or her fresh love, sexual fidelity isn't irrational. After all, early in a relationship, not only is the sex still good, but we are also in the mode of strategic self-presentation, preventing us from sharing our more personal, emotional aspects.

What is ironic about this progression, however, is that while emotional and economic connectivity increases the longer a couple is together, the desire for (and the act of) monogamy is strongest in the romance phase of the relationship. It begins to wane through storming and carries on diminishing through norming and performing. For example, if you talk with most long-term couples about finances, you will find that an economic pattern emerges. When two people begin to date, they do not generally have access to each other's bank accounts and they do not maintain or even desire to maintain joint expenses. In fact, the only real financial decisions reside over who pays for a date. However, the couple eventually cohabitate and begin to divide their expenses. It is here that the financial responsibility of one partner affects the other. Normally in this stage each maintains his or her own bank account; one's money is one's own money. However, with enough time (usually years) couples eventually cease to consider what was purchased on whose account. They cease to tally just who paid for what and begin to look at their money as a collective—which eventually leads to having a joint account. This is the economic part of the norming stage. Another way to state this is that if Dick takes Jane's credit card to purchase new wheels for his car after 20 years of marriage Jane pays no attention. But if Dick takes Jane's credit card and purchase new wheels after dating a week, Jane calls the police.

The same blending process is true with our emotional matriculation. For example, when my partner and I first began dating, we each had friends and family we sought for emotional support. These friends were our default sources. For example, if during the first week of our relationship Grant had lost a grandmother, he would have sought support from his immediate family and his long-term friends, not me. However, if something tragic like this were to occur today, his initial source of comfort would be me. This isn't because we are socially expected to seek comfort primarily from our partners, the way we are socially expected to only seek sex from our partners; it is instead an act that occurs as a natural product of our increasing emotional investment with each another. Both of the economic and emotional aspects of our relationship connectivity have grown as a product of our years of being together. These issues are not troubling or aggravating. I do not feel that I am being oppressed because of our economic and emotional exclusivity.

Whereas most couples find that their economic interdependence and emotional mutualism grow in time, in contrast, they (oddly) expect and desire sexual fidelity from the very moment that they begin dating. This feels right because it fits with the hegemonic ideal and our initial sexual desires and biological responses. However, the elevated rates of oxytocin that bind one to his or her new partner begin to fade and each partner increasingly desires sex with others. This might be particularly true for youth.

I recognize that sexual desire might decrease as a function of age, but for the men in my study, the longer they are in a relationship, the more they desire sex with someone else. Where committing to sexual fidelity was the rational choice at the start of a relationship, it ceases to be an effective sign of commitment and becomes an increasingly illogical and burdensome commitment as love and emotional intimacy grow.

Thus, questions I ask in this chapter center on what emotional cost occurs for the restriction of men's sexual activity with others after the sex in one's own relationship grows boring. In this chapter I am interested in knowing what feelings of sexual oppression occur when we are prohibited from doing what our bodies increasingly desire and what negative relationship-harming emotions are generated in the monogamy gap. But I begin by discussing a somewhat surprising finding. Normally, open relationships are critiqued for exposing one to the risk of sexually transmitted infections. In this chapter I draw from research to show how monogamy also poses a risk.

SEXUALLY TRANSMITTED INFECTIONS

It seems self-evident that monogamy is the most likely form of relationship coupling to keep one free from sexually transmitted infections. Monogamous partners should be able to have condom-free sex without issues apart from pregnancy. However, this fails to account for the problems associated with cheating. Because cheating is so heavily scrutinized, men and women who cheat are less likely to tell their partners when they cheat, opening them up to infection. One does not generally say to their partner, "Honey, I had sex with someone else last week, so you should get yourself checked." Thus, the institution of monogamy might not protect one from disease the way we commonly think it does.

Research on heterosexual undergraduates suggests that only about 10% use condoms consistently (Prince & Bernard, 1998). This number is even less among sex buddies (Civic, 1999; de Visser & Smith, 1999, 2001). However, college students in monogamous relationships are the least likely to use condoms (Mahoney, Thombs & Ford, 1995) and the most frequently stated reason for the failure of undergraduates to use condoms is monogamy. Once there is a degree of implicit trust between partners, there is an expectation of monogamy that leads to the diminution of condom usage.

Instead of using condoms, most heterosexual college students rely on oral contraception, because to request that one's partner use condoms is to question his or her loyalty to monogamy (Pivnick, 1993). In other words, for one partner to suggest that condoms are necessary implies that he or she does not trust the other—and this "trust" is thought (artificially) to be the foundation of a romantic relationship. Asking one's partner to use condoms therefore undermines the relationship (Wight, 1992).

But it is important to recall that cheating was the norm among my participants. Therefore, an empirical question of importance (and one not fully addressed with this research) is "What is the risk of infection when one is engaging in high-risk sex with one's 'monogamous' partner" (Lehmiller, 2009; Nichols, 1990)?

The literature on infection control suggests a strong relationship between rule breaking and risky intercourse—almost as if once an individual breaks a self-imposed rule (such as cheating), one permits oneself to break other rules as well, like condom usage (Cochran & Mays, 1987). For example, Bearman and Brückner (2001) show that heterosexual youth who take virginity pledges are one-third less likely to use contraceptives when breaking their pledge than youths who did not take the pledge. This is one reason why the state of Texas failed miserably in preventing teen pregnancies through implementing programs in which kids took pledges to refrain from sex until married. Instead, teenage pregnancy skyrocketed.

Hammer et al. (1996) suggest that when monogamous couples have sex without condoms, they do so not because they expect monogamous sex to ensure the safety of their sexual health, but because they fear questioning their partner's trust and commitment by asking him or her to use condoms. If, however, people break the rules (in this case, cheating), they tend to break other rules as well (in this case, condom usage); thus, it stands to reason that men who cheat (of which most do) are less likely to use condoms. This means that it is foolish for one to expect that monogamy will protect one from infection. This may help explain why Newmann et al. (2000) found that 88% of women infected with HIV in South India are in what they believed to be monogamous relationships.

Not only are men unlikely to use condoms when they cheat, but they are also unlikely to tell their partners that they have cheated. In a recent survey of American university students, Vail-Smith, Whetstone, and Knox (2010) find that not only did 30% of the men they surveyed admit to cheating, but that only one-third told their girlfriends that they had. They write:

> Furthermore, because only 33.2 percent of those who report cheating disclose their infidelity, most of those at risk because of their partner's behavior do not even know they are at risk. For this group, there was little protection in "monogamy." Because of the high occurrence of cheating, those in monogamous relationships should reassess their degree of commitment to condom use during sexual encounters with each other (p. 18).

This means that there is only an illusion of safety with monogamous relationships. Barry Adam (2006) suggests that the monogamy gap sets up a situation that may leave a partner vulnerable to infection. This supposition is supported by more recent research in Western cultures.

In a recent study in Ireland (Shiely, Horgan, & Hayes, 2009), researchers found teenage girls and women with only one sexual partner were more likely to contract sexually transmitted infections than those having multiple partners. For females, having just one partner in the past 3 months increased the risk of acquiring a sexually transmitted infection. Meanwhile, women who had had two partners in the previous 3 months were 28% less likely to contract a sexually transmitted infection than those who had been monogamous. Women with more than three partners in the previous 3 months were 18% less likely to have a sexually transmitted infection.

For men, a univariate analysis found that having two partners in the last 12 months (compared with 0–1 partners) elevates the risk of sexually transmitted infection diagnosis. However, having three or more partners is associated with a lower risk. This trend has also been observed in other surveys of British sexually transmitted infection clinics (Hughes, Catchpole & Rogers, 2000).

Another way to examine this is to suggest that those with multiple sexual partners decrease their chances of infections. This may be because those who permissively partake in recreational sex are more likely to use protection, compared to those who cheat (Hammer et al., 1996). Those who have more sex seem to approach it from a more rational basis, because they are outside the monogamy bubble. They are prepared with condoms and avoid risky practices. They become responsible sexual citizens.

Supporting this contention, the British study, which analyzed 15,000 patient records from three sexually transmitted infection clinics, found that more sexually experienced women were more aware of the risks of sexually transmitted infections. Because of their awareness and sexual frequency they were more likely to use condoms. In reporting on the study titled "Monogamous Women at risk of More STIs," in the online version of the *Sunday Times* (October 4, 2009), a consultant in infectious diseases at Cork University Hospital said:

> Some people who are more sexually active are probably more aware of the risks they are taking and will therefore go out prepared. If they are going to a nightclub and are anticipating that they may have a casual contact, they will go prepared, whereas people who are inexperienced are maybe too shy to ask somebody to use a condom, or to bring it with them. That's the main reason we felt that being more sexually experienced actually protected you.

More evidence to support this proposition comes from Canada. Although I cannot find the peer-reviewed article from which a September 9, 2009 article in Canada's *Globe and Mail* is based, the article reports upon similar results. The article suggests that large numbers of unmarried, sexually active Canadian adults are not using condoms because they think that monogamy is a reliable form of protection. However, even if these men were not cheating, they opened themselves to infection because they were serial monogamists, having sex with only one person at a time, but having unprotected sex! In other words, monogamy might have been a safer strategy for having unprotected sex in the 1950s, when premarital sex was taboo. But monogamy is no guarantee today. Ignorance, and a lack of symptoms (which can often have long incubation periods), lead these people to falsely believe that monogamy will protect them.

In another finding, Rotermann and McKay (2009) asked 19,455 unmarried, sexually active Canadian adults aged 20 to 34 who were not living in common-law arrangements, "Did you use a condom the last time you had intercourse?" They found that more than 50% of women and 40% of men said they had not used a condom. The study found that condom use declined steadily with age, despite the fact that the risk of infection did not. One researcher said, "The 20-year-old uses condoms less often than the 16-year-old, and the 25-year-old uses condoms less often than the 20-year-old, and all the way up the line." Supporting this, one-third of respondents said that they had multiple sexual partners in the previous year, either concurrently or one after the other. The main reasons for going without protection pivot around a false sense of security. Other studies have found similar results.

Most recently, a study of gay couples in San Francisco interviewed 566 gay couples to find that 45% said they were monogamous and 47% said they were in open relationships (Hoff et al., 2010). However, in 8% of the couples, one partner thought the relationship was open and the other thought it was monogamous. This finding, that a sizeable minority of partnered gay men are confused as to whether their bond is monogamous or not—likely because the mandates of monogamy make it difficult to discuss—is dangerous because if one is having sex with someone outside the relationship, and the other doesn't know about it, it could be an opportunity for risk of infection to that partner.

This collective body of research therefore implies that while one might think they can trust their monogamous male partners, sociologically speaking they cannot—and most likely should not (Adam, Sears, & Schellenberg, 2000; Mutchler, 2000). And, although I did not study women and their sexual relationships here, this edict likely works the other way, too (Wiederman & Hurd, 1999). Men thinking that condom-free sex with their ostensibly monogamous girlfriends is safe may also be jeopardizing their health. Logically, this is true of gays and lesbians, too. Essentially, trust in monogamy may lead partners to unwittingly choose unsafe sex (Adam, 2006; Sobo, 1995).

RELATIONSHIP TERMINATION

One of the motivations for doing this research was a number of couples I know who permitted the unreasonable expectation of monogamy to break them up. Take, for example, Scott and Darren, who had been together 13 years before Scott cheated on Darren with an 18-year-old he met at a club. Darren found out about the episode, and he broke up with Scott. Thirteen years of otherwise blissful marriage were eradicated, and the couple even had to sell the house in which they together paid a mortgage. Thus, the divorce was financially disastrous and emotionally ruinous.

Why, I question, would a couple with so much love and history together split up simply because one had recreational sex? This is the unreasonable situation that monogamy places us into. We place too much at stake for the expression of a biological desire. It was not "falling out of love" that broke this couple up. It was not irreconcilable differences. It wasn't even that one of them was having a romantic affair. It was nothing more than one member of the 13-year dyad had sex with a highly tempting individual. He felt guilty about it the following day, told his partner, and soon enough found himself living alone in an apartment.

Similarly, I talked with an 18-year-old who told me about the emotional devastation his father caused his family after cheating eight times on his mother. This again was not an affair; it was simply a man rectifying the monogamy gap through cheating with 8 different women. The boy maintained intense anger toward his father for splitting his family up. In his eye, his dad cheated and it was therefore a predetermined, intentional act to divide his family. When I explained to the boy that his father likely entered the monogamous relationship in good faith, but that in time monogamy grew trying—that it was monogamy that failed his father, not his father that failed the family—he began to let go of some of his anger.

These stories, and hundreds of similar stories I have heard from my friends and students, are all-important reminders that it is the expectation of monogamy that breaks families up—not cheating. If we did not demand sexual fidelity of our partners, we would save many families from the process of guilt provoking, shaming, and ultimately separating parents. Studies, including a nationally representative survey (Amato & Previtti, 2003), show that infidelity is the major reason for divorce (Amato, 2003; Amato & Rogers, 1997). Worse, parental divorce is associated with lower quality marriages of their offspring (Amato, 1996). This, in turn, raises susceptibility to the children of divorced parents divorcing themselves.

Perhaps the most memorable story comes from Aspen, who met his girlfriend during his freshman year. He described her in absolutely glowing terms. "She was everything to me," he said. "She still is."

> I did everything for her. Not because I wanted something, but because it made me feel good. . . . We were inseparable. My family loved her, and her family loved me. . . . We went on family holidays together, and we lived together my sophomore year. . . . It was amazing, we had total domesticity. We decorated the apartment together, we talked about marriage even… There was no doubts that she was the one for me.

All of this relationship bliss came to an end when he cheated on her at a soccer tournament away from home. "We were out drinking with other teams [including women's teams] and there was this girl. I don't even remember her name." He added:

> It's not like I even tried to hide it. I called her that next day to tell her. I apologized and apologized, telling her how awful I felt. I cried, a lot. She told me not to expect her to be there when I got home. I called her over and over again on the way home, but she wouldn't pick up. I must have left ten apology messages on her phone. When I got to the apartment, she was gone, and all of her stuff was gone, too.

It has been a year since she moved out, and she has still not spoken to Aspen about it. She only relayed through friends that she was not coming back. Aspen desperately misses her. "I still can't think about dating other women. She was my best friend, and it's all gone."

The question I ask is, is this a reasonable reaction to casual sex? Were Aspen and his girlfriend best served by the contract of monogamy? How many fine relationships, how many families need to be torn asunder because we equate sex with so much? It is easy to stand back, fold one's arms across one's chest, and proclaim, "Well, that's what one gets for cheating." But does the punishment really fit the crime? Should it be a crime in the first place?

Ultimately, our emphasis of evaluating monogamy as the litmus test of a relationship seems to be failing us. Our emphasis on sexual fidelity places an unreasonable ultimatum on a relatively unimportant variable. If one is truly concerned with protecting marriage, if one is truly concerned with protecting kids from the consequences of divorce, it is monogamy that needs to be critically examined—not cheating.

THE OPPRESSION OF POSSESSION

Almost all of the men in my study who tried monogamy for more than 6 months report that monogamy instead tried them. Only a handful of men remained happily monogamous, and it was only those still in the first few months of a relationship that suggested that monogamy came easily to them. But even those who *manage* monogamy successfully for a few years indicate that monogamy does not guarantee them a lifetime of sexual joy.

At one level, men understand this. I think it is fair to suggest that most men "intellectually" are capable of thinking about it. For example, I received an e-mail from one of my graduating students recently:

I am getting married in 10 days. I am nervous and excited because I have wanted to marry her for a long time but know how hard marriage is going to be at times. I am praying that I can be interviewed as an anomaly in your studies on monogamous relationships in the future.

Still, others simply understand monogamy as frustrating, upsetting, and burdensome. Barash and Lipton (2009) write:

Nearly everyone has experienced the pulls and pushes of extramonogamous temptation: being pulled toward another and/or pushed away from an unfaithful partner. And rare indeed is the person who hasn't been affected, nearly always for the worse, by the extramarital transgressions of someone close to them. Few experiences are more disruptive—emotionally, financially, personally, and also laden with impact that reverberates throughout a family, often for years, if not decades (p. 53).

My proposition is that within the monogamy gap, the explicit and implicit denial of the opportunity to have sex with others is intellectually understood, but it nonetheless *feels* like oppression. Few of us like to be controlled, and this makes it difficult when our personal desire for monogamy begins to wane.

RESENTMENT

Although the men in my study did not explicitly state that they resented their partner, this emotion was oftentimes evident. For example, in a sarcastic tone, Nigel said, "I'd love to be having sex with other women, but I can't. I have to go home to my girlfriend." This was particularly the case when other guys were talking about hooking up with women. While out clubbing with a group of university soccer players, several of the guys were talking about who they wanted to try and pick up. Looking down at women on the dance floor, one player said, "That chick is hot. I'm going down to work on her." He left me and CJ alone, looking down on those dancing. "Why, don't you go down and dance with someone?" I asked. "I can't," CJ said. "I've got a girlfriend," in a disappointed tone.

I later asked CJ how he felt about not being able to be one of the guys—not being able to sow his oats. "It sucks. If I didn't have a girlfriend, I'd have been out there working the dance floor." He added:

> You get a girlfriend and say goodbye to being one of the guys. I can't have sex with other women, which sucks, but I can't even do things that might be perceived as—you know—the beginning stages of having sex. I love my girlfriend, but sometimes I think I should dump her just so I can be free again . . . but you can't have your cake and eat it too.

What these men describe is the loss of sexual freedom. Accordingly, as a sociologist, what is interesting about their descriptions to me is that they do not view with joy, or even contentment, the fact that they have 'voluntarily' given-up casual sex in order to retain the emotional benefit of longer term coupledom. Instead, they lament their inability to have that coupledom alongside extradyadic sex. Monogamy, to these men, exists as a form of forced sexual incarceration. Worse, as university students, they exist within a peer group that partakes in the thrill (and oftentimes success) of seeking out sexual recreation.

I call this sexual incarceration because they have not freely chosen to give up the pursuit of recreational sex. This is why they do not rejoice in watching their mates hit on women on the dance floor from a safe distance. Instead, they were socially compelled to give up this freedom. Regardless of how they intellectually view monogamy, they experience it as oppression; and oppression breeds resentment.

Understanding monogamy as oppression is not a new proposition. Hyrum (1885) wrote:

> Monogamy being partial in its privileges, and oppressive in its prohibitions, like every other oppressive and unjust thing, provokes resentment and enmity, and cannot be thoroughly maintained and honestly observed. Human nature is constantly rebelling against it, and is persistently asserting its inherent and inalienable right to all the benefits of love and marriage, of which this system has deprived it (pp. 166–167).

Men also felt resentment at missing out on their university experience. As their friends went out "on the pull," men partnered for over a year had to stay with their girlfriend. As they continually decline their friends' invitations to nights out, these friends ask them less and less—a cycle develops. For example, Ben told me, "I don't really get to do many things. I'm with my girlfriend all the time, and if I go out with others, she gets jealous." Even when Ben is permitted time away from his girlfriend, he discusses feeling electronically leashed to her.

> So let's say I'm allowed to go out with some of my friends. That's great and all, but she's so jealous that I might meet some other girl that she restricts me.

I can't dance with other girls so I can only dance with the guys I go with, and I can't really talk to girls there either. So it's like I'm allowed to go out, but with serious restrictions. . . . Worse, she still leashes me electronically. I'll get texts from her all night long. "What you doing?" "How's it going?" "What time do you think you're coming home?" And I know she is just sitting at home stewing in jealousy that I'm out having fun and she's not. I just know she's thinking that I should be spending more time with her. And I know she's worried that I'm "Oh no" actually talking to other girls . . . I love her, but I've lost so much freedom. I'm only 19, it's not supposed to be this way. I'm supposed to be having the time of my life, not answering to someone. I feel like when I was 15 and my mom was asking tons of questions about who I was going out with. It makes me wonder if I'll ever have the freedom to just make my own choices.

Monogamy is not entirely responsible for Ben's feeling of being controlled. But I question just how much more open Ben's girlfriend would be if she did not fear that he might hook up with someone else. How much better would it be if she simply expected him to pull (make out) with others on the dance floor as part of his having a good time that night? If she knew that her partner was hooking up, and had her permission, it would likely relieve some sense of the oppression that Ben experienced.

Monogamists will balk at this proposition of monogamy being oppressive and generating ill feelings toward one's partner. They will argue that we are seemingly free to enter into monogamous relationships and can therefore choose to avoid them. They will contend that we are well aware that we will want sex with someone else, but know that with the commitment of a relationship (and thus monogamy) we will not act upon it. They will maintain that if we do not desire monogamy, we should not commit to it in the first place. At a surface level they are correct. But there are also serious faults with the monogamist's argument.

First, it is important to consider just how we are cajoled into monogamous relationships through cultural expectations that provide no real alternative. If one feels romance for another, the chances of having it returned are low if the person suggests that he or she does not want to be monogamous. Sacrificing sex with others is palatable because they are enjoying the sex that comes with the onset of a relationship, and the couple's future is distant, and thus out of mind.

This corresponds with men's hormonal yearning for monogamy in the romance phase, too. Recall that men are hormonally predisposed to monogamy through the oxytocin and arginine vasopressin system. In time, however, our biology relinquishes the desire for monogamy. Our carnal fantasies desire gratification from outside the relationship. Accordingly, we agree to monogamy because we are duped into wanting it. It is only later that we come to realize that monogamy generates relationship stress.

Giving up sex with others is considerably easier when one is enjoying current sex, and when one is duped into believing that the sex he or she enjoys will be forever lasting. This is perhaps one of the greatest myths I encounter in my daily conversation with people: the belief that the neurological excitement of sex with one's partner will not fade—and that if it does fade it is one's own fault.

Shelton (2008) calls those who eschew the idea of monogamy as being established against our biological desires *romantics*, suggesting that they scoff at the notion of needing multiple sex partners and insist that, if they are not sexually satisfied, they have just yet to meet the right person. But human beings are not dogs. We cannot enjoy the same food night after night. This is recognized as a punishment. So what stops us from doing this? Why are open relationships so rare despite monogamy being so plain and repetitive? The answer is largely found in avoidance of what is thought to be an even more unpleasant emotion: jealousy.

11

Jealousy

One factor that both monogamous and open relationships have in common is that jealousy is often a source of emotional discontent. Monogamy is not a guarantee against jealousy. Quite the opposite; the constant policing that monogamy requires structures jealousy into it. Thus, in this chapter I examine how monogamy structures jealousy into a relationship and how open relationships can help each member of the couple unlearn jealousy. I first give recognition to the psychobiological explanations of evolutionary psychology, before dismissing them and discussing how we learn what to attach jealousy to, and why monogamous relationships likely engender more jealousy than open sexual relationships.

EVOLUTIONARY PERSPECTIVES ON JEALOUSY AND CHEATING

Several evolutionary psychologists theorize a biological basis for jealousy. They theorize women to be more upset about emotional infidelity than men because men and women are thought to have faced different threats to their ability to procreate within their ancestral history (Buss, 1995; Daly, Wilson, & Weghorst, 1982; Symons, 1979). Fertilization occurs within the female; thus, an ancestral man could never know for certain that a child was his own. Fred Flintstone did not have access to a DNA test; thus, if Wilma Flintstone was impregnated by Barney Rubble, Fred could spend (read waste) resources on genetically unrelated children, thus decreasing his reproductive fitness.

It has therefore been hypothesized that men developed a specific innate psychological mechanism that responds to the threat of sexual infidelity with intense jealousy. This jealousy (presumably coupled with men's propensity for violence) is thought to thwart another male from having sex with their mate. This has even been linked into theorizing that men are more likely to commit physical spousal abuse toward their partners (Daly & Wilson, 1983). According to this theory, the propensity to grow enraged over infidelity is "just" part of a man's biological makeup.

Men's greater tendency toward expressing jealousy through anger and aggressive behavior is a well-documented phenomena (Daly, Wilson, & Weghorst, 1982; Geary, 1998; White & Kowalski, 1998). Supporting this, Buntin, Lechtman, and Laumann (2004) use the *Chicago Health and Social Life Survey Design* to show that heterosexual men's rates of violence against their female partners is between 10% and 62%, depending on the part of the city they studied. Paik, Laumann, and Van Haitsma (2004) suggest that sexual jealousy among young men plays an "important role in elevating the likelihood of intimate-partner violence among dating and cohabitating couples" (p. 233).

Conversely, an ancestral woman faced no threat of a man pretending to have her baby (cuckoldry) because a woman could fool a man into thinking it was his baby despite the fact that she was impregnated by another. Regardless of who fertilized her, any child she bore was obviously her own. Women were therefore not under selective pressure to form a sexual jealousy trait. Instead, they faced a different threat; her chosen mate (regardless of whoever impregnated her) might expend his resources on another woman's children. Accordingly, evolutionary psychologists suggest that women developed an innate psychological mechanism to respond to a mate's *emotional* infidelity—the assumption being that a man who is in love with a woman is likely to expend resources on her (Harris, 2002). As Daly and Wilson (1983) put it:

> A Darwinian perspective on sexual jealousy suggests the hypothesis that it will prove to be a sexually differentiated state in people . . . because of the asymmetrical risk of cuckoldry. While women may be expected to be jealous of their mate's allocation of attention and resources, for example, they do not have the same rationale as men for being concerned with specifically sexual fidelity (p. 182).

This view of jealousy as a sexually dimorphic adaptation has great intellectual appeal, seemingly linking an important aspect of human emotion to the ultimate force shaping living organisms. It is therefore not surprising that this theory is discussed in social psychology textbooks. It has also received a great deal of attention in books and articles written for the general public (Harris, 2003).

There exists some (limited) evidence to support this theory. Most of it comes from American university students, where they are asked to imagine a mate's hypothetical infidelity, both sexually and romantically. They are then asked which is more upsetting: imagining their partners having sexual intercourse with another person or falling in love with another person. Perhaps unsurprisingly most women predict that emotional infidelity would be more upsetting than sexual infidelity (Buss, Larsen, Westen, & Semmelroth, 1992; DeSteno & Salovey, 1996; Harris & Christenfeld, 1996), but men actually appear to be evenly split in their responses. In trials of the study, 40%–60% suggested that sexual infidelity would be worse than emotional infidelity.

Also supporting the notion that men and women experience jealousy differently, Moi (1987) examined gendered differences in jealousy, finding that women primarily experience jealousy as loss, while men experience it as anger against the rival. Perhaps an example from my study will illuminate this gendered perspective.

Aaron, in his second year at university, had a girlfriend of 4 years. Aaron is careful not to have his girlfriend visit his university; instead, he expresses to her that he takes pride in being the chivalrous one (not his word) to pay the train fare and make the 3-hour trip to visit her. There is, however, an alternative motive for Aaron's traveling. Aaron cheats on his girlfriend, often two or three times a week. He takes no shame in his cheating; instead, he brags to his friends about it.

I asked him about how and why he cheats. It is clear that Aaron has cheated so much that he no longer (or perhaps never did) feels guilt over it. I asked, "Why don't you just open the relationship up?" "No way," he responded. When I asked him why not, suggesting that it would make a lot more sense, he said, "No fucking way am I going to let some guy fuck my girlfriend."

What was truly significant about this exchange, and something that's hard to explain in writing, was the visceral nature of his reactions. The idea of another man having sex with "his" girlfriend brought an intensity to his response that made even me momentarily feel that I might be physically attacked.

I met Aaron for a pint of beer with some of his mates a few weeks later. One of the other boys asked Aaron what he would do if he found out that his girlfriend was cheating on him. Again, Aaron lost his composure, saying that he would break up with her. When one of his mates razzed him about his double standard, he grew angry. He recognized the double standard but would not emotionally accept it.

Stories like this make gender an important variable in dealing with anger. However, the evidence for the alleged evolutionarily account of gender difference is debatable. It is unclear that the reported differences are biologically determined as opposed to being socially constructed. For example, gender differences have rarely been noted in reports on global measures of jealousy in infants and toddlers (Hart & Carrington, 2002; Hart et al., 1998). However, I recognise it is possible that testosterone plays a part in activating the jealousy system and that would not be expressed until adulthood.

Supporting the view that jealousy is not hardwired differently according to gender, in a review of the topic Harris (2003) failed to find a robust sex difference across a variety of data sets. Although the speculations offered by proponents of this form of Darwinian explanation about jealousy are intriguing, according to Harris, they do not seem to be right (Harris, 2003). Further supporting this argument, Mullen and Martin (1994) found that, in contrast to the theory that gendered differences in jealousy exist as a product of evolutionary psychobiology, men and women in New Zealand were equally likely to have been physically assaulted by a jealous partner after cheating. Furthermore, more than 70% of the men from China, Germany, and the Netherlands report that emotional infidelity would be more upsetting than sexual infidelity (DeSteno & Salovey, 1996;

Harris & Christenfeld, 1996). Thus, I maintain that jealousy over cheating is most likely a product of culture—at least it is not pure genetic hardwiring.

JEALOUSY IS NATURAL, BUT JEALOUSY OF SEX IS NOT

Jealousy may or may not appear differently in men and women, but it most certainly is a natural emotion. The best evidence that jealousy is hardwired comes through the work of Hart, Harrington, Tronick, and Carroll (2004), who find what appears to be jealousy in infants who are as young as 6 months. This work shows that there is some form of negative emotion in the infants when their mother directs her attention toward what appears to be another baby, as opposed to a book.

According to an e-mail conversation with jealousy expert Christine Harris (June 22, 2010), of the University of California, San Diego, "If there are hardwired triggers it would be on a more basic level—such as loss of attention, but clearly development, experience, and culture greatly influence jealousy reactions." Thus, my take on jealousy is that it is an innate human emotion that may be expressed naturally over some things, but that it is likely mostly to be expressed through the cultural learning of what acts to be jealous of. In other words, I first recognize that the ability to feel jealously exists, but that we most likely learn what to associate the feeling with. This is not unlike other emotions. For example, if I am playing soccer and someone pushes me, I am not as angered as I would be if I were just walking down the street and being pushed; context is everything in the expression of emotions.

Beginning from the assumption that, at its core, jealousy is just one emotion available to human beings but that we must learn what to attach it to (Frijda, 1986), many psychologists approach jealousy from the perspective of emotion theory. Although these theories vary, collectively they stress the importance of interpretation and appraisal of a diverse assortment of threats in the elicitation of jealousy (Harris, 2003). In particular, emotion theories view romantic and sexual jealousy as the result of perceptions that someone from outside the relationship poses a threat to that relationship (Parrott, 1991; White & Mullen, 1989).

But what is perceived as a personal threat will, to a large extent, be influenced by the values of one's culture. Jealousy does not solely concern infidelity. Social-cognitive theorists (who use emotion theory) hypothesize that the same basic processes of jealousy are exemplified in multiple other (nonsexual) human relationships (parent–child relationships, friendships, etc.). Accordingly, psychologists emphasize the importance of two factors that increase the likelihood of arousing jealousy (Harris, 2003). The first is when relationship rewards are threatened. The second is when some aspect of a person's self-concept is challenged by someone outside the relationship. For example, White and Mullen (1989) defined romantic jealousy this way:

> Romantic jealousy is a complex of thoughts, emotions, and actions that follows loss or threat to self-esteem and/or the existence or quality of the

romantic relationship. The perceived loss or threat is generated by the perception of a real or potential romantic attraction between one's partner and a (perhaps imaginary) rival . . . (p. 9).

This is not a particularly new way of examining jealousy. In (1931), Margaret Mead suggested that threats to self-esteem are at the root of jealousy. Similarly, others emphasize the importance of threats to aspects relevant to one's self concept (Mathes, 1991), self-definition (Parrott, 1991), and self-identity (Salovey & Rothman, 1991), as underlying triggers of the experience of jealousy. It is thought that these threats are particularly salient in romantic relationships because these relationships are potentially rich sources of personal rewards (Turner, 1970; White & Mullen, 1989).

Harris (2003) suggests that there is an association between jealousy/anger and fear/sadness. When one focuses on the potential loss of a mate, sadness *or* fear may be elicited, whereas focusing on the sense that the rival has wronged one may elicit anger *or* jealousy. She says, "The extent to which one experiences jealousy over a mate sleeping with someone else will depend on appraisals for why he or she is doing so and how it reflects on one's own self and one's relationship rewards" (p. 122). This means that if a culture prescribes that it is appropriate for a member of a dyad to sleep with someone outside that relationship, a jealousy threat is minimized or eliminated (Wood & Eagly, 2002).

FREEING OURSELVES FROM THE BURDENS OF SEXUAL JEALOUSY

It is a poor reflection of our culture's emotional intelligence that in our monogacentric culture, we do not readily understand how open sexual relationships can free us from the burdens of jealousy. Instead, we are taught that infidelity is such a violation of our love that we are to be angry, demoralized, and humiliated. This, of course, is socially constructed. Harris (2003) concludes, "What is considered illegitimate or arbitrary will vary greatly across individuals and cultures. In short, the elicitation of jealousy, like other emotions, is likely to arise from cognitive appraisals rather than simple innate hard-wired triggers" (p. 122).

The current configuration of the social construction of jealousy means that it is monogamous couples who experience jealousy more than those in open sexual relationships. However, the operation of hegemony once again means that we fail to analyze it this way. Few people bother to ask what the negative ramifications of monogamy are on jealousy; instead, they ask these critical questions about those who are in open relationships.

Robinson (1997) also writes about how monogamy structures jealousy. This jealousy is something of a Catch-22. Couples feel jealousy over the mere idea that their partner might have sex with another, often even feeling jealousy when their partner socializes with an attractive person. However, jealousy is what traps them into further jealousy. Jealousy prevents people from further exploring nonmonogamous alternatives. And while the men in this study recognize this (when I point it out to them), they nonetheless feel that the petty, ongoing jealousy they have currently is better than the extreme jealousy they would feel if their partner were to engage in extradyadic sex. William said:

> Oh yeah, I'm jealous all the time. I constantly wonder who it is she's out with, what she thinks about other guys. Of course you can't say that, can you? You can't just say, hey I'm jealous. Because that would show that I don't trust her.

Accordingly, rather than monogamy freeing one from jealousy, the institution of monogamy is upheld by it. Robinson (1997) writes:

> Kingsley Davis, in the 1950's, argued that monogamy produced jealousy, not jealousy monogamy—but this did not lead him to critique the concept of jealousy—instead it entailed an acceptance of it on the grounds that jealousy performs a function in that the absence of jealousy would naturally lead to promiscuity and therefore the breakdown of society (see Moi, 1987) (p. 148).

Most of the men in my study also took this perceptive. The men feared jealousy from their girlfriends or boyfriends having sex outside the relationships, or from even thinking about sex outside the relationship. They then used their fear of jealousy to police their partner's behaviors and limit the social arenas they could experience. Feeling a sense of jealousy led men to read their partner's text messages, to make sure they were not growing too close to another person. Others logged onto their partner's Facebook or MSN pages and carried on Internet chats under the guise of being their partner. Jealousy influenced them to unduly question their partners about their doings.

Jealousy is a vexing human emotion. It festers in your gut and eats at your sanity. Jealousy comes out in all types of destructive ways. I know this because I used to be an extremely jealous person. I recall once being so attracted to one of my heterosexual male roommates that I grew intensely jealous anytime he would even mention finding women attractive. My jealousy then peaked the first time he brought a girl into his room. Like most people, I could not permit myself to admit to jealousy back then. For some reason our culture frowns upon the feeling of jealousy; thus, the experience of jealousy comes out through anger. Accordingly, I found reasons to be mad at him. And because she was preventing me from having him (as ridiculous as that is) I also grew mad at her. Ultimately, my anger caused him to move out.

The point is, when one is extremely jealous, one acts and says things that push the object of one's affection away. A better approach is to admit that one is jealous, and then to permit the individual to experience the "act" that is the source of your jealousy. Through a desensitization process one can learn to undo one's jealousy. This approach worked for me.

When I grew jealous of my next friend, I admitted that I had a crush on him and I told him not to change his behaviors. I knew that this would only reinforce my jealousy. Instead, I learned to talk about and use affirmations of "I am mellow" to reduce jealousy feelings. I would admit to feeling jealousy, if and when I did. I did not permit him to change his behaviors on the account of my jealousy. Doing this would instead privilege and reproduce jealousy. In other words, if people "get what they want" through the expression of jealousy, they learn to use jealousy to get what they want on other fronts. This leads to a cycle where one gets more and more jealous as a way to manipulate others into conceding to their desires. This is simple behaviorism. Thus, when the women in my study controlled their partners' behaviors in order to avoid jealousy they instead constructed jealousy; and people do not appreciate having their behaviors controled because someone else is jealous. Sean said:

> I hate it when she tells me what I can and cannot do. She gets real jealous real easy, so because of that I can't hang out with my friends, or go out with groups that include girls in them. If I say, "I'm going to lunch with some classmates," she wants to know who? Or she will be like, "Are any of them girls?"... I then have to account for how I am either not attracted to any of the girls or in some way relieve her jealous fears.

Thus, Sean permits his girlfriend's jealousy to anger him, but he still permits his own jealousy to control her; and this likely angers her. This is how monogamy reproduces and exacerbates jealousy. Just because Sean felt unreasonably controlled by his girlfriend's jealousy does not mean that he has learned from the toils of jealousy. When I asked him if he allows his girlfriend to go out, as the only girl, with a group of guys, he said, "Fuck no. Absolutely not. I trust her, but I can't trust other guys."

12

Liberation from Monogamous Missionary Sex

Relationships are not fixed; they are ever-changing, fluid, and constantly in the state of becoming something new (Deleuze & Guattari, 1999). Still, there are predictable stages and events that characterize *most* relationships, and a key finding of importance considering relationship progression for monogamy and cheating is declining sexual desire for one's partner.

In this chapter I first explicate the research which proves that sexual frequency declines as a couple ages. I show that this is related to relationship duration and not just a result of the natural process of chronological aging. However, in this chapter I also show how changing notions of morality have, perhaps paradoxically, accelerated the rate at which a couple habituates to their monogamous sex.

First, the increased amount of time that one is in a relationship correlates with a greater likelihood that one will grow bored with the sex and therefore cheat. Second, the earlier age upon which we start consuming sex (real and cyber) and the proliferation of sexual variety available to us in both real (via hooking up) and cyber ways, combined with the increased social permission to masturbate to this pornography (and hook up with those we meet on line), has meant that monogamous sex looks considerably more boring than it ever has.

In other words, I suggest that men today grow habituated to monogamy more quickly than their fathers and grandfathers did. I describe this as a process related to increased ability to have sex before marriage, increased availability of sexual imagery, and the increased social acceptability of masturbation. Thus, this chapter suggests that as our society becomes more sexually liberated, monogamy becomes a less harmonious fit. I describe this process through what I call *relative sexual deprivation theory*.

THE LAW OF DIMINISHING SEXUAL RETURNS

There is an old saying that if a newly married couple puts a penny in a jar every time they have sex within the first year of marriage, and then take a penny out of that jar every time they have sex after the first year, there will be enough pennies in the jar to last them the rest of their marriage. The humor and wisdom of this adage is of course the reality that sexual desire for one's partner fades in time, and therefore sexual frequency with that partner also dwindles. This is something I describe as *the law of diminishing sexual returns* because the more time you invest into a relationship the less sex it yields.

My thesis is simple: Most men in sexually and emotionally exclusive relationships cheat in order to secure more neurologically stimulating sex. It is my argument that when men who maintain high intimacy and commitment cheat, it is not because they fail to love their partners; instead, it is because their sexual passion has diminished—an unavoidable event.

Even if one's partner remains aesthetically appealing, the somatic desire to have sex with that partner inevitably wanes—perhaps a little, but most likely a lot. Blumstein and Schwartz (1983) tie this phenomenon in with two sources of aging, one's own aging body and the age of the relationship:

> While the aging process takes its toll on sexual frequency, the process of living together for many years exerts a separate influence. Even though a couple in a new relationship will have sex quite often, partners are still affected as the years pass and they are aware of their declining sexual activity. They naturally wonder how much is due to inevitable physical changes and how much is due to a waning interest in each other (p. 198).

Commenting on the literature concerning decreasing sexual frequency across both cohorts and generations, Willetts, Sprecher, and Beck (2004) write:

> The decline in sexual frequency with age, found consistently across studies, seems to be due to psychological, social and biological factors associated with the aging process (Call, Sprecher, & Schwartz, 1995). Decreases due to habituation, or the reduction in novelty because of being with the same partner, are also likely to occur, but habituation may explain primarily the decrease that occurs early in marriage or a marriage-like relationship, which is the specific period of time that has the greatest decrease in sexual frequency (p. 70).

This decrease in sexual frequency is not, as earlier studies seemed to suggest, related to marital quality (i.e., lower sexual frequency does not indicate less marital satisfaction). Supporting this, Call et al. (1995) use a multivariate analysis on a national sample to show that decreasing sexual frequency is the result of marital habituation and *not* decreased relationship satisfaction. Schwartz and Rutter (2000: 132) write:

> Sexual decline is generally understood as the consequence of habituation. All evidence about sexuality indicates that passion is fueled by novelty, uncertainty, achievement of someone's love, and desire. Marriage itself mitigates uncertainty, and the need for achievement of someone's love. Thus, marriage itself reduces some of the prime motivations for sexual arousal.

Further supporting the hypothesis that declining sex in a relationship is related to habituation, Kinsey, Pomeroy, & Martin (1948), Kinsey et al. (1953) found that not only did yearly marital intercourse decrease by age cohort, but also infidelity (which he reports at about half of all married men and a quarter of all married women) increased among men and women in their 40s, suggesting that extramarital sex accounted for 10% of their sexual encounters. Instead of reading this as people cheating frequently, I think it more attributable to infrequent sexual activity with their spouses.

One can read this, perhaps, as men and women experiencing a midlife crisis and seeking sex to relive their youth. One can hypothesize that, for these couples, they have fallen out of love and that is why they cheated. However, there is a more plausible explanation: These men and women have been in a monogamous marriage a long time, and they desperately crave sex with someone else. They desire outside sexual stimuli so much that even among the *women* who cheated, 50% did so again. In fact, the average woman who cheated did so five times. (Kinsey did not catalog the frequency of men's cheating beyond whether they had at least once cheated or not.)

This does not rule out that men cheat for other reasons, too. For example, men who exist in relationships with low commitment and/or intimacy might cheat for more romantic ideals, and some men (including some in my study) might also cheat because they have low emotional investment in their new partner. But most of the men in my study did not cheat because they grew apart emotionally or because they had only very limited investment in their girlfriend/boyfriend when a better opportunity came along. These are not the type of cheating episodes that are either the most common in this research or the most interesting.

I am explicitly concerned here with the type of cheating that occurs when men do love their partners, when they maintain high emotional intimacy and commitment with them: relationships that are characterized as being in the norming and/or performing stages in my relationships development model. I am explicitly concerned with understanding more about horny men who love their partners and yet crave extradyadic sex.

The assertion I make—that couples are destined to lose their sexual passion for one another—is enhanced by my second assertion: that this is increasingly true of today's youth, compared to the previous generations.

ASSERTION 1: IN TIME WE LOSE OUR SEXUAL PASSION FOR A MONOGAMOUS PARTNER

It is unrealistic to expect continual, highly energetic, passionate, exploratory, and riveting sex with just one partner. A decrease in passion is an unavoidable consequence of being a human being. It is simply part of the human condition of adaption to neurological stimuli. This is not a simple supposition. It is borne out in my research.

Few of the participants cheated within a month of dating. Instead, cheating generally began after 3 or more months. Mike, for example, said: "No. I had no desire for sex with other women at first. All I could think about was her." But after these elevated levels of passion and romance declined (sometimes plummeting) matters began to change for these men. Dan said that although he had always fantasized about other women, he used to be content to have sex only with his girlfriend. Referring to his earlier sex life, he said:

> It was hot . . . real hot. But in time, it just lost some of its appeal. We did things to spice it up, and we still have something of an active sex life, but I can't say that some other girl wouldn't be nice from time to time.

Similarly, Jon said, "When I first started dating her I thought she was so hot I wouldn't want any other woman for the rest of my life, but that's not what happened." This was true of both straight and gay men, and this finding is replicated in other research on men as well (Harry, 1984). I am not the only academic to suggest that there is a law of diminishing returns when it comes to one's investment in a partner for sex. A recent book by Christopher Ryan and Cacilda Jethá (2010), *Sex at Dawn*, makes the point so well that it became a *New York Times* best seller.

You can explore the dozens of self-help books at your local bookstore to find numerous books/chapters that offer "good advice" for keeping the sexual spark alive. The point remains, however, that neurological passion dies as a relationship progresses. Despite efforts to spice it up, there is very little that you can do to keep it new. Conversely, no research—ever—has shown that sex becomes better, more exciting, and more frequent as the years of one's monogamous relationship progresses.

Further highlighting that a diminishment in sexual frequency and intensity is a normal and functional process of growing intimacy and commitment to a partner, there is ample empirical support from multiple other large-scale academic studies. These studies not only augment my research, but they perhaps better explicate my point. This is because I did not acquire numerical data concerning declining sexual frequency with my participants. While almost all of the men described a decrease in sexual activity over their relationships, I did not ask all of the men how many times a week/month they had sex. This is partially because I am a qualitative researcher and I am less skilled in this form of research and tabulation. But it is also because of the extreme complexity of asking this type of question. What counts as sex? Is it intercourse only? Does massaging someone you find attractive count? And how does one fairly compare sexual frequency rates of cohabitating couples, noncohabitation, and those who maintain long-distance relationships? The more one questions these variables, the more complicated things get.

However, large-scale studies of sexual frequency do exist. And as problematic as they are (the nature of the questions is limiting; the informants are generally lumped in together regardless of how long they have been with their partners; and they each ask and report on sexual frequency using different types of statistics), these studies might nonetheless tell us something about decreasing sexual activity over the course of a "marriage." These studies are also perhaps more accurate because we can assume that they avoid some of the problems that a population of university students presents (temporary locations, long-distance relationships, existence in a rich sex market, etc.).

When it comes to studying heterosexual married couples' frequency of copulation (an oversimplification of the types of sexual activities a couple might engage in), Kinsey (1953, p. 394) conducted the first, pioneering study. Kinsey and his colleagues found that married, heterosexual couples aged 16–20 had intercourse 3.7 times a week, and that this number slowly decreased over age cohorts (which also reflects the aging of one's relationship). Kinsey reported that those aged 36–40 indicated two sessions of intercourse a week, and those 51–55 reported having 1.2 sessions of intercourse a week. Interestingly, those aged 56–60 reported just 0.8, suggesting that sex greatly decreases in one's late 50s. These statistics necessarily conflate two variables on sexual frequency: one's sexual drive (which might perhaps wane with age) and the boredom of sexual habituation that occurs as the age of the monogamous relationship progresses.

In the next national study, Blumstein and Schwartz (1983) found the same decreasing age-cohort effect and similar rates of intercourse frequency. Blumstein and Schwartz suggest that sex between long-term married heterosexual couples does not disappear from their lives altogether, finding that in only 15% of the cases does it drop to less than once a month—although these couples report that their sex is not as "energetic" as it once used to be.

Blumstein and Schwartz (1983) add to the analysis a study of gay male couples—something that was likely impossible to do in Kinsey's day. Here, they show that gay male couples are more predisposed to growing bored with sex than heterosexual couples. They write (1983): "Gay men have more sex often in the early part of the relationship than any other type of couple. But after ten years, they have sex together far less frequently than married [heterosexual] couples" (p. 195).

It is likely that gay men have more sex than heterosexuals in the early phases of a relationship, which causes them to grow desensitized in fewer years. However, it might also be that because gay men share similar emotions about sex (compared to the divergence that men and women in heterosexual relationships might feel), gay men are more honest about their declining sexual activity and are therefore less likely to simply go through the motions in order to fulfill a social role.

Gay men are perhaps less likely to pressure unenergetic sex onto each other, without feeling that a decrease in passion is indicative of a decrease in emotional intimacy. This honesty is also more likely to influence gay men to seek extradyadic sexual pleasures outside their relationship, which will then reduce the amount of sex they report having with their partners on Blumstein and Schwartz's study. This is not something Blumstein and Schwartz account for, but it can nonetheless be gleaned by their noting that gay men are much less likely to exist within monogamous relationships.

A monogamist might argue that these statistics show sex does not die with relationship duration. Those wedded to the idea of monogamy being the only "right" way of being in a romantic relationship are likely to suggest that just because sex declines in frequency with age, it can still be just as good. Accordingly, those looking to deflate my argument will undoubtedly use these preceding statistics to argue that heterosexual marriage *is capable* of delivering a lifetime of sexual pleasure, even if the frequency is somewhat diminished. However, I point out that there are several important considerations to take into account when analyzing statistics from large-scale studies like Kinsey, Blumstein, and Schwartz; Laumann et al.; or the Hite report (in England).

First, these studies do not account for *quality* of sexual interaction. Just because one is engaging in sex does not mean that one is enjoying it. Second, at the time these studies were conducted sex was not as voluntary between couples as it is today (women had much less sexual agency in Kinsey's time than they do today). Having sex was part of the obligation of a couple (particularly on the part of women). Third, there has been an attitudinal shift (a true paradigm shift) concerning the availability and increasing morality of recreational sex, pornography, masturbation, and other aspects of sexual practices today (Dines, 2010). I argue that these changes serve to reduce our sexual intercourse with our partners because there are many more other exciting options available today.

In the next section I unpack my argument as to why it may be more difficult for youth today to keep their monogamous sexual lives thrilling, exciting, and long lasting compared to how their parents or grandparents may have kept their sexual passion alive. I suggest that the pornication of society, the early age at which we begin sex, and the marvelous psychosocial effect of the Internet have made us all grow somewhat desensitized to monogamous sex. But instead of problematizing the pornication of our culture, I celebrate it, suggesting that it both liberates and improves our sexual selves.

CULTURAL PORNICATION VIA THE INTERNET

There have been wholesale changes to our sexual and gendered society over the last two decades, changes that add to the massive overhaul of our attitudes toward sex and our sexual practices since Kinsey and his colleagues conducted their studies (Kinsey, Pomeroy, & Martin 1948; Kinsey et al. 1953). These changes have come from many social influences: the decreasing religiosity of our social worlds, women's liberation, gay liberation, and the advancement of technologies of culture—particularly the Internet—which has ushered in a democratization of sexual desire (Attwood, 2010; McNair, 2002).

Pornography aesthetics have, in recent years, moved from the skin magazine under the bed to an accepted embeddedness in multiple aspects of today's popular culture. As sex has become less stigmatized, mainstream media texts and other cultural practices using pornographic styles, gestures, and aesthetics have become more prominent in all aspects of commercial culture—and this leads to a further erosion of sex as stigmatized. This process, which Brian McNair (2002) describes as a "pornographication of the mainstream," (I just use "pornication") has developed alongside an expansion of the cultural realm of pornography, which has become more accessible to a much wider variety of audiences through the Internet. This is much different than how boys used to consume pornography (Attwood, 2010).

Whereas teenage boys once traded baseball cards, today they trade digital pornography clips obtained free from Web sites. Where once they sneaked a peek at their Father's *Playboy*, today they have access to pornography on their cell phones. Instead of pages of still shots of normally posed nude individuals, the world of interactive and dynamic pornography has come to fruition. The Internet provides anyone the ability to instantly access a display of sexual variety—of any type in all manners. Here a whole range of bodies have sex in all combinations, styles, mixtures, manners, and video quality. But bodies also copulate with all forms of once highly taboo sexual object choices. Any sexual fetish can be located in the cyber world, and a few hours of exploration might subject one to images that one previously had no idea he or she would be aroused by. Whatever you desire to see—people being urinated on, toe sucking, self-sucking, BDSM, chubby people, older people, group sex, animal sex, scat, objects of all sorts being inserted into anuses and vaginas, public sex, oral sex, facials, incest,—it can all be found on the Internet.

Furthermore, for the first time in history, rather than simply looking at an erotic drawing, reading an erotic text, or salivating over an erotic photo, today it is possible to interact with the subjects of our desire. We can sex text from our cell phones, masturbate to the text and/or Web cam images of a friend on MSN, or find a plethora of people to have sexual chat and/or Web cam with that we don't know, found in any number of sex-related chat rooms. If you want, you can pay to watch professionals online, too. We can upload our own pornography to amateur Web sites and take delight at knowing that others are fantasizing about us.

There are no age controls for these Web sites, and there is no need to register a credit card. Accordingly, Dines (2010) suggests that kids today access pornography on average at age 11. But pornography is undoubtedly popular with a large swath of the population; after all, *sex* remains the most popular word typed into search engines. Thus, whereas governments used to control porn in a misguided attempt to prevent it from unduly influencing its citizens' minds into sexual deviance (Rubin, 1993), today's governments cannot control it. The Internet has ended such prohibition—efforts to the contrary are futile.

I am not critiquing the panoply of sex and sexual variety on the Internet. I think it wonderful. It provides what some feminists concerned with pornography have been calling for all along: not an abolition of pornography but an explosion of the subjectivities of differing kinds of people in pornography (Ellis, O'Dair, & Tallmer, 1990). This explosion of pornography has reshaped and greatly expanded our cultural/sexual pallet of opportunities: Gone is the expectation of heterosexual missionary sex (Segal, 1994). The Internet has sparked a revolution of sexual practice, but it has also sparked a revolution in the liberation from oppressive norms.

For example, the Internet has been useful in reducing cultural homophobia through making homosexuality (and gay sex) visible. Today's Porntube.com generation see, early and often, sexual images that arouse or entertain them. Whether accidentally or intentionally, my students tell me that they view video clips of gays, lesbians, and others once stigmatized by the Victorian cult of heterosexual boredom. Often a heterosexual cannot find his or her preferred images of heterosexual intercourse without filtering through the images of the acts once so socially tabooed. Curiosity of the other, or perhaps a desire to simply see what others enjoy, tempts the heterosexual-minded young person into clicking on the link and watching what their mothers and fathers despised so much. In viewing gay sex they grow desensitized to it. In fact, as I find with my heterosexual male students after showing them gay pornography in my sociology of sexualities class (and anonymously surveying them), some of them are even aroused by it. Thus, I propose the Internet has been instrumental in exposing the forbidden fruit of homosexual sex, commoditizing and normalizing it in the process.

Also highlighting how the Internet has been useful in democratizing sexual desire, it has provided lesbian, gay, bisexual, transgender, and other forums to organize for political action; forums to share life narratives; and forums for heterosexuals to ask sexual minorities "anything" about their sexual lives. Clearly, the Internet has been beneficial in making visible these lives to the "normal" heterosexual world. The Internet has taken away the fear for us to ask about one's sexual orientation, too. For example, MySpace asks for one's sexual orientation; Facebook asks whether one is interested in men, women, or both; and both of these Web sites make this part of the basic information package one can publicly present to the world. This has severely reduced the notion that homosexuality (particularly) is a "private" affair; thus, it has helped reduce heterosexism. It is increasingly less acceptable to assume that one is straight.

These trends have resulted in some measurable changes to our attitudes and behaviors regarding other forms of sexuality, too. There has been a lessening of the double standard of stigma associated with women having premarital or recreational sex (Bogle, 2008; Tanenbaum, 1999; Wolf, 1997), and there exists a strong culture of hooking up among today's youth (Bogle, 2008). Facebook even permits one to say that he or she is in an open relationship.

The Internet has also impacted upon our sexual behaviors with our partners. The commoditization of extreme pornography makes yesterday's stigmatized bedroom activities normal, perhaps mundane. Thus, the range of sexual behaviors we can partake in and discuss with our friends is greatly expanded, and this gives us more opportunities to expand our boundaries of what is gay/straight, degrading/invigorating, dangerous, or boring (Subotnik, 2007).

If there is a downside to all of this sexual availability, however, it is that these combinations of changing sexual mores and the lessening of stigma around sexual practices has also led to a quicker desensitization to monogamous sex with our partners. Key to my argument, that the panoply of easy sexual imagery (and sex itself) reduces the timescale we can have sex with our partners before becoming desensitized, is not just the availability of these images and acts, but the social permission to masturbate without stigmatization to them.

I argue that just as the Internet has been instrumental in eroding cultural homophobia and making gay sex more palatable (or even titillating) to hetero-sexuals, it has also been vital in decreasing the amount of sex that married couples have together. This is not because of the nature of the pornography, how-ever; instead it is because of the ability for one to enjoy sexual fantasies through *masturbation*.

MASTURBATION AND MONOGAMOUS SEX

Masturbation has, as Laumann et al. say (1994), "a troubled history in Western cultures" (p. 80). This is very much an understatement. In fact, at the core of mas-turbation's Latin meaning is the word "abuse." Over the centuries it has been asso-ciated with a variety of evils. Held as a moral sin, masturbation has been perceived as a corporeal threat to health for centuries. Even in the last century it has been associated with a variety of psychological and medical illnesses—far too many illnesses and psychological abnormalities to list here. Important to this research, however, is that during the time Kinsey (1948; 1953) conducted his research, mas-turbation continued to be socially perceived as moral weakness (Moncy, 1986).

This resonates with my own experience decades later. I recall multiple conver-sations in which my high school friends (early to mid-1980s) stigmatized others through accusations of their masturbating. This social mindset also existed in my young adult years (late 1980s and early 1990s). I recall taking a university sexuali-ties course in 1988, where the professor positively discussed masturbation. However, none of the students admitted to actually doing it, including me. I sat terrified that someone might ask if I had. This is because, back then—the apex of homophobia that characterized the 1980s (Anderson, 2009)—masturbation was linked to homosexuality. Boys assumed that it would take a "fag" to enjoy it. I was deeply closeted and thus concerned to be thought straight. I therefore did not admit to masturbation until after I came out of the closet.

Cross-sectional and longitudinal studies based on middle-school and high-school males in the 1980s and early 1990s support my experience. They show that only about a third to less than half of males report having ever masturbated (Halpern, Udry, Campbell & Suchindran, 1993; Udry, 1988). In 1994, Laumann et al. found that 37% of the men interviewed said that they had not masturbated even once during the last year. And an unimaginable 41% of youth aged 18–24 said that they too had not masturbated, not even once, during the previous year as well. Laumann et al. write: "Even today masturbation is considered variously as a sin, as a sign of social or psychological incompetence, as evidence of a lack of willpower, or only appropriate for adolescents and people who do not have sex partners" (p. 80).

But to the young men reading this book, an anti-masturbation culture does not resonate. Young men today do not have to "admit" to masturbating; instead, it is assumed that all young men (and increasingly women) just do masturbate. Highlighting how matters have changed, only 6 years after the Laumann study (which found 63% of men admitting to masturbating once in the previous year) Gerressu et al. used data from a 1999–2001 survey (published in 2008) to show that 95% of men reported having masturbated at some point in their lives and that 73% reported masturbating in the 4 weeks before their interview, with 51.7% saying they had done so in the previous week.

More recent research highlights even higher rates of masturbation. For example, research conducted in 2008 on 886 boys in seven middle-schools of British nationals found that boys began masturbating at about 12 years old, and by the time they were 19 years old 93% were admitting to masturbating (Unni, 2010). In a recent study published in 2008, Meston and Tierney (2008) show that 97% of white undergraduate men say that they have masturbated. They also found a few racial differences, with Hispanic men saying that they masturbate at 93% and Asian men at 89%. These high rates of reported masturbation (compared to previous studies) are illuminating of the changing social attitude toward masturbating, not only because they are higher than previous research but because they are derived from Texas, a conservative and religious state.

In the most up-to-date research (not yet published), Michael Bailey found that of the 276 undergraduate men he surveyed, the average male student masturbated 17.6 times per month. The largest group, however, were those masturbating more than 30 times a month. The message I take from my undergraduates in Britain (as well as with the men I researched in the United States) is that young men are more worried about whether they masturbate enough to be considered normal, as opposed to fearing they are the only one to indulge in such wondrous pleasures. In a very real sense, masturbation has gloriously come out of the closet. Highlighting this, Kontula writes (2010):

> Over the last decades, the rate of Finnish people who masturbate has truly exploded. The proportion of male respondents jumped from 74 to 97 percent . . . The figures for the youngest respondents are actually somewhat higher. In 1971, only approximately 60 percent of middle-aged men had occasionally experimented with masturbation. Thereafter the experimentation and practice of masturbation has progressed rapidly from one generation to the next . . . Masturbation frequency increased substantially with each survey. For example, the proportion of respondents in the youngest age group who had masturbated during the preceding month grew between 1971 and

2007 from 36 to 85 percent for young men ... Of those who had masturbated
in the last 24-hour period, the proportion of young men had jumped from
4 to 29 percent (p. 99).

Not only do today's youth masturbate more often but they also talk publicly
about it. They share conversations with others about how often they jerk off; some
even talk about what techniques they use. For example, last semester one student
asked (in front of the sociology of sexualities class) why it was that his wanking was
better while rubbing his nipple. Similarly, when I was describing that anal sex feels
good for men because the prostate is rubbed from the inside (pushing the ejaculate
out harder), one young heterosexual man asked if that was why it felt better when
he fingered himself while masturbating. These types of conversations were also
commonplace with the American men I studied in my ethnographies of the soccer
teams. There was much talk about masturbation techniques. There was no shame
in saying, for example, "Right guys, I'm going home to rub one out." When I que-
ried them about their sexuality, asking if they "ever thought of guys when jerking
off," few said they had; but none protested that they did not masturbate.

This social discourse around masturbation is found on the Internet, too.
Those looking to hone their masturbation skills might check out www.advanced-
masturbation.com, www.letsmasturbate.com, www.jackinworld.com, www.male-
masturbation-techniques.com, www.a2zmasturbation.com, www.askmen.com,
www.the-penis.com, www.aboutmasturbation.com, www.ivillage.com, www.
advancedmasturbationtechniques.com, www.onanibcs.com, www.mymasturba-
tion.com, www.secretsofmasturbation.com, www.masturbation-passion.com, www.
masturbationpage.com, www.knowhowmasturbate.com, www.mysecrethealth.
com, www.mymalesexuality.com, www.holisticwisdom.com, www.greatmastur-
bationtips.com, www.allsexguide.com, www.jackintech.com, and www.hardys-
masturbation.com.

These are, of course, only a partial listing of the Web pages devoted to masturbation that end in .com. We can also list the Web sites devoted to masturbation in
the domain name that ends with .net, or for the more conventional, simply click
on Wikipedia, since there are even masturbation techniques discussed there.
Desire a visual? Just YouTube "masturbation."

Finally, and just to highlight how normal masturbation is today, on one site there
are around 20,000 videos that guys have posted of themselves performing autofel-
latio or self-sucking (and what percentage of guys can do that?). If that many have
posted videos of that, how many have posted videos of generic masturbation? On
one page alone I found 30,000 videos of guys masturbating. All of this is surely more
exciting, more pleasurable, and more satisfying than an aging, crumpled magazine.

GAY MEN MASTURBATE MORE

It is also quite likely that gay men masturbate more than straight men (Gerressu
et al., 2008; Laumann et al., 1994). The statistical finding that gay men masturbate

more might simply reflect the fact that gay men are more used to discussing "sensitive" subjects than heterosexual men, and therefore are less inhibited in admitting it on a survey. Or gay men might just enjoy masturbation more (it is, after all, the equipment they prefer); or it may reflect a psychological process of desiring more sex as a result of being closeted for a number of years.

The reason gay men masturbate more might also have to do with epigenetic occurrences that give gay men more testosterone. Incidentally, this has also been found to give them larger penis sizes. Exemplifying this, Blanchard and Bogaert (1996) used self-reported studies of body dimensions of 844 gay men and 4,104 straight men, gained from the Kinsey Institute, to determine that gay men come later in the birth order, have an earlier onset of puberty, and a lower body weight. Blanchard then went on to determine, using much of the same sample, that of the 935 "exclusively gay" men and 4,187 "exclusively straight" men, gay men had larger penis sizes (Bogaert & Hershberger, 1999). Gay men's penises were thicker (4.95 inches versus 4.80) and longer (6.32 inches versus 5.99) than the sample of white men collected between 1936 and 1962.

While measurements were self-reported, the mean difference between the two groups should be valid unless it can be shown that gay men (and these would have been mostly closeted gay men) can be shown to exaggerate more than straight men, which nobody has researched. Either that or the Kinsey (1948) sample is misrepresentative. Many scholars like to critique the Kinsey sample, but I maintain that it is our best large-scale study of human sexuality to date.

Regardless of whether one accepts the penis size study, a large number of other researchers have found multiple biological differences between gay and straight men (Henry, 1942). This is a source of academic interest (and agitation) that goes back to the days of Magnus Hirschfeld (1914). This means that if someone is trying to answer the question as to whether sexual orientation is something we learn or are born with, the answer is clear. It is something we're born with. Even the majority of sociologists (who are trained to believe that everything is socially constructed), agree with this proposition. In 2006, research on hundreds of American sociologists found that nearly 60% supported an essentialist position (Engle, McFalls, Gallagher, Curtis, 2006). Important to how this might impact monogamy and cheating, one difference is that being gay might come along with a healthier libido than heterosexuals have; this also makes monogamy for gay male couples more unrealistic.

ASSERTION 2: TODAY'S YOUTH HABITUATE TO MONOGAMOUS SEX FASTER THAN OLDER GENERATIONS

The point here is that when masturbation was socially taboo (as it was until approximately the late 1990s), many married men likely sought regular sex with their wives because it was the *only* mechanism of sexual outlet. This propped up the figures of sexual frequency with one's partner and likely extended the couple's sex life (as poor as it might have been). If men used to be shunned away from masturbation, it might help explain why Safilios-Rothschild (1977) found that half of married couples had sexual problems or incompatibilities. Perhaps they were having either unwanted sex (after sexual habituation) or they were having poor sex, because they had not masturbated enough to understand their own sexual patterns and pleasures.

My argument is that our newfound permission to masturbate, combined with a new vessel for material to masturbate to (the Internet), has had profound implications in terms of giving men more sexual outlets than before. Whereas masturbation and pornography were once understood as signs of depravity, they have come out of the closet and have been thoroughly integrated throughout our culture. It follows, then, that if there are other/alternatives to the same old boring sex with one's partner, we will seek these alternatives, forcing a quicker habituation to monogamous sex.

INCREASED MASTURBATION LEADS TO DECREASED SEXUAL FREQUENCY WITH ONE'S PARTNER

It makes sense that when masturbation is stigmatized, when it is viewed as an indictment of love, couples will have more sex with each other. But if masturbation is instead socially and personally acceptable, it will erode at the frequency with which a couple has sex. As the stigma about the panoply of sexual activities that were once taboo decreases, there is less need, want, or desire to have sex with one's partner. Why would one want the same old sex, night after night, when one can find idyllic bodies having sex on the Internet for free? And if one gets tired of simply fantasizing about having sex with someone other than his or her partner, one can join any number of Web sites devoted to seeking out casual sex; one can even join nearly 8 million others on AshleyMadison.com, a Web site specifically devoted to help people cheat. Alternatively, Craig's list is well-known for this as well.

Accordingly, I hypothesize that if one were to ask young men today the same questions about masturbation and sexual frequency that were asked a half century ago (in the same manner as Kinsey investigated), these young men would be much more likely to indicate that they have lower rates of sexual frequency with their monogamous partners. And while I cannot definitively support this from my own data (because I did not systematically collect and analyze it this way), I make this assertion from the dozens and dozens of conversations I had with these men where it *seemed* that for those in my study (18–22 years old) who were coupled for over 2 years, they were having on average less heterosexual sex with their partners than Blumstein and Schwartz found with their 65-year-old respondents! This doesn't mean that these men want sex less; it means they won't settle for the same old boring habituated sex. Blumstein and Schwartz (1983) support this hypothesis by showing that people who have had more premarital sexual intercourse are also likely to have more extramarital intercourse. Thus, early experience (variety) of sex leads to desiring yet more sexual variety (unless, of course, this is a function of higher sex drives), and this is not something monogamy can facilitate.

My suggestion is that as our culture loosens up sexually, we expect more sex; we have sex earlier; we have sex with more people; we expect more diverse sex; and we expect to have some of the sexual fantasies handed to us by the media and advertisers. Thus, even though we commit to monogamy, we do not necessarily want it. Why would we, when we see what else we can have?

While I cannot definitively state that each generation is decreasing in monogamous sexual frequency, other researchers do inadvertently help make my point. Supporting my theory that the increased pornication of society leads to decreasing sexual frequency with each passing decade (in addition to cohort age), Laumann et al. (1994) use *The National Health and Social Life Survey* to show that married couples suggest they have sex less than the married couples in the Kinsey or Blumstein and Schwartz studies.

A few years later, Smith (1998) used *General Social Survey* data to show that sexual frequency between married couples was now down to 61 times a year. He also showed that sexual frequency had declined similar to other studies. Smith found that this number is elevated by couples married less than 3 years and that sexual frequency also decreases as cohorts age (a long-standing and consistent finding). For example, Call et al. (1995) shows that those married under 2 years report sex at 11.7 times per month, but that frequency declines with each subsequent age cohort. And when examining the same issue among married Chinese couples, Cheung et al. (2008) showed that 50% of men aged 19–29 have sex once a week or less. These are much less frequent rates of sex compared to studies of Western men. They also show that by the time a couple gets to 61–70, 100% have sex four or less times a month.

Surveying 4,000 American couples, Berkowitz and Yager-Berkowitz (2007) suggest that 15%–20% of American couples have sex fewer than ten times per year. They note that the absence of sexual desire is the most common sexual problem in the country. Ryan and Jethá (2010) link this to the 118 million prescriptions written for depression in 2005, in America alone.

In case you had a difficult time following all of those statistics, the essence of what I am saying is that with each subsequent investigation into the sexual frequency of monogamous couples, we find decreasing rates of sexual frequency. As the decades pass, the same age cohorts of monogamous couples are reporting less, not more sex in their partnered relationships. The table below uses large scale investigations of American sexual practices to show a decrease in the quantity of heterosexual married sex over the previous four decades.

Ostensibly, this seems at odds with the increased sexual liberation of our culture. One might think that the more sexually liberated our culture becomes the more sex we would have with our partners. But I suggest that what is occurring

Table 12.1

1953	Kinsey	16-20 years old	Sex 192 times a year
1995	Call	Married for less than 2 years	Sex 140 times a year
1998	Smith	Married couples of all ages	Sex 61 times a year

here is that we are having less sex with our partners because after the romance period (with its heightened sexual passion) wears off, masturbation (to the great variety of free pornography, Web-camming, or chatting) is more accessible and enjoyable. I also point out that the Internet, and a culture of hooking up, also gives men more opportunity to cheat. This adds up to more quickly habituating monogamous sex.

All of this pornographic availability also means that older studies of sexual frequency were inflated. First, in times of high homohysteria (Anderson, 2009) men were more likely to boast of their sexual frequency in order to gain heterosexual capital and distance themselves from being thought gay—particularly if discussing their sex lives with a sex researcher. Thus, the reported rates of sexual frequency may not reflect reality. But now that homophobia is decreased, men no longer fear being homosexualized the way they once used to (Anderson, 2009), and they may be more likely to report their rates of sexual intercourse more honestly.

Second, rates of reported sexual intercourse in decades past were higher because this was the *only* acceptable outlet for men (and women) to have sex: pornography, masturbation, and hooking up were all taboo. If one could not masturbate without the wife's disapproval, heterosexual sex was the only safe choice. So for those who use the Kinsey or Blumstein and Schwartz's statistics of ongoing sex found decades into a monogamous relationship to support monogamy as providing abundant sex, one must ask: *(1)* are these rates artificially inflated through boasting? And *(2)* if they are real, do they speak to the quality of this monotonous, monogamous sex? Finally, we should ask, if men had the opportunity for other sexual outlets, as they do today, would the rates have been as high? I think not. Instead, as the pornication of our society has given us more sexual opportunities, people desire sex with their partners less, and with others more.

Supporting my theory that the pornication of our culture promotes monogamy, the most recent *General Social Survey* data concerning cheating show that 34% of those asked admitted to cheating in 2002, while in 2006 that number rose to 40%. The table below highlights four trends that I hypothesize impact our rates of (declining) sex in marriage.

All of the social-sexual changes I mention (particularly relating to the Internet and pornography) are sure to be described by social conservatives (functionalists) as the declining significance of morality. For example, in her book *Pornland: How Porn Has Hijacked Our Sexuality* (2010), Gail Dines argues that the more men watch pornography, the more they want pornographic-style sex (something which

Table 12.2

Availability of pornography	increasing
Acceptance and frequency of masturbation	increasing
Acceptance and frequency of pre-marital sex (hooking up)	increasing
Cheating	increasing
Sexual frequency with one's partner	decreasing

I agree with). She also argues that men quickly grow habituated to sex with their partners because they see an immense variety of industrial-strength sex on the Internet (agreed). Dines adds that sex with one's partner looks boring or uninteresting compared to the sex they see on the Internet, and that this leads some men to lose sexual interest in their partners altogether (no argument there). In time, she argues, men would rather have masturbatory fantasies to Internet pornography than have sex with their partners (my study bears this out as well). Her argument is that most women do not want the kind of sex reflected on the Internet and that the problem with pornography is that it normalizes that which is actually a minority preference for many women, who would rather kiss tenderly and hold their partners (and here is where we depart views). She clearly has not talked to the women in my classes!

To be clear, while I agree with Dines and use her conservative views to support my theory that the Internet has withered at marital monogamy, I have *serious* issues with Dines' work. She is a conservative, sex-negative thinker. Whereas she finds pornography degrading and harmful to relationships, I find it liberating. I also disagree with her perspective that pornography is not the same as sex, which she suggests is because pornography is an industrial product that commoditizes human needs and sells it back to people in an oftentimes unrecognizable form. I disagree with this because much of today's pornography is user created. In fact, the pornographic movie industry is under great threat because people are shooting and posting their own pornography instead. One of my friends shot his own porn film, posted it, and it has been viewed 7.6 million times.

There is little actual research (albeit there is plenty of speculation) on women's preference for female-produced pornography (Attwood, 2010). In 2007, Michael Bailey's lab conducted an unpublished trial study of potential erotic stimuli, using neuroimaging, and found that most women (especially lesbian women) preferred lesbian porn produced for lesbians, as opposed to lesbian porn produced for heterosexual men. Thus, this suggests that the reason that most porn is produced for heterosexual men (followed next by homosexual men) is because men are substantially more visually stimulated (erotically) than women.

Whatever one's hypothetical position on women and pornography, research has shown that porn made by and for women looks remarkably like the heterosexual porn made by men (Rubin, 1993).

Whereas Dines argues against the virtues of the Internet, I argue that the Internet has brought a great democratization of sexual desires to us (McNair, 2002). It is alive with real people acting out sex in ways that real people desire. The Internet validates real people's sexual proclivities outside of heterosexual, married missionary sex and it has been particularly helpful for gay men and lesbians, who do not have their own sexual lives reflected back to them in the media the way heterosexuals do.

All of this ties in with my work on cheating in a very logical way. First, as long-standing sociological research shows, the increased amount of time that one is in a relationship correlates with a greater likelihood that one will grow bored with the sex and therefore cheat (Allen et al., 2005; South, Trent & Shen, 2001; Treas & Giessen, 2001). Second, the earlier age upon which we start consuming sex (real and cyber) and the proliferation of sexual variety available to us in both real (via hooking up) and cyber ways, combined with the increased social permission to masturbate to this pornography and hook up with those we meet online, has meant that monogamous sex looks considerably more boring than it ever has. I explain this with *relative sexual deprivation theory*.

RELATIVE SEXUAL DEPRIVATION THEORY

Vanneman and Pettigrew (1972) have suggested that we tend to decide how well-off or deprived we are, not from any absolute, but instead from how we compare ourselves to others. Relative deprivation theory determines that we decide on what we deserve and what we should expect by looking at other people. We then compare ourselves with this standard.

Even multimillionaires who live in housing tracks with those who make more money feel less than. This is because we tend to look up to those who are doing better than us, not down to those lesser off; this is relative deprivation theory at work. I apply a sexual perspective on relative deprivation theory in this section, noting its application to monogamy and cheating by examining the moral-sexual zeitgeist upon which Kinsey conducted his research and comparing it to today's moral-sexual zeitgeist.

Consider the relationship between acceptable sexual activity and morality in the 1950s to today. In the former, sex of almost any form was socially stigmatized, unless one was in a heterosexual, married relationship. When boys and girls dated, for example, they did so without any sexual contact (even a kiss goodnight) for several dates before gradually moving to the lost word of "petting" (rubbing bodies without intercourse, and usually with clothes on). Before the sexual revolution, people progressed very slowly in their sexual/dating relationship. It might take weeks to engage in kissing, several more before groping over the clothes, and a male getting to feel the real breasts of a woman was a notable occurrence. These days, things occur much faster. Schwartz and Rutter (2000) say, "Petting is now foreplay. Touching and stimulating occur, but the expectation is that partners are preparing for intercourse" (p. 94). And even if, back in the 1950s one did have sexual inter-course, sex was confined to just this partner. Worse, other forms of sex with this partner were morally (and perhaps legally) prohibited (i.e., oral sex, anal sex).

Now, if you were a 19-year-old, horny, straight male who could not have sex because you were not married, and you could not masturbate without depressive guilt because you believed the preposterous myths about the ills of masturbation, and you had to sink considerable emotional and financial investment into a girl to stand the chance of someday having a feel of her breasts, you would compare yourself to those who were getting more sex (or even any sex) and think you were deprived. You would "look up" and compare your miserable sexless state to your 19-year-old married friends, who were bragging about how amazing and wonderful sex with a woman was. You would probably think to yourself, *Man, if I could just find a woman to marry I'd be so happy, I'd never complain.* Thus, it is likely that partners in the 1950s *did* have much more heterosexual intercourse with each other than partners do today: They were kept from it before marriage, oral sex was constructed to be degrading, and masturbation was taboo.

Conversely, if you are a 19-year-old, horny, straight male today, you might look to your monogamous relationship, with its routinized and invariant sex, and consider yourself sexually deprived. This is because today's youth are capable of hooking up with multiple sexual partners without the emotional and financial investment their fathers put in to gain sex (Bogle, 2008; Stepp, 2007). Single young men today have sex without investment.

This is not to say that all college students are hooking up frequently; in fact, recent research on over 800 heterosexual students at one university found that in the last year only 60% of the men (and women) had hooked up (Owen, Rhoades, Stanley & Finchman, 2010). However, when one accounts for the fact that part of the remaining 40% are those in monogamous relationships or those who choose to abstain from hooking up, and when one accounts for the socially and physically awkward, it indicates that a sizable portion of university students who want sex are getting it. This is certainly the case at my university; and this is probably even more true of gay men who have an easier time acquiring sex (Rotello, 1997).

Youth today are also capable of experiencing other (perhaps more extreme) forms of sex that were never available to those in the 1950s. For example, using data from the *National Survey of Family Growth*, Leichliter, Chandra, Liddon, Fenton & Aral (2007) found that 34% of men and 30% of women ($N = 12, 547$) reported participating at least once in heterosexual anal sex. The percentage was even higher among 20- to 24-year-olds, peaking among 30- to 34-year-olds, which may suggest heterosexual anal sex becomes part of the sexual repertoire as individuals age. However, when this is compared to older studies, it is evident that anal sex is on the rise for heterosexuals. A 1992 survey showed that 25.6% of men and 20.4% of women reported lifetime heterosexual anal intercourse (Mosher, Chandra & Jones 2005). These, like so many other alternative forms of sex, are likely underreported (Halperin, 1999).

But sexual diversity goes beyond this. Heterosexual men might even be fortunate enough to possess the proper sexual capital and social networks to have threesomes, either with two women, or even with one of their male friends. In fact, in previous research on a select group of heterosexual male undergraduates I found 40% had engaged in threesomes with two men and one woman (Anderson, 2008).

The availability to pursue (even if one does not acquire) this type of sex (when single) might just give the illusion that being single provides a richer sex life than having a monogamous partner of a year or two. Many of the men in my study suggested that, while they would not break up with their girlfriends, they were nonetheless jealous of their single male friends. Ricardo said:

> I go out with my friends, and sometimes it just sucks. They will be working the place, looking for women to score with; bringing them home; and having sex with some hot new girl. But I can't do any of that. I can't even partake in

the thrill of the hunt. All I can do is sit and watch . . . and listen to their stories of their fun while I return home to masturbate to some thirty second clip that stalls halfway. . .

My analysis suggests that being in a monogamous couple today (well after the romance phase wears off) is *not* where the fun is. The sex in a monogamous relationship might be good (even amazing) for the first few months, but eventually men in these relationships find that they desire sex outside of monogamy. They desire the kind of sex that they see on the Internet, the kind they hear that their friends are enjoying. Eventually, habituation sets in to such a degree that these monogamous men rarely ever want sex with their partners (even if this habituation takes 3 or more years), but they do want, as desperately as men wanted to feel a woman up in the 1950s, sex with that girl they found on the Internet or that girl they saw at the club. Today, it is the long-term coupled monogamous man who looks up to those who have it better. When it comes to sex, relative deprivation has switched in the previous 60 years.

Ricardo would, of course, have the best of both worlds should he be permitted to have (exciting, thrilling, and exploratory) recreational sex with others; if he could have the type of sex he sees modeled to him not only on the Internet but with his very own friends—if only he could have *this* type of sex and then return home to the warmth, intimacy, and love of his personally intimate relationship with his girlfriend. But he is not permitted this. While our culture has progressed to permit all forms of sex when one is not in a relationship many of the old rules of 1950s-style sex still apply to monogamous couples. It is still socially unacceptable to bring others into the sex; it is unacceptable to seek sex outside the relationship; and it is still unacceptable for almost all men in this study to have cyber-sex with someone on the Internet. Many men in my study even reported that their girlfriends were not happy about them masturbating to the thoughts of other women (although most suggested they never discuss it with their girlfriends). Thus, the only real progress for heterosexuals in partnerships in this 60-year period is that today they can have monogamous relationships without marriage, and they can explore other forms of sex with their partner (i.e., oral sex, anal sex, or even the man being digitally penetrated) within those relationships.

Compare this to the monumental change for an uncoupled heterosexual man. He has moved far away from a position of not being permitted any actual sex in any form, or even being able to masturbate without undue social and psychological reprise. And, even if he was able to shake off the shackles of such a sex-negative society and enjoy himself through masturbation, the pornography available to him back then paled in comparison to the cyber-real sex that is available on the Internet today (which will soon be available in 3D). Accordingly, maintaining the commitment of sexual fidelity to one's partner today is perhaps considerably more difficult than it has ever been.

However, my study shows that all of these social-sexual changes have not negatively impacted upon how men emotionally relate to their partners—in fact, in other research (Anderson, 2009) I show that the improvements to our culture that permit heterosexual men to express more feminine emotions and distance themselves from macho attitudes enhances the relationships they have with women—however, it has severely impacted upon their views of what a lifetime of monogamy means. I therefore argue that today's men likely want extradyadic sex more than men of previous generations. My argument is that because of the advancements in feminism, and the voice and stake of equality it has given women, heterosexual men might actually love their girlfriends more today; but that they nonetheless grow bored of the sex more rapidly. Thus, they find themselves looking, but not fully admitting to themselves that they are looking for other sexual outlets. It is here that the internal war begins.

There is one final variable to consider concerning my relative sexual deprivation theory. Despite the growing acceptance of casual sex for men and women in society, men still receive more social capital for having sexual expertise/experience than women. Men still receive the praise of their fellow male peers for having lots of sex, more than women. But, importantly, it is not lots of sex with the same woman that earns men this credit. It is having sex with many women. So men who "shag around" on the weekends, men who hook up, are given more social credit than those who are in a monogamous relationship (Bogle, 2008; Stepp, 2007). In short, young men who have sex with lots of different women receive celebratory, congratulatory, and idealized praise by their peers; while men in monogamous relationships are patted on the back for their choice to "settle down" early.

All of this sexual availability and reversal of praise has meant that when one considers one's sexual positioning within a context of relative deprivation, monogamy today may place one closer to the bottom of the stratification looking up to those who are single or in open relationships. One in a monogamous relationship might have some grounds to complain. The only difference is that the monogamous man can achieve extradyadic sex if he really wants to. All he needs to do is cheat.

PART FOUR

The Reality of Cheating

13

Prevalence of Cheating

In their book concerning the anthropological genesis of families and relationships, *Sex at Dawn*, Ryan and Jethá (2010) suggest that cultural events beginning 10,000 years ago "... rendered the true story of human sexuality so subservice and threatening that for centuries it has been silenced by religious authorities, pathologized by physicians, studiously ignored by scientists, and covered up by moralizing therapists" (p. 2). Yet despite an impressive withering at the centuries of sexual taboos in the previous few decades in Western cultures, monogamy has prevailed as the only acceptable all-important litmus test of a dyadic relationship. Culturally, monogamy reigns supreme.

But despite the mandates of law, despite the cultural prohibitions that brand those who cheat as unloving sluts, despite the hegemonic religious, cultural, and political power in shaping negative attitudes toward nonmonogamies and promiscuity as acts of deprivation, cheating still frequently occurs. Culture seems capable of programming our ideas and attitudes about what we ought to and ought not to do sexually, but it is less effective in controlling our actual behaviors than the propagators of monogamy desire.

Culture is incapable of controlling our innate sexual desires, and thus culture is ultimately incapable of ceasing cheating behaviors. And this fact is not just about monogamy: It relates to heterosexuality, homosexuality, bisexuality, genetic sexual attraction, pedophilia, or any sexual "fetish," drive, or impulse. This is not a failure to cast off our animal instincts; it is instead a reflection that there is a gap between what we are told about sex, what we feel about it initially, and what we ultimately end up wanting. The monogamy gap I spoke of in Chapter 10 exists not just for a few, but for us all—at least at some point in our coupled lives.

Our cultural failure to lift the veil of monogamy, exposing it to the reasoning of daylight, permits monogamy to throb on our consciousness as a conservative ideology—and as most conservative ideas do, to thwart progress toward our liberation and happiness. Monogamism, based in poor science and sloppy reasoning, exists as the single greatest cause of relationship dissatisfaction and emotional confusion in our lives. This is not because there is anything intellectually wrong with desiring sexual fidelity; instead, it is because there is something *biologically* wrong with it.

This chapter examines the findings of multiple other researchers' work into cheating. It highlights that cheating is an increasing event, due to changing cultural norms and practices, and it highlights the variables that influence cheating.

KINSEY

If there was ever a cultural moment in which all of the conservative principles of Christian fundamentalism and puritanical reasoning were impactful in the modern Western world during the 20th century, it would likely be in America, during the years following World War II. During this "idyllic" 1950s era, men and women were thought to be abstinent until marriage, and even sex among married couples was silenced. It was not until the late 1960s that the first married couple were even shown in bed together—wearing pajama tops and bottoms. Perhaps older readers will recall how Lucy and Ricky from *I Love Lucy* (1951–1957) slept in separate beds; as did Fred and Wilma Flintstone from *The Flintstones* (1960–1966); and Mr. and Mrs. Howell from *Gilligan's Island* (1964–1967). In the next decade we were hidden from the bedroom of Mr. and Mrs. Brady from *The Brady Bunch* (1969–1974). This was certainly the age of God, capitalism, and the American Dream. Yet all was not so idyllic behind the scene.

In 1947, Alfred Kinsey founded the Institute for Sex Research at Indiana University, now known as the *Kinsey Institute for Research in Sex, Gender, and Reproduction*. Kinsey's research on human sexuality not only laid the groundwork for the academic discipline of sexology, but it provoked immense controversy in the conservative 1940s and 1950s. This is because Kinsey (1948) studied not only youth and adult sexualities but also those of children—showing they were capable of sexual stimulation and orgasm. Kinsey also brought homosexuality out of the closet, showing that 10% of his 6,013 men had had some form of gay sex.

There are some ardent detractors to Kinsey's work—most of whom are not sexologists. These folks argue that Kinsey's data (on multiple findings) are skewed because they are overrepresented by prisoners and prostitutes; because Kinsey classified some single people as married who were not (cohabitating) and that he included a disproportionate number of homosexual men in his sample, which they think may somehow have distorted his studies. He is also critiqued for his heavy-handed interviewing tactics. Some suggest that he bullied participants until they said that they had, for example, had homosexual sex.

However, much of this criticism stems from what research protocol prohibits us from doing today. Kinsey did what he had to do in order to get the data. And nobody has been able to do anything nearly as thorough ever since. For all the complaints about Kinsey, his data remain the best we have.

Regardless of whether one agrees with the methods that Kinsey used, his landmark research raised cultural understandings that sexuality was much more complex than conventionally thought. Kinsey, with his volumes of research on human sexuality, opened the door for multiple other scholars to follow.

Some will argue that Laumann et al. (1994) instead represent the best study of sexuality: It is reported to use more of a random sample, and it also used face-to-face interviews. But the Laumann sample is half the size of Kinsey's, and it did not use the same interviewing technique that Kinsey did. Furthermore, it had a response rate of 78.5%, so nearly a quarter of those asked to take the survey refused to. While this is speculative, it seems reasonable to infer that people who had cheated or were gay were more likely to refuse to take the survey.

Kinsey was to human sexuality what Einstein was to physics. He sparked a revolution in the study of human sexualities, and together with those studying it from psychological, sociological, and/or biological disciplines we have developed a truly impressive bank of empirical research concerning sexuality. So Kinsey was the first to show us that despite the "civilized" nature of God-fearing, apple-pie-eating, baseball-loving, middle-class white Americans, they were still cheating. Many others have followed.

LITERATURE ON CHEATING RATES

Culture cannot prevent what our genes desire, and so monogamy only remains a hegemonic ideal. Considerable research since Kinsey details the fact that most monogamous relationships are monogamous in name rather than deed. Demaris (2009) says, "Regardless of the quality of the marital relationship, temptations to be unfaithful constitute an ever-present danger for married individuals" (p. 598). And because this cheating is generally undisclosed, most couples live within non-consensual nonmonogamous relationships, instead of the monogamous relationships that they expect (Duncombe, Harrison, Allan & Marsden, 2004).

As I discussed earlier, cheating rates are extremely difficult to determine. This is because they rely upon differing definitions of what it means to cheat. Researchers have also struggled with both the conceptual and operational definitions of cheating and infidelity. While sexual intercourse seems to be universally included, others include thoughts or emotional bonds with others (Allen et al., 2005). Older literature on young (unmarried) men shows that dating infidelity included extra-dyadic kissing as well as intercourse (Roscoe, Cavanaugh & Kennedy, 1988). This is congruent with older research on married men (Buunk, 1980; Edwards, 1973). However, given that heterosexual men in my sample now kiss other men as a fraternal bonding mechanism (Anderson, Adams & Rivers, 2010), "kissing" does not work as a catch-all category, as it can be sexual or nonsexual depending on context; and context is something quantitative surveys fail to capture.

The largest obstacle to analyzing cheating rates, however, remains self-censorship. People are simply afraid to admit to what is stigmatized. This is even true in surveys. As an example, I recall taking a survey in my college sexualities class. Here I checked the box that said I was straight. I knew damn well that I like guys, and that I like guys only. But I was so vexed by my shame of being gay (an emotion entirely culturally produced) that I could not bring myself to mark the box saying that I was gay. To my senses today, this seems ridiculous. The research was after all anonymous, but then that is the power of stigma. Whether it be admitting to one's self that causes the self-censorship, fear of being caught (that the survey is not truly anonymous), or some other unique reason, stigma prevents real rates of cheating (or any other condemned act or behavior) from being known.

It is therefore extremely difficult to suggest what figures about cheating most accurately reflect contemporary society. This is why Kinsey was so heavy-handed in his interview techniques; he was battling his own informant's self-censorship in an age of immense social functionalism. In this culture of God and country, it is amazing that Kinsey got anybody to admit to cheating at all.

All of this shows the impossibility of conducting a random sample on a taboo subject, and it suggests to me that Laumann's sample (using a population probability sample) is no more representative than Kinsey's. Indeed, the Laumann study was sent out only to households, excluding those in college, boarding schools, the military, the homeless, and so on.

In the next section I present the findings from a large number of studies. While each study can be critiqued (as can mine), it helps us view the relationship between monogamy and cheating from a broader perspective. That is to say, although there are faults with these studies, collectively they paint a picture that cheating is widespread. And whatever aggregate of "cheating" percentage one desires to concoct from these conflicting reports, chances are the actual rate is much higher.

STATISTICS

Kinsey, along with his colleagues Pomeroy and Martin, suggested in their (1948) book, *Sexual Behavior in the Human Male,* that on the basis of his data it is probably safe to suggest that about half of all the married males have intercourse with women other than their wives at some time while they are married. The next Kinsey Report, *Sexual Behavior in the Human Female* (1953), added that by the age of 40 years, 26% of married women interviewed had reported sexual encounters involving intercourse with men other than their husbands. Thus, Kinsey et al. (1953, p. 437) found about half of all married men and a quarter of all married women have "committed adultery."

Laumann et al. (2004) comes up with some of the lower rates of cheating. Their work suggests that just 25% of married men report having at least one extramarital "affair." And this word "affair" might be taken as having an extramarital emotional relationship, not just cheating sexually, something young men are less likely to have engaged in compared to simply having extradyadic sex.

Tafoya and Spitzberg (2007) find similar figures for women, showing that 21% of women have cheated in marriage. However, countering Tafoya and Spitzberg (2007), in a nationwide study of female sexuality in the United Kingdom, Hite (1991, p. 395) found that 70% of women have had sex outside their marriage. In her following study (1993) she found that 72% of men had cheated on their wives. Vangelisti and Gernstenberger (2004) find that married men cheat at rates of up to 60% or 70%. Smith's (1991) study uses *General Social Survey Data* to show that 70% of married men have adulterous sexual relationships. Other population-based probability samples suggest that between 1.5% and 3.6% of people have cheated on their married partners within the previous year alone (Choi, Catania & Dolcini, 1994; Leigh, Temple & Trocki, 1993; Smith, 1991).

LaSala (2004a) found that of the 60% of gay men who reported being monogamous 45% had cheated (with a median of 5 cheating episodes), and 17% had done so in the last year. Thus, of the 121 gay coupled men LaSala interviewed, a total of 81 (or 67%) admitted to having extradyadic sex.

Gay men likely cheat at higher rates than heterosexual men. This is because of the ease and accessibility of sex in the gay community. Blumstein and Schwartz (1983) found that 82% of gay men had been nonmonogamous during their relationships. For many, this occurred with partner consent, but that 43% had cheated because there was no agreement. Blasband and Peplau (1985) found gay men cheat at a rate of 74%, while Harry (1984) found that, whether through agreement or not, 66% of gay men have extradyadic sex within a year, and this number extends to 90% by the fifth year of a relationship.

For university-aged gay men, Peplau and Cochran (1988) surveyed 128 gay males to find that of those in relationships (which was only 41%) 54% said that they had sex with someone other than their partner in the previous 2 months— and this was during the AIDS crisis. It is unclear, however, as to whether this is the result of cheating or whether it is the result of open relationships.

Rates of heterosexual undergraduate men who cheat can also be quite high. First, male college students appear to cheat at higher rates than do their female college student counterparts (Hansen, 1987; Wiederman & Hurd, 1999), although this could also reflect women's elevated identity management about cheating when filling out a survey. For this population, the lower end of the cheating spectrum comes with Feldman and Cauffman (1999), who only found that one-third of their male participants have cheated. But this study is problematic because it is not clear how participant's understood cheating in this study. They may, therefore, have only answered positively if they had cheated through vaginal sex.

At the other end of the scale, Wiederman and Hurd (1999) find that 68% of the 299 university men selected for being in a long-term relationship have cheated by kissing. Oral sex was also high. Here 47% gave oral sex to the person they were cheating with, while 53% received oral sex. Finally, Wiederman and Hurd (1999) report that 49% of male undergraduates have cheated by intercourse.

Once undergraduate men cheat by performing any of these activities, eight out of ten do so again (Wiederman & Hurd, 1999). In fact, the men who cheated by having vaginal sex were more likely to repeat their cheating (85%). Collectively, this means that whether it be through kissing, fondling, oral sex, or vaginal sex, 75% of the heterosexual men in their study (compared to 68% of the women) had cheated in one form or another. These are high statistics considering that the average age of the men in their study (as with mine) was just 19. These findings therefore suggest that despite being culturally stigmatized, cheating may be closer to the rule than the exception for undergraduate males (Wiederman & Hurd, 1999).

In summarizing their review of the cheating literature, Luo, Cartun, and Snider (2010) suggest that the variance in these studies is due to three factors: the idiosyncrasies of the sample, the time frame during which extradyadic sex was considered, and the way it was operationalized in each study. They suggest that one of the most important determinants of the obtained prevalence rates of cheating is the degree to which the samples are representative of the population. In conducting a meta-analysis on these studies, they show that nationally representative, random samples find a lifetime cheating range from 1.2% to 37.5%, whereas in community and college convenience samples, the overall rate appeared to be much higher, 16.5% to 85.5%. However, they also suggest that there was a systematic difference in the operational definition of cheating between the random and the convenience samples: Whereas the national samples tended to focus on sexual interactions, the community samples and college samples have considered a wider range of behaviors that can be classified as cheating.

VARIABLES THAT INFLUENCE CHEATING

Treas and Giesen (2000) contribute to this literature by highlighting that some men are more likely to cheat than others. They use a nationally representative survey of Americans to control for the variables that constitute this "gendered" effect and find a higher likelihood of sexual infidelity among those with stronger sexual interests; those with more permissive sexual values; those with lower subjective satisfaction with their partnered relationships; those with weaker network ties to their partner; and those with greater sexual opportunities. With these factors controlled for, gender differences are substantially reduced or eliminated. In other words, if women also maintain stronger sexual interest, more permissive values, and weaker ties to their partner, they cheat as much as men.

But Treas and Giesen's (2000) research also highlights that if men are more likely to cheat because of opportunity (existing within a sexual marketplace and good looks), the rates of cheating are thus minimized by ability to cheat. It is therefore important to consider that just because one has not cheated does not mean that one would not if the opportunity arose (Greeley, 1991).

It is obvious that people with fewer opportunities for extradyadic sex must go to greater lengths to have it. But "opportunity" reflects a myriad of variables beyond what Treas and Giesen can be expected to account for. Research has shown, for example, that those who work away from the home are more likely to cheat (South & Lloyd, 1995) as the workplace offers access to potential partners (Lawson, 1988), particularly for people who attend overnight work-related travel (Wellings, Field, Johnson & Wadsworth, 1994). People from big cities are more likely to have extradyadic sex than those from small towns (Smith, 1998), because big cities offer more anonymity. And, when one combines fortunate human capital (good looks and youth) to the anonymity of big cities, yet further opportunities are provided.

Highlighting how anonymity, youth, and decreasing stigma against sexual activity influence casual sex, years ago one of my 17-year-old high school runners was driving down the 55 freeway in Southern California in stop-and-go traffic. He smiled at a woman (likely in her 30s) who flirted back. After exchanging sexually suggestive smiles, she waved him to follow her off the freeway exit. She parked in a remote area, got into his car, and gave him a blow job. He didn't know who she was, and because they live in Southern California (with 16 million other people), it is unlikely that they will ever see each other again. This would not happen in Wapakoneta, Ohio.

Because it is clear that opportunity for casual sex strongly influences men to cheat, it should be noted that the elevated rates of cheating among gay men are a reflection of the fact that gay men maintain *much* greater opportunity for casual sex, and therefore increased opportunity to cheat. Not only are there a variety of cruising spots (where men go to have sex in isolated parks at night) in almost any Western city, but almost all major cities have bath houses as well. Here, one simply pays a small entrance fee in order to cruise around the spas, steam rooms, or other facilities looking for people to have sex with. One can, if he wishes, join in an orgy or rent a private room with no ceiling so that others might be turned on by the moans. These facilities not only exist all over the Western world, but they are even found in some Muslim countries (see www.bathhouseaddict.com for a directory). For gay men (and boys) less inclined to have sex outside of the home, www.gaydar. com, www.gaydar.co.uk, www.gay.com, www.manhunt.net, www.adam4adam. net, www.ladslads.com, www.fitlads.net, Grindr, Bender, or Qrushr (for the Iphone), as well as scores and scores of general and specialist Web sites, provide gay, bisexual, or curious men the opportunity to find recreational same-sex sex. Thus, gay men are provided with the infrastructure for recreational sex in a way that heterosexual men can only be jealous of.

Another obvious variable to rates of cheating, however, concerns one's *desire* for sex. Even when all else is equal, individuals with more sexual experience are likely better at picking up subtle cues that one is sexually interested in them. In his book, *The Game: Penetrating the Secret Society of Pick up Artists*, Neil Strauss (2005) teaches men how to pick up women for casual sex. Strauss highlights that there is both an art and a science to acquiring casual sex. Thus, one's ability to cheat is dependent on a myriad of variables, including practice.

IT IS NOT ALWAYS CLEAR WHEN A RELATIONSHIP BEGINS

There are of course many advantages to a culture that permits men and women to have casual sex outside of a relationship. There are some emotional disadvantages, too; but these seem primarily limited to women who hook up. Fielder and Carrey (2010) find that some women feel depression after hooking up—evidence that the double standard of sexual recreation has not yet been eliminated. Consistent with their study men reported no negative emotional consequences to hooking up, with the exception of the caveat that hooking up means that it is not always clear whether one is on a date or simply having casual, emotionless sex. Danny, for example, told me that while he hooks up with women regularly (assuring me that he's followed his father's advice in always using a condom), matters get tricky when it is not certain whether it is a hookup or a date:

> If I just meet a girl at a club and bring her back to mine, it's pretty clear it's just a hookup. But if I meet a girl elsewhere, and we talk for a while first, it blurs the lines of whether it's a first date or a hookup. Generally speaking, however, you know whether it was a hookup or a date in the next day or two. It really depends on the text that you send; or what she sends.

Tom says that if the ensuing text messages lead to meeting up socially it is to be anticipated that it is a date. From this point onward, monogamy is expected of that person:

> Yeah, if you hook up with someone and then meet up with them a few days later. If you do any of that romantic stuff, dinner, or a movie, or whatever, you're dating. And then the expectation is that you're not having sex with anyone else . . . It doesn't matter really whether you've formalized it or not. It's like monogamy kicks in by the act of seeing them again. And from that point on, cheating is not cool.

Rich says that he too finds discrepancy in whether his sex is "hooking up" or the first act in monogamous dating. But he finds that the discrepancy lies with a divergence between his views and those of the women he sleeps with. This is consistent with research on hooking up, showing that—although matters are rapidly improving—men are still more free to engage in it without social stigma than women are (Bogle, 2008).

Rich is known among his teammates as being a player. They tell me that he "scores" all the time. "I hook up with a lot of women," Rich tells me. But sometimes they think it's more than that:

> I don't know why. I don't ever say, "Hey, let's date." I just meet them and have sex with them. Sometimes I never hear from them again, but sometimes, man, they just can't get it through their heads that it was just sex. They text and text and text. It gets annoying. But I think the deal is that they kind of have to rationalize to themselves that it was a date so they don't think that they're being slutty . . . if they are having sex and there is the aim of developing a relationship, then it's okay. But if they are just hooking up for fun, then some people might call them hoes or whatever.

Rich tells me that he understands this dynamic—that he feels for the women he sleeps with. Because of this he will often engage them in a series of text messages, knowing that the girl he slept with (particularly if she left a party in front of friends to have sex with him) will tell her friends about their growing texting relationship. "Eventually," he says, "I'll find some reason why we're not compatible, so that she can be let off the hook with her friends and not be thought a slut."

Rich is not the only highly promiscuous individual I researched. A number of men I interviewed had dozens of sexual partners. One said, "I lost count around 70," and this is even more elevated for gay men. One of the youngest I interviewed was just 18; at the time he entered university he had already had sex with 48 guys. But even these highly promiscuous men (with rare exception) maintain that while it is okay to have casual sex without intent on the development of a relationship, once that relationship starts, the casual sex must end.

CAN IT BE CALLED CHEATING IN THE "FUZZY DAYS" OF A RELATIONSHIP?

All agree that when one is dating, extradyadic sex must not exist. But cheating sometimes occurs before a committed relationship has grown. In other words, cheating sometimes occurs when a relationship is formalized but the couple has yet to engage heavily in the romance phase. For example, despite David's understanding that "cheating is not cool," he nonetheless finds himself doing it a lot. "So if I meet up with her after hooking up, she's expecting monogamy. But if I find someone I like more, I'm hooking up with her. That's when things get fuzzy."

I asked David, "So if you meet a girl, have sex, meet her again the next day for dinner but have sex with some other girl that night, are you cheating or not?" He replied, "I don't know. It's not like we decided to date. We didn't formally say, 'Hey, let's be boyfriend/girlfriend,' but then monogamy *is* kind of expected."

This fuzziness occurred with other men, too. Victor, for example, said that he once was dating a girl a few times, "But I really wasn't that into her." He added:

> I think I was just dating her because it was a secure source of sex. She was politically conservative and I'm liberal. I just didn't think she was smart enough for me, either. But it was fun, you know, to have the hot sex and do the romance thing.

Because Victor was not overly "into" this girl, he found it rather easy to cheat on her and then break up with her when a better prospect came along. "So I met this other girl," he told me. "And she had it all going on . . . I dumped the first, and I've been with the other girl ever since."

This zone of not knowing, however, is not explicitly what I am concerned with in this research. Instead, I am concerned with men who have moved beyond this fuzziness and are in definite, defined, and monogamous relationships that exist well into the romance phase. And it is here I show that despite revering monogamy, 78% still cheat.

14

Spontaneous Cheating

Buss (1995) suggests that we have behavioral evidence that infidelities and short-term mating occur in every culture, just as long-term mating is also a universal norm. University undergraduate men in my research are no different. Most desire extradyadic sex, and they are well placed to transition their desires into action. This is because they inhabit social spaces that make spur-of-the-moment cheating more likely. Potential sex partners can be met in dorms, classrooms, sporting facilities, university social spaces, clubs, and pubs. These environments provide more opportunity for men to cheat compared to when they were back home, because they are away from adult surveillance and they exist within an alcohol-soaked social culture. There is more opportunity here for spontaneous sex than just about any other point in their lives.

Highlighting this, in 2005 I arrived to teach at my new university in Bath, England. During the first day of class I asked my new students (all athletes and all in their first week of university) to tell me something about themselves, to describe something they passionately loved and something they equally hated. Most waxed about loving particular musical groups or activities, or they espoused their love of football. Hoping to protect their identities in the romance phase of group formation (strategic self-presentation), hate was reserved for broccoli or boy bands. But Harry was different. He said, "I hate cheating." He elaborated that he had only been at university a week and already people were cheating on their boyfriends or girlfriends back home. I asked Harry why he thought this was so. "Because they can," he said.

About a third of my students indicated that they had a partner back home. When I asked how many had cheated on that partner in the first week of university life, two hands went up. It seems perhaps Harry was right. A significant proportion of my students had admitted to cheating within a week of arriving at university; others were likely to be denying it publicly for fear of repercussion.

Unlike American universities, first-year British students begin university a week before classes—something known as fresher's week. Here they attend one drunken social event after another. The week provides them the opportunity to get to know their new flat mates and the layout of the university. But the university also stands to make a lot of money from the copious amounts of alcohol purchased by students who've just turned 18 (the age of consumption in the United Kingdom).

The first week of university is expected to be one of the best weeks of their lives. Not only are they away from parental regulation, but they meet hundreds of other youth, and they have a week to party. And, perhaps for the first time, they can bring someone back to their room, anytime. They might even find sex through one of their 12 flat mates in their mixed-sex halls. Why would they not have spontaneous sex?

But it is not just the lack of adult surveillance that influences these behaviors. It is also a collective monitoring of one's peers. As with the United States, heavy drinking is considered indicative of youthful independence; it is a form of social bonding (Gough & Edwards, 1998; Graham & Wells, 2003). For some, the body's ability to endure and withstand the effects of heavy alcohol is considered a masculinizing "achievement" (Peralta, 2007). However, a latent effect of this consumption is that alcohol serves as a disinhibitor—a negation of the ego that normally protects from long-term emotional damage of behaviors that will cause guilt, stigma, and shame.

Thrown into an orgy of young, hot, alcohol-fueled bodies, how tempting must it be for these puerile youth to cheat on their partners back home? This is particularly the case when they must at some level question whether their new long-distance relationship will work (most don't). Accordingly, those who come to university coupled in spirit are surrounded by single, available men and women. Furthermore, everyone (coupled or not) is in a state of strategic self-presentation. This amplifies their sexual appeal. They will never spend so long fussing with their hair and clothes as they do that first week of university life. Combined with their youthful bodies, not yet ravaged by years of university drinking, this means that these young men and women are at the apex of their cultural sexual appeal. There is an expectation of sex, there is alcohol, and there is anonymity to influence cheating. There is even a place to do it. Harry, as it turned out, was a keen observer of social events.

Harry needed look no further to find cheating than to those in his flat. I called Harry to interview him about his recollections of his first year of university (he is not included as one of the 120) when writing this chapter. After laughing about his moralizing statement he reminded me that while his public proclamation kept him from cheating on his girlfriend, it did not stop his girlfriend from cheating on him. He found out that she was one of those swept into the atmosphere of sex and revelry during the beginning of her university life. I asked him to remind me why he was so bothered by the cheating that, at a time when everyone else was in strategic self-presentation, making light-hearted comments to their new classmates, he took such a moralist stand.

"You've got to remember," he told me: I just met all these new people in my hall, six guys and six girls. And of course we ask each other who has a boyfriend or girlfriend—as you do. So within the first night of us all sitting around getting to know each other, our relationship status is out there. So, I'm expecting that those with a partner to be the ones to go to bed early, to let the single people look to get to know each other. But that very night I saw one of my new hall mates take a girl into his room. And I knew he had a girlfriend. By the time I met you a week later I had seen so many people who said they had a boyfriend or girlfriend cheating, it just really pissed me off. It's like don't say you're going to be monogamous if you're not.

But as strident as Harry was in attempting to persuade his peers into being faithful to their partners back home, he fought a losing battle. Year in and year out I ask my incoming 18-year-old students who has cheated on a partner at least once (after removing those who have not had a partner from the sample). Each year more and more students stand (yes, I ask them to stand). This year (2010) 56 students said that they had cheated, and 17 said that they had not. This, mind you, is only in the first few weeks of their university life.

I could fill pages upon pages of the cheating stories men in this research told me. However, I instead present a few stories that summarize the experience of men who cheat in what I call a spontaneous manner. These are typical stories of the spontaneous cheater. In relating these stories to you, I aim to provide an understanding of how this type of cheating emerges, under what conditions, and how the men deal with it.

LEWIS'S STORY

Lewis's dad cheated on his mom. Lewis found out about it when he was 12. He talked extensively about the devastation this cheating caused his family. His mom divorced his dad, and this hurt the family financially as well.

> It was real tough on us. I saw the damage that cheating causes. Our lives were never the same. We went from living in a nice house to an apartment. We didn't see our dad very often, and I didn't really want to, either. I had this idyllic family before my dad cheated, but after, it was all destroyed.

Lewis said, "I'm very against cheating." Nonetheless, Lewis *has* cheated. "I have done it. I won't lie to you."

Lewis met his girlfriend during the last half of his first year at university. They got on well and began hanging out within a few days of meeting. "We were walking down by the lake, and I just asked her if she wanted to go out with me." Lewis said that they spent the rest of the school year in relationship bliss, but that over the summer they fought a lot. "It was really stupid stuff," he said. "To be honest, I can't even tell you what we were fighting about, but we fought a lot."

By the time the next academic year came Lewis and his girlfriend were in something of an on-again off-again relationship. He believes that this may have something to do with why he cheated:

I was at a party with my friends. My girlfriend was visiting her mom, and there was this really fine girl. She was flirting with me. I kept seeing her looking at me, and then we did that stupid cheesy smile thing, like we were in fucking grade school or something. . . . I was really horny.

After some social maneuvering to get closer to her without making it obvious, Lewis eventually joined the group she was with. "It was one of those things where I'd try to steer the conversation to something that we had in common so that I could exclude others. You know, hoping they would leave." Lewis said that eventually others left, and he was left alone chatting with her. Then, when almost everyone else had fallen asleep, they began to cross the line between flirting and cheating.

There were like guys sleeping on couches and stuff, and we were talking. So I was all, let's go outside so we don't wake them. And we started walking, and just kept going. And we were down by the lake, oddly enough the same spot that I asked my girlfriend out. And it was so warm and nice and dark.

Lewis spoke in a softer voice, "I wish I hadn't." When I asked him what he did with her, he told me that they began making out. Eventually he lay on top of her, mostly clothed. Each undid their belts, but because Lewis was not expecting to have sex he did not have a condom. "I just thought I'd rub it around the area a bit, but it just sort of slipped in."

Lewis told me that he planned on pulling out before ejaculating, but in that moment he failed. "I felt bad right after. Like the moment I came I just felt bad. And that made it awkward . . . I was freaked out for lots of reasons . . . I was just shaking, like uncontrollably, I was so worried I just couldn't stop."

"She assured me she wouldn't get pregnant, that she was on the pill." Lewis tried to play off his anxiety, "but she could tell I was bothered . . . she told me not to worry about it, that she wasn't going to tell anyone. But I still stressed." Lewis said that despite having cheated, knowing the devastation that it caused his family, he decided not to tell his girlfriend. "What good would it do to tell her? She'd just break up with me, and we would both be unhappy."

I asked Lewis how his mom learned that his dad had cheated. "Did he tell her?" Lewis answered, "No. My mom found out because he left a condom wrapper in his pants pocket." Despite Lewis's cheating, he still judges his dad for it. "He was married. He had kids. There was much more at stake."

I asked Lewis, "Honestly, do you think that if you were married to Laura that it would have changed the events of that night?" Lewis grew a bit angry, "Absolutely." He added, "I'm still monogamous, because that's what we are."

FRANK'S STORY

Frank is a heterosexual soccer player from a Catholic College in the Midwest. He said that, like Lewis, he cheated not without intent but simply out of the opportunity and desire. Like Lewis, he also cheated at a party.

Frank was talking with a girl who sat down on the couch next to him. "I was already pretty gone," he said, referring to the amount of alcohol he had drunk. "My girlfriend was at the party too, so I just played polite. You know, I didn't flirt or smile too much." Frank told me that his girlfriend came over to him, likely as a way of politely letting the other girl know that he was taken. "I introduced her, telling her that we shared a friend in common, and then my girlfriend left to go talk with her friends . . . but I could tell she was keeping an eye on me."

Frank says that he was called to the top of the stairs where some friends were, so he left the woman on the couch. But he kept looking and glancing back down the stairs to her. "Eventually I found a reason to call her to the top of the stairs. I was talking there with her and some other guys, when I saw my girlfriend go outside to smoke." Frank said, "And I just knew that I had a few minutes while she was outside . . . she was giving me the look, you know. I just knew she wanted me." Frank pulled the woman into the bedroom adjacent the hallway:

I was only going to kiss her. Just a bit, and then move back into the hallway, into the same spot as I was before so it wouldn't look like I had moved or anything when she came back. So I started making out with her and it progressed. Next thing I know I had my hand up in there, and I started fingerbanging her and she was all over me . . . I swear it was like less than two minutes before we were on the bed going at it. And then the door opened. I just saw this sliver of light and I so knew I was busted.

Frank said that it was indeed his girlfriend who walked into the room. And when she saw him on the bed she left the party crying. I asked him if she broke up with him because of it. "Yeah, man," he said in a very sad tone. "I really liked her, too."

After the incident, Frank's girlfriend went home and put up on her Facebook wall that she broke up with him and why. "I paid for it," Frank said. "I mean, I really paid for it . . . I couldn't get a date for the life of me. This is a small college and everyone knew what happened. It's not just that I cheated, I cheated in front of her. Like how stupid could I have been?"

I asked Frank why he cheated. "I have no idea," he said. "I mean clearly there was a thrill in the game I played to get it on. You know, it's like having sex outdoors, it's more exciting because you can get caught. But I don't know why, really." I then asked Frank, "Did you seek those kind of sexual thrills with your girlfriend at the time? You know the outdoors sort of stuff?" He answered:

We used to, yeah. But not that much toward the end of the relationship. We weren't really having much sex. I just didn't have the drive for her. Don't get me wrong, I loved her. I loved her a lot. I'm still really upset that I did that.

She was like 'the one' for me. And I'm not just saying that. I'm not being some stupid kid who thought he was in love when he wasn't . . . It's been like two years now, and I still miss her, bad.

THOMAS'S STORY

A freshman in college, Thomas says that he has only cheated once. Thomas, who had been with his girlfriend for 4 months, was out dancing with his friends when they began flirting with a group of girls. Thomas said, "I met this girl and my first thought was I want to fuck her tonight." Thomas danced with her, grinding her from behind. "I just freaked her, rubbing her from behind. And then I turned her around and started making out with her. We were just getting it on. Fuck it was so hot."

Thomas danced with her for a while, and then went to buy some drinks. Thomas pretended not to have a girlfriend and he told me that after minimal conversation he went back to making out with her in the upstairs bar. "It was like an hour of just passionate kissing, and then I asked her if she wanted to go back to my place."

After the sex, Thomas lay in despair. "I had never thought I would cheat. I always looked down upon guys for being slags for cheating. I don't know why I did it really. Maybe subconsciously I wanted to know what it was like." He added:

I think that somehow I thought that, through cheating, I would find out just how much I loved her. Like maybe if I felt really guilty afterwards it would mean that I really loved her and it would be good that I cheated. So I did.

Worse than the guilt he felt afterward, however, was the fear. "The moment it was over I felt fear. Like, oh shit, what have I done? type of fear. Like, oh shit what if she finds out?" Thomas has not cheated again. Although he has been tempted, he remembers the fear he felt after cheating the first time. "I don't want to go through that again," he said. "It's just too scary."

MAX'S STORY

Men not only cheat on their girlfriends with girls but sometimes they cheat on their girlfriends with other men. Seven of the gay men I interviewed for this book have at some point also had some form of sexual interaction with straight men. And sometimes these straight men have girlfriends. For example, Max was camping with his family when he met a group of six teenage boys. "They were just gorgeous," he said:

I first saw them when I walked across the campsite to get to the shower blocks. They were running around topless playing rugby, and they were so good looking. I just had to befriend them. So when they were sitting on the swings, I joined them.

Max says that he spent the rest of the day with them. In a more private moment, one of the boys, Robbie, asked Max if he had a girlfriend back home. "I said no, of course. Then he casually asked me if I had a boyfriend. I said, 'No, but I am gay.'"

As the evening grew late, Robbie told Max about his girlfriend, expressing surprise that he had not yet cheated on her. Max said, "He stopped, turned to me, and said, 'I want to try something, but I don't want the others to know about it.'" Robbie then leaned over to kiss Max, and then pushed Max to his knees to give him oral sex.

Max said, "As into it as he was," Robbie began to stress about it immediately after. "He kept saying, 'You can't tell anyone.'" Max repeatedly reassured Robbie that he would not tell anyone. But even after the camping trip was over, Robbie continued to text Max, asking him not to tell anyone. "It's ridiculous," Max said:

> I live two hundred miles away, it's not like I could tell anyone who knows him anyhow. He went from being totally playful with me before I sucked him off to being timid around me, and he sort of avoided me the next day. I don't know why he freaked out so much.

THE "OH SHIT, OH SHIT, OOOOOH SHIT" ORGASM

You may have been shocked by the risks some of the men in my aforementioned cheating stories took. Frankie cheated on his girlfriend at a party his girlfriend was also attending, while Robbie let Max perform oral sex on him in the woods, even though his friend could have come and easily caught them in the act. A psychologist might explore these issues from a Freudian perspective, suggesting that these men took calculated gambles because they subconsciously wanted to be caught. Perhaps they might suggest that Frankie wanted to end it with his girlfriend, or that the boy Max performed oral sex on wanted to come out as bisexual or gay. However, I see things quite differently.

I maintain that only nature could compel us to take such risks. I argue that our somatic desires for sex wither at our self-restraint—compelling us to partake in socially dangerous sexual behaviors. This reminds us that we are not always fully in charge of our own destiny, particularly in the moments before orgasm.

Our biological makeup compels us to seek short-term, selfish pleasures that have at least some basis in our long-term survival. Whether it be a lust for food or sex, regardless of what society or our own sense of morality tells us, our agency erodes to resist our bodies' constant campaign to partake in carnal delights.

I have heard this transition from sexual thrill to fearful dread from so many men over the years that I have grown to call it the "oh shit, oh shit, ooooh shit" orgasm—as in, "that feels good, that feels really good! Oh my, what have I done?" The point is that men's horniness influences them to have sex that they might not have otherwise. Brad, who had sex with a minor, illustrates the point well:

> I met this girl once. She was the sister of one of my roommates, and she came over to see her brother. I thought she was fine from the moment I saw her, and we got to talking a bit. When she left, she told me to add her on Facebook. So I did. I knew I shouldn't be talking with her online; I knew that I was only really talking to her because I was so into her. But I thought *hey it's not illegal to talk*. . . So I continued talking with her, and one thing leads to another and she asks me if I have a girlfriend, and I told her that I did. And she wanted to know about sex, what it was like and stuff . . . .

Brad told me that over the course of several nights he used their Facebook chats about sex as fuel for enhanced masturbation. "I didn't want to actually do anything with her. I'd have way too much guilt about that and I was afraid of—you know, going to jail. But you know, we talked about sex a lot, and that got me going." He continued:

> One day we were talking and I told her I was going to be at an ice-skating rink that night, and she typed, "OMG I'm going to be there, too." I told her that it would be good to meet her, but that there would be no kissing or anything on the count that I was taken and she was my roommate's sister.

After meeting the sister at the ice-skating rink, and talking a while, Brad was off-ice, playing video games. The girl came over and said that she wanted a photo of her with him in the camera booth. "I knew I shouldn't have. Like I knew what was going to happen but I did anyhow." Brad made out with her in the camera booth, and then the girl said that she had to go home. Brad offered her a ride.

> I told myself that I had already violated the monogamy rules by kissing her. So I thought I could just make out with her in the car more. I wouldn't be doing anything else, and the damage had already been done. So why not enjoy it more?

Brad pulled the car over in a semi-isolated place and began making out with her. But her hands began to spread down his body and onto his crotch. Brad did not stop her. She unzipped his pants and performed oral sex on him.

> It felt so good. I was so totally turned on. Probably because it's taboo and all. But it was good, and she really knew what to do. But I was scared that we'd get caught. And then when she started blowing me, all I could do was look around to make sure nobody could see. I was ready to start the car and drive off if anyone came. But the closer I got to cumming, the less I cared about it. I stopped worrying about the fact that she was 15.

All of this changed the moment Brad achieved orgasm:

... the moment I came, like the moment the orgasm subsided, I was freaked out. *What the fuck have I done.* This chick is 15 and she's sucking me off? I was so scared. I was scared for weeks, maybe months; that she'd tell someone.

Nobody has found out, but Brad still fears that she will tell someone when she's older:

I still fear that she's going to get older and somehow feel that I was responsible. I mean, she was only 15. If she gets a boyfriend someday she could tell him about it, or she could tell her brother because he is still one of my best friends. And you know damn well that if she tells him, he's going to seek revenge by telling my girlfriend. So I'm still worried about it. That's a lot of stress for an orgasm.

Brad's story illustrates how a moment of sexual bliss can yield years of dread. What I find interesting about this story, and the dozens (if not hundreds) of similar stories I have heard, is just how easily we as human beings are led to follow our nature in pursuit of sex—despite the socially or even physically imposed or inherent risks that can last a lifetime.

It also highlights what all men know about orgasm: that we have a "point of no return." Men can readily stop masturbation in the first few moments, but eventually we reach a threshold where the orgasm becomes the most important thing in the world. At the second before ejaculating, if one's mom walked in the guy wouldn't be able to stop. This might also help explain why the withdrawal method serves as a lousy form of birth control. Men might think that they are going to pull out just before orgasm, but they often don't.

For example, Nick said that while hooking up with a girl once, he didn't have a condom. Yet he still had sex with her. "I knew I shouldn't but I was so compelled to. I justified it at the time, thinking that she was clean and that there was no way I could get an STI from her and that I would just pull out." Nick told himself that he wouldn't cum inside her, that instead he'd pull out and cum over her. "But the closer I got to orgasm I just stopped caring about the repercussions. I just laid into her and let it go all up inside. But the moment after I did, I was just like, oh shit. This is not good." Nick was right. It was not good. A few weeks later the girl told him that she was pregnant. At 20, Nick became a father with a girl he had never met and, sadly, now intensely dislikes.

The point is that when our bodies crave sex they have a way of turning off the intellect that normally governs the rational side of our thought processes. We recognize that we are doing what we should not, but the consequences somehow seem dim. It seems okay—somehow worth it. We are, in effect, drugged by sexual desire.

I earlier said that "culture cannot normally prevent what our genes desire." I propose that this is also/often true of our willpower to resist what our genes demand. Freud described this as part of our psychic apparatus: that our psyche was divided into three parts, an id, an ego, and a superego. In short, the id is the impulsive, demanding immediate pleasure-seeking part of ourselves, the part that disregards social consequences. The ego, however, seeks longer term pleasure—actions that will benefit one in life and career. It is the job of the superego to adjudicate between these two drives. Whatever the actual processes of these mechanisms are, it is clear that humans struggle with competing desires.

How many times have you eaten a chocolate bar that your somatic hunger drive desired (id), but that you did not want because of the added body fat (ego)? I propose that the "oh shit, oh shit, oooooh shit" orgasm operates under this principle. Our reasoning, our defense against long-term grief, is subdued by the petulant child that is the id. From a more psychoevolutionary perspective, the id represents inherent compulsions and drives—orders from thousands of years of honed survival drives—that our bodies carry out. The ego, on the other hand, represents culture and society, moral reasoning and culturally constructed notions of what is right and wrong.

Daily, multiple inherent biological drives compete with our socially constructed notions of decency. The moment that candy bar is eaten, the moment that orgasm happens, it is our culturally constructed ego that dominates because the inherent drive has been satisfied. We feel guilt because society tells us that we *should* feel guilt. We feel remorse and shame because our instinctual actions (eating chocolate or having extradyadic sex) have been socially coded as such. Once the id is at rest, the moralizing of the ego takes full force.

This Freudian battle seems to land disproportionally on the side of what our genes desire when temptation is easy to obtain (such as food) and less with sex. But the id nonetheless wins out from time to time. But whereas one can run a few miles to make up for the candy bar, the consequences of orgasm can be much more severe.

The point is that the desire for sex is so much a part of our nature that men unwillingly risk love, their families, careers, and in many but not all Islamic countries, even their lives for it. It *is* human nature to pursue sexual pleasure. Freud called this the reality principle. And it is certainly true that in order for us to function as a society many of the id's desires require obedience to the ego. When it comes to an inherent, biological drive as strong as sex, millions of years of evolution have equipped our ids with a tool that the ego cannot always handle: the ability to silence our reality principle temporarily. Alcohol further serves to silence the ego. Thus, once we have that orgasm, and our deep-seated drives for sex subside, we awake to the moral reality of our times that this is not socially acceptable: oooooh shit!

CHEATING FOR SEX, NOT LOVE

The type of cheating thus far described in this chapter summarizes men as horny. They have normally grown bored with sex with their partners, or desire it with others even if not totally bored with their partners. They find an opportunity, and oftentimes use alcohol as a disinhibitor in order to break down their socially imposed barriers. These men cheat, have their "oh shit, oh shit, oooooh shit" orgasm, and this then leads to a campaign to conceal their indiscretions. If they are caught, they blame circumstances and alcohol, as if they had not strategically (even if subconsciously) maneuvered themselves into positions to make cheating more possible.

A typical example comes from Jon, who knowing that a particular woman was interested in him, volunteered to walk her back to her room after a party. In reflection he said, "I know it was a stupid situation to put myself into, but I was drunk." And when asked if he would have readily volunteered to walk someone home to their dorm that was not sexually attractive to him, he answered, "No. I think I would have stayed and had another drink."

All of the cheating men, gay or straight, told themselves that they would never cheat again. Some have not, but most say they either have cheated again or can now imagine themselves doing such again.

But what is notably missing from these narratives is that these men did not describe being dissatisfied with the emotional relationship they maintained with their partners. These men were not shopping around for new partners. "No," Tom said. "It had nothing to do with wanting her as my girlfriend whatsoever. Not even in the slightest. It was about the thrill of the sex." Thomas, Aspen, and Ricky all concur with Lewis, who said:

> I love my girlfriend. I would never want to hurt her. I don't really know why I did it. I just wanted to. But it was never about dating the other girl. I didn't even really care about her at all. I just wanted her, if you know what I mean.

It should not therefore be assumed that men in my study cheat because they are uninterested in their relationships. While research certainly finds that men are more likely to date because they are after sex in the first place—something which is now decreasing because of a positive cultural movement of hooking up (England, Fitzgibbons Shafer & Fogarty, 2008), particularly for men (Fielder & Carey, 2010)—men are not immune from the pain of breaking up, and at least the men in this study did not eschew relationships because they were only after sex.

Indeed, research in developmental psychology suggests that an emotional connection to a romantic partner provides an important social identity, contributing to a positive self-conception; and that being in a relationship serves as a mechanism of social integration during this tumultuous late adolescent period of life (Meirer & Allen, 2008; Montgomery, 2005). This same research finds that young adults seek companionship, emotional security, love, and physical intimacy from romantic partners, with the ultimate goal of finding a long-term mate. These findings apply equally to men as they do to women. Collectively, cheating for these men was about having their sexual, not emotional, desires met. Furthermore, and important to this research, their cheating did not lead them to contest the value or utility of monogamy.

In the next chapter I show that as men learn to handle the postorgasm dread, and rectify the reason they cheated, they oftentimes cheat again. I show that their cheating stories slowly grow to be more calculated—less spontaneous—but that nonetheless these men still love their partners. The calculations behind their cheating might change, but the reason for their cheating does not.

15

Cheating Out of Love

My data suggest a pattern concerning cheating, particularly cheating out of love. Prior to being in a sexual relationship, men in this study thought they would be happy with monogamy. And after entering into a sexual relationship participants were satisfied with monogamy, maintaining sexual fulfilment that comes from early relationship bliss (Aune & Comstock, 1997). At this stage, most continued to view those who cheat as immoral, and they rarely considered that they might themselves one day also cheat. I have suggested that this heightened early romance validates the myth that monogamy is sexually fulfilling, making it easier for men to commit to. However, the participants' monogamous sexual fulfilment is mostly short lived, and eventually most participants desire recreational sex with others— even if they still somewhat enjoy the now routinized sex with their partners.

Men in my study first handled the difference between wanting extradyadic sex and monogamy by masturbating to the thoughts of others, which normally includes using pornography. They then begin fantasizing about having sex with someone else, even while having sex with their partners. As sexual habituation takes hold, and the couple comes out of the storming stage, even the thrilling make-up sex wanes. Men find themselves stuck between both wanting monogamy emotionally while also wanting the type of compelling stimulation that comes with recreational sex—the kind they see on the Internet and hear about from friends. They look up to those who have more and better sex (relative sexual deprivation) and not those who are getting less. Their initial strategy of fantasizing about others or spicing up their sex lives holds less appeal: They desire the real thing, so that cheating grows increasingly tempting.

Initial cheating episodes almost always occur under the influence of alcohol. Here, men begin by just experiencing the thrill of moving themselves closer to another. This leads to a very minor infraction (perhaps a kiss), which permits them to engage in prolonged kissing because, if caught, the consequences are about the same. Kissing leads to touching, and the march toward orgasm proceeds. Thus, each micro interaction leads to another slightly more egregious sexual act. Men are thus carried into sex acts that result in orgasm in a way that they might not otherwise be if someone they were flirting with simply said, "Let's fuck."

After cheating, most participants attributed their failings as something that "just happened"—as if they occurred in an alcohol-induced social vacuum. Subsequent conversations, however, usually reveal intent on cheating, even if subconscious. These men placed themselves into situations where their agency gave way to chance of sexual activity.

While interviews with these men suggested that most participants primarily cheated because of the sexual monotony that comes with long-term sexual exclusivity combined with a high sex drive, other research supports my findings, showing that early age at first intercourse, as well as greater number of previous sex partners, are also indicated with increased rates of cheating (Forste & Tanfer, 1996; Whisman & Snyder, 2007). The important factor here is that men with a higher libido are more likely to desire sex with multiple people and are therefore more likely to cheat. Thus, I have suggested that the rate of cheating I find (78%) is likely higher than those of other studies because my participants are young.

I described other structural variables that make cheating more likely as well. As others have shown, these include separate habitation from one's partner (Paik et al., 2004), working away from the home (South & Lloyd, 1995), and gender-integrated living situations (Anderson, 2008a). All have influenced the rates of cheating. Other influences surface from participants' access to a direct sexual marketplace, like a university (Laumann et al., 2004) and a cultural hypersexualizing of men's gendered masculine identities at this age (Klesse, 2006).

In this chapter I add to the literature on cheating with a discussion of premeditated cheating. Here, I suggest that after men cheat spontaneously, they are more likely to plan cheating. For these men, I suggest that they make a rational choice in weighing the opportunity (the reward of extradyadic sex) against the cost (risk in being caught) with cheating. They weight this against the opportunity (the reward of extradyadic sex) agasint the cost (of having a partner break up over the mere proclamation of interest in an open relationship) of staying with their partners and asking to be in an open relationship (Reiss & Miller, 1979). In this research, men overwhelmingly thought that the best chance of them acquiring extradyadic sex and retaining their partners came through cheating—not asking their partners to be in an open relationship. This suggests that men who plan ahead to cheat—not those who have emotional affairs—ultimately do so because they love their partners and desire to remain with them. They love their partners, desire to keep them as their emotional lover, but also desire sex with others. Because they fear losing their partners should they express to them a desire to be in an open relationship, they view cheating as a rational choice to have their desires met.

CHEATING AS A RATIONAL CHOICE

The basic principle of rational choice theory is the assumption that even highly complex social phenomena can be understood through breaking down individual actions into the steps of which they are composed. The argument is that these individual steps have been made by individuals who have undergone some form of decision-making process. Key to understanding rational choice theory is that "rational" here means something quite specific. It is not "rational" in the sense we use it in day-to-day life, meaning "sane" or "logical." Rather, the rational here refers to a *decision-making process* that has been undertaken before an action is done.

It may not be rational in the conventional sense to leave the car engine running as I dash somewhere to do an errand, but it is a "rational choice" in the theoretical sense because I have weighed up the chances of my car being stolen against the time I save. The validity of my decision is not important—the fact is that I made one. People do not simply act because society tells them to. While people are influenced by society's norms, they also calculate risks and benefits; they pursue a profitable balance of rewards over costs. For example, if you have worked all your life to be a professional cyclist, and you know that all the other cyclists are doing steroids, and therefore taking steroids is necessary to win, you may choose to take steroids, even if there is a risk of being caught. It is a rational decision, even if the consequences (if caught) might end up making it seem foolish.

Rational choice theory works well with economic models because financial rewards are relatively easy to tabulate. But the quantity and value of social approval or social stigma is less easily measured. Still, this does not mean that we do not calculate risks and benefits of social interactions. In the case of the cyclist, he knows he will not medal without the drugs, but that if he takes the drugs and wins the race, he has a 50% chance of being caught. This is still better than a 0% chance of winning without the drugs. Cheating is therefore rational.

In relation to chatting somebody up with the intent of having sex with him or her (in this case someone who is not cheating), we weigh the risks: embarrassment, losing face in front of friends, and lowering our sexual ego if rejected. On the other hand, we ask ourselves what the reward might be if accepted: social praise, raising our sexual ego, and standing a much better chance at acquiring sex with that person. Depending on what is more important to the individual, saving face or gaining sex, will likely determine the outcome of his or her actions.

Thus, the final step in my dyadic dissonance theory comes through analyzing these men's cheating behaviors through rational choice theory. Here, I argue that we need to theorize about extradyadic sex in terms of anticipated costs and gains. As Reiss and Miller (1979) suggest, we need to hypothesize a "'reward–cost balance'" for sexual permissiveness.

The hegemony of monogamy explains why we desire monogamy through desensitization to partnered sex; relative sexual deprivation theory explains the drive for extradyadic sex in an era of pornication; and cognitive dissonance theory explains the way we will normally handle this dissonance. But when circumstances present themselves, so that there appears to be a better chance of not getting caught in cheating, rational choice theory explains the act of premeditated cheating.

But the way I use rational choice theory does not perfectly explain the spontaneous cheating I described in the previous chapter. I argued that spontaneous cheating is the result of an overwhelming biological desire to have sex—and that men don't put much thought into how they will acquire it. Spontaneous cheating was not the result of rational processes; most of the times the men described irrational situations—in this case, defined by situations that are likely to have their cheating divulged. There is of course still a choice with spontaneous cheating: At some point, there is still a choice to cheat. Even though the circumstances have not been planned and they do not rationally choose to put themselves in them, when they arise there is still a reward–cost choice to make about whether to have sex in the room with your girlfriend downstairs or take the blow job in the park at the camp site. I argue, however, that after cheating once or twice in this spontaneous manner, men begin to make a reasoned argument to themselves about why they should cheat, and how they should do it to minimize the chance of being caught.

Men feel guilt, fear, and anxiety after cheating the first time, yes, but when they realize that they can cheat and get away with it, they begin to consider cheating as a way to rectify the monogamy gap. They begin to understand that cheating is a way to keep their partners while simultaneously having thrilling sex.

LIAM'S STORY

Liam is not one of the official 78% of the men who have cheated in my research— although at last count Liam has cheated 13 times. How he came to this position is fascinating, yet common. The only difference between Liam and the others who frequently cheat by habituation and premeditation is that Liam came to cheating later than most of the men in my study.

Liam was one of the students whom I grew to know more personally from this research. He had been with his girlfriend since before coming to university. When they graduated from sixth form (British equivalent of a high school) he and his girlfriend headed to different universities. "I can see why guys do it," Liam told me. "I see why guys cheat. Guys are horny bastards, aren't they?" He added, "But I'm not going to. I haven't and I won't. You've seen my girlfriend," he said, "I've got too much to lose."

At the time of interview, Liam also suggested that he was having impassioned sex. This was something made easier by the fact that he only saw his girlfriend once or twice during the university semester. Longing for each other and having much less sex than couples who attend the same university, Liam said he was enjoying his sex life, "Yes, it's good." He added:

> Well, she wouldn't do it for a while. It took like maybe 3 months before I fucked her. We did other stuff so it was okay, but I was her first . . . I am also quite large, so even when we began having sex it's not like we were having sex.

In the last few months of sixth form (high school) they were having lots of sex:

> I knew I'd be going to [names university] and she would be going to [a different one] so I was trying to get in as much [sex] as I could. We were doing it all the time, everywhere. I was like a horny little rabbit just going at it . . . By the time summer was halfway through, we settled down.

I asked Liam about whether or not he fantasized about other women:

> I don't think I ever just thought about her. I did a lot when we were going out but not having sex. Particularly after she'd blow me, which never makes me cum, and then I'd have to wank to finish. Or if we were making out and then she had to go, I'd rub one out to the thought of her. But it was never exclusively. If I hadn't seen her in a few days I'd simply watch porn and think of whomever I saw there . . . .

Liam never had guilt about masturbating to the thoughts of other women: "I am human, you know. You can ask me not to have sex with someone but it's ridiculous to ask me not to think about someone else." Still, Liam never told his girlfriend about his masturbatory thoughts. "Don't be ridiculous. There are some things better left unsaid." And when asked about what he would say if she did ask, he answered: "Dunno, really. I guess it would depend on how she asked it."

During the first week of Liam's final year at university we met in the university bar for a chat about our respective summers. Because Liam was one of the few undergraduates I knew who was with his partner for years without cheating, I asked how things were going. It was here that he told me he had begun cheating:

> The first was a drunken time at a party. She wasn't even hot, but I did it anyway. I took it on her word that she had no diseases, but I didn't use a condom. Maybe it wasn't the best idea I ever had.

Liam then began to tell me about his fears that his girlfriend would find out, because there were people at the party who are friends with her. He then (effectively) described having an "oh shit, oh shit, oooooh shit" orgasm.

His initial cheating opened the door to more. He has now cheated 13 times. When I asked how he does it, I was taken by the calculated manner, the forethought he put into his cheating:

> I first find out what university they go to. And if they go to mine, I don't flirt. If they go to another university, I give them a fake name, and I never give out my Facebook. I don't even give them my mobile number.

Liam said that most of the girls he sleeps with know he's cheating. "They don't mind," he said. "Oftentimes I think they like it." Liam felt guilty about cheating after the first few times, but he suggests that his guilt has decreased. I therefore asked him about discussing with his girlfriend the possibility of having an open relationship. Liam answered, "I'd hate her sleeping with other people, so I would say no. I wouldn't change our relationship. That way she won't sleep with other people and I can carry on [cheating]."

JAMES'S STORY

In his second year of university, and despite having a monogamous, long-term girlfriend back home, James frequently cheats on his girlfriend. I wondered how he did so without his girlfriend finding out, why he did, and what he thought about opening his relationship up:

> At the start I wasn't cheating on her. But after a while it felt like I was getting the same old thing. I just needed some other sex. So, yeah, I find girls from time to time to hook up with. Okay, I find lots of girls to hook up with.

James was with his girlfriend for 2 years before coming to university and he did monogamy for 6 months before he began cheating. He has now cheated over 20 times. I asked him how he does it:

> In a word, Facebook . . . When I was at home I used to befriend lots of girls and add them on Facebook. But they were all from my town or friends of my girlfriend. It didn't matter though, they'd still flirt with me. . . . When I got to university I was adding everyone I met, but my girlfriend was also looking at photos of everyone I met and bugging me about them . . . . You see where I'm going with this?

James said that after being at university a few weeks his Facebook life was causing his girlfriend to question him about his posts, asking who the new girls were that he added. That is when James came up with the idea of making a fake Facebook account (using a pseudonym) that his girlfriend didn't know about:

> I made this account, put up a bunch of photographs of myself, and didn't add any of my friends. When I meet a girl, if she goes to another university, I add her. I then add her friends, and their friends. I have this whole fake persona thing going, and I say that I'm single, and it works well . . . I look at the friends of every new friend I add. If they have my girlfriend as a friend, I unfriend them. Simple as that.

James says that he is more calculated in his sex now, too.

> I always use a condom and I always have sex at their place. I never bring them back here. So if I'm going to one of their rooms at [names other university]

it's all good, but if I had them here, people would be like "Hey James" and it would blow my cover.

"All of this, just to have sex? I ask. "Why not just be in an open relationship?" James grew strident. "My girlfriend would never go for that. She would flip out if I approached her with the idea of an open relationship."

CHEATING OUT OF LOVE

Men cheat for a variety of reasons. For example, unloving men, and those near ready to break up with their partners are certainly more likely to cheat. These men would have the privilege of being indifferent toward cheating because the cost of being caught is not great.

I also recognize that some men cheat as a process of getting back for indiscretions that they feel their partners have committed against them. For example, Gottman (1993) describes the process of a couple's progression toward divorce as a "distance and isolation cascade" that brings verbal assaults and a sense of being overwhelmed by the other's negativity (p. 64). Later stages find spouses spending less and less time together, and finally cheating. An extreme example of this type of cheating is described by Brown (1991) as an "out-the-door" affair. Here, one partner pursues an extramarital relationship specifically to force a partner to end an unhappy marriage. But these are not the type of scenarios that are reflected in the narratives of the men I studied. The aforementioned might account for some married couples, but it does not seem at play here. Instead, I suggest that my participants cheat out of love.

It is important to understand the narratives of Liam and James because their stories highlight the rationale of the cheating frameworks for this demographic of men. That is, each in their own way highlights that he is not cheating because he fails to love his partner; these men are cheating because they want extradyadic sex. None of the informants maintained that they cheated in preparation to break up with or because they no longer loved their partners. Liam remains with his girlfriend of over 5 years now, and James lasted over 3 years with his girlfriend.

I have no doubt that a number of readers will suggest that, at a deeper level, these men cheat because they fail to love their partners. And I have no doubt that I will be accused of not investigating their deeper psychological states. Supporting this, a number of researchers have shown that dissatisfaction with one's relationship might be associated with extramarital sex (Brown, 1991; Vaughn, 1986). However, other studies also fail to find this association (Maykovich, 1976). Thus, cheating might be an indication of relational dissatisfaction (particularly among married men and particularly if carrying out an affair). Even men who carry out affairs are likely to still love their partners, but it does not indicate that just because someone cheats, that he does not love his partner.

Although some participants expressed more love for their partners than others, none of the cheating informants maintained that their cheating, whether it be spontaneous or premeditated, resulted *from* a lack of love. And with the exception of a few who thought that cheating might serve as a test of their love (i.e., if I cheat and I feel bad it means I love her) early into their relationships, these men said that they did not cheat as a way to look for a new partner. Instead, most expressed that the reason they cheated came from a compelling desire for extra-dyadic recreational sex, despite their genuine romantic interest in their partners. I believe them.

What I am suggesting is that it is far too simple an understanding of the relationship between men, sex, and love to suggest that the answer to one's cheating lies in a lack of emotional investment in one's partner, or even to suggest that it can be prevented through a campaign of continually spicing up one's sex life. Matters are much more complicated.

This finding might anger some readers, but the evidence suggests that these men do not cheat because they are romantically unsatisfied; instead they cheat because they are romantically satisfied but sexually unsatisfied with sex with the same person. Thus, a subversive interpretation of monogamism is to suggest that these men cheat because they *do* love their partners—they are simply too afraid to take the chance of losing their partners by expressing a desire for recreational sex with others. Accordingly, I suggest that cheating is part of monogamy. Like the now archaic word *feal*, which meant both "faithful" as well as to hide or conceal, for most people monogamy is to say one thing while doing the other. On the front stage, monogamy is supported and affirmed, but in the backstage, something entirely different occurs.

The other side of the cheating equation is that those who "were cheated on" are expected to be so socially damaged that they are compelled to break up with their partners. I recognize that a mate who learns of a partner's infidelity is likely to, as Treas and Giesen (2000) say, "respond with emotionally-draining recriminations, tit-for-tat infidelities, physical abuse, the withholding of couple services (e.g. sex, companionship, monetary support), and even divorce" (p. 50). So even if they don't find their partners calling the relationship off, divulging one's cheating opens the door for the likelihood of major relationship turmoil.

This, and the threat of losing their partners, is why most of the men who cheated did not tell their partners about their cheating. Why would they? Honesty is not the litmus test of a relationship. The litmus test of a relationship concerns monogamy. So, when some articulate, "I was more mad because he lied to me about it than having actually done it," I suggest that this is untrue. We are more upset about the act than the covering of the act. Our friends tell us to break up with someone when that person has cheated on us; they are less likely to tell us to break up with someone because that person has lied to us.

BREAKING UP

Harris (2002) shows that just over half of couples who experience a divulged cheating episode break up because of it. Furthermore, she shows a significant gender difference in who terminates the relationship. Her study shows that 94% of women (evenly split between straight and lesbian) said that they were the one to end the relationships, but only 43% of the men (also evenly split by sexuality) said they ended their relationship because of cheating. In other words, women are twice as likely to terminate a relationship because of sexual cheating: Women police monogamy more.

I therefore believe the heterosexual men I interviewed when they told me that they feared that if they told their girlfriends about their cheating their girlfriends would break up with them. From this data one can only draw the conclusion that these men rationalize that they are better to live with the strain of guilt than they are to be honest about their indiscretions. Coming clean is, statistically, likely to end things.

This standpoint has some real-world application for those who have been cheated on. As controversial as this will sound to those once cheated on, it is important to realize that his cheating was realistic proof that he loved you. If he did not love you, he would have broken up with you. The fact that he cheated indicates that he loved you and wanted to stay with you.

Of course, one can argue that these men should constrain themselves from cheating, but that does not change the circumstances of whether (or how much) they love their partners. It does not change the finding that cheating is quite often a rational choice in weighing the odds of the opportunity–versus the potential cost to have their growing desires for recreational sex met, while not jeopardizing their relationship status by honestly expressing this desire for extradyadic sex to their partners.

Of course, just because one makes a choice does not mean that he is free of guilt and shame following his actions. Indeed, many of these men deeply regretted their choices, particularly when they lost a partner that they loved.

16

Consequences of Cheating

EMOTIONAL CONSEQUENCES OF CHEATING

While the focus of my work was to explicate monogamism and the reasons men of this demographic cheat, I do not wish readers to think that cheating is consequence-free. Thus, in examining some of the damage that occurs after cheating, it is noteworthy that almost all participants who admitted to cheating expressed a lingering anxiety that their partner would find out. This unanticipated fear is particularly true for those who also feared that logistical factors could threaten to expose their secret. For example, Dan attended a party with his friend Ryan, where he met a woman from another university. The two kissed in a vacant room, but not without Ryan's noticing. Dan said:

> I had insane fear the next day. You know, that she would find out I wasn't where I said I was. But then I began to forget about it, you know. Like I didn't think about it all the time. . . . Still, whenever my girlfriend was around me and Ryan together, I totally stressed that he would fuck up and say something about it.

Dan also said that his cheating generated a further unintended consequence. Dan later felt himself wanting to detach from Ryan's friendship, but he felt he couldn't for fear that Ryan might be more inclined to reveal his secret.

Cheating participants also feared the social ramifications should their friends or family learn of their cheating. Paul said:

> The guilt sucks, but it's not like I killed someone or anything . . . . But try telling that to her friends (laughs). My friends [presumably male] might be more understanding of it, but her friends [presumably female] would be pressuring her to break up with me.

Paul's response indicates that how individuals evaluate (judge) cheating may be gendered (DeSteno & Bartlett, 2002), but more important, he highlights the cultural pressure for cheating victims to end their relationships. The result is that women are oftentimes socially compelled to break up with their cheating boyfriends, even if they do not personally wish to; breaking up serves as an identity protection mechanism from a monogamist culture. Not to break up with a partner after he cheats on you can be considered a sign of weakness.

In addition to the fear and anxiety that these men express, each cheating participant also maintained a varying degree of guilt. Paul said that while he maintained no guilt when masturbating to thoughts of other women, after once having vaginal sex with another woman he felt tremendous and overriding guilt, guilt that still remains over a year later. "I can't forget about it," he said. Yet despite the guilt and fear of discovery, Paul has yet to tell his girlfriend—he is too afraid of the consequences. "If I tell her, she will certainly break up with me."

Interestingly, despite his guilt, and because his cheating has not been discovered, Paul claims to feel little reason *not* to cheat again. "If she finds out about the first one, she's going to break up with me. So why not do it with her [the same girl] again?" This is consistent with other literature on cheating, which finds that once men (or women) do cheat, they are likely to continue cheating (Wiederman & Hurd, 1999).

These emotional consequences highlight how monogamy places men into a Catch-22. If they remain monogamous, they suffer from the pain of wanting sex with others, taking out the frustration of not being able to have it on their partners, and constantly comparing themselves to those who are getting more stimulating sex. However, if they cheat, they feel anxiety about their cheating, fear, and guilt that lingers for months or years. Monogamy makes these men damned for doing and damned for not doing. Thus, I do not want readers to come away from this book thinking that I am advocating cheating. These are choices that individuals must make on their own.

MEDICAL CONSEQUENCES OF CHEATING

Monogamists might read this account and question the correlation between recreational sex and sexually transmitted infections. First, I admit that I do not provide statistics of sexually transmitted infections here. I fully acknowledge that sexual recreation, like so many other forms of thrilling recreation, carries a measurable risk. However, I do not acquiesce to the propagators of sexually transmitted fear-mongering, either.

One can take risk prevention seriously in his or her extradyadic sex. In doing so, one can greatly curtail this threat, even eliminating the possibility of HIV transmission or unwanted pregnancy. Furthermore, by substituting sexual intercourse with mutual masturbation, frottage, and oral sex, a substantial further reduction to the possibility of acquiring sexually transmitted infections can be achieved. Being vaccinated for hepatitis and human papilloma virus (HPV) are also intelligent decisions to ward off disease.

I also remind readers that being in a monogamous relationship is no guarantee against sexually transmitted infection, either. Monogamy is mostly an illusion (Adam et al., 2000; Mutchler, 2000). As I earlier pointed out, trust in monogamy (thinking that condom-free sex with one's ostensibly monogamous partner is safe) may lead partners to unwittingly choose unsafe sex (Adam, 2006; Sobo, 1995). Thus, the empirical question to be addressed is, what is the risk of infection when one is engaging in high-risk activities with one's "monogamous" partner compared to what is the risk when making informed choices about safe sex in an open manner? This is a question for other researchers to answer. But for those reading now, I simply maintain that if one is prepared for and strictly practices safe sex, what one should worry about on the way to a hook up is not whether you will get a sexually transmitted infection, but whether you will get into a car accident on the way. This is to say that we place too much fear on the health implications of sex, and not enough fear on the health implications of playing competitive sport (Anderson, 2010a) or driving. For more on how we tend to fear all the wrong things in life, I highly recommend reading Barry Glassner's (revised 2010), *The Culture of Fear: Why Americans Are Afraid of the Wrong Things: Crime, Drugs, Minorities, Teen Moms, Killer Kids, Mutant Microbes, Plane Crashes, Road Rage, & So Much More.*

17

Counter Currents

I have taken 17 chapters to spell out the intricacy of my dyadic dissonance theory. But it remains just a theory—a proposed explanation for an observable phenomena. It is not a law, and not all men are destined to cheat. Almost a quarter of the men in my study have not yet cheated, and some of the men (albeit very few) express no desire for sex with others. This means that some men do (at least for a few years) defy the odds. In this chapter I provide a narrative from Luke, who has not cheated, and I analyze it for the possible reasons as to why. However, ultimately, I propose that neither sociologists, psychologists, neuropsychologist, evolutionary psychologists, or biologist know why most people cheat, and yet why some men (even those who have high sexual capital and ample opportunity) do not.

LUKE'S STORY

Luke, 19, met his girlfriend when he was just 14. "I was with my girlfriend for four and a half years and I have never cheated." I questioned Luke extensively about whether he had even ever kissed another girl. He has not.

Luke's case fascinates me. Why is he the exception to the rule? In examining his narrative, I first eliminated sexual capital. Ugly men have less opportunity to cheat (Treas & Giesen, 2000) and therefore they are less likely to do such. Luke, however, is exceptionally good looking. He even informs me that he has had opportunities to cheat.

I also wondered if perhaps he refrained from cheating because of a religious disposition. But Luke informed me that he is an atheist. Nor is he from a small town where it is too dangerous to cheat because of the small social networks. Luke also has plenty of friends who do cheat. Furthermore, Luke attends university (a rich sexual marketplace) and his girlfriend lives back home, providing him even extra opportunities to cheat. Despite all of this, Luke insists that he has not wanted to cheat, not just because of his sense of morality, but because his sex has always ". . . been good, never bored."

I wondered if Luke's excellent sex life with his partner might be a reflection of having infrequent sex, which keeps it more stimulating. But Luke says that he lived just 10 minutes away from his girlfriend when they were back home, and that they normally had sex six times a week.

Still, there are some reasons why Luke might be different. The first is that Luke had not had sex before this girlfriend. Thus, like the men of the 1950s, he doesn't know exactly what he's missing. He has had one partner, ever. Second, Luke dated his girlfriend for 7 months before having sex. And sexual habituation might set in slower for those who wait longer in the face of temptation. Third, Luke and his girlfriend are still very young and very good looking. Perhaps he would feel differently about his monogamy if he found his partner less attractive? Fourth, and perhaps most relevant for those looking to extend their monogamous sex lives, he and his girlfriend are open about his use of pornography.

Luke is free to masturbate to the images of multiple other women, and this might help add enough diversity to his somatic imagination to help make his sex with his girlfriend less routine. I hypothesize that this openness permits him to do such without feeling guilty, which permits him to avoid attaching negative emotions to his girlfriend the way one would if he had to be secretive about his interest in pornography. In other words, he has less reason to cheat because he is not being held back from his fantasies. He is only prevented from acting on his fantasies.

Still, (very few) other men in my research have met this same criteria, maintaining permission to masturbate to pornography, and yet they do cheat. I do not therefore wish readers to come away from reading Luke's scenario and think that because years of monogamy appear to be rewarding for Luke, they will for you as well. Statistically speaking, this is unlikely.

Ultimately, it's also possible that the constitution of some people is such that they are happy with monogamy. Sociologists have very little to say about why some people resist the temptation to cheat better than others, but neuropsychologists are beginning to look at the ability to override impulse (to cheat) as a function of "executive control," something associated with the frontal lobe (the last part of our brains to evolve). Rittera, Karreman van Schie (2010) show that men who are not cognitively taxed are more likely to consider sex with someone other than their partner, than someone who is distracted. They also propose that people may be less able to resist temptation to cheat when they are emotionally exhausted or drunk.

I suspect, however, that remaining monogamous has more to do with someone's constitution than their micro-policing of desires. There are some people who eat the same breakfast each and every morning. Not only are they content with this, but they look forward to their "usual." It may very well be that there are, for some unidentified reason, some people who are better designed for monogamy, when the vast majority are not. Currently, there is no way of knowing how to identity these people. What is interesting about the 25% of men in my study who did not cheat (remember that these men are still quite young, and thus they may very well end up cheating someday), is that when I told them that I was finding about 75% were cheating, and suggested that this was probably true of undergraduate women too, they believed that their partners were part of that 25%.

18

Conclusions

This research has been a long time in the making. I have used hundreds of secondary sources (other researchers' work) in analyzing the 120 interviews I conducted on a group of undergraduate men (gay and straight) who were selectively chosen because of their elevated ability to cheat. I choose men who maintained high sexual capital and existed within a rich sex market not only because access to this group was convenient for me as a professor, but because I was looking to elucidate why men value monogamy, why they cheat, and how they rectify their views of monogamy despite it failing them.

My research breaks down disciplinary boundaries, drawing from sociology, anthropology, evolutionary psychology, neuropsychology and biology. I show that the collective body of these works are rather synergistic in highlighting the inadequacies of monogamy as a social institution. Whereas sociologists and biologist might disagree all sorts of other matters, when it concerns monogamy, we use different modes of analysis, but essentially we all show that monogamy is a failed institution. The collective of this research has permitted me to theorize the social processes that take young men from a disposition of expecting monogamy of themselves, to valuing monogamy but nonetheless cheating. I call this *dyadic dissonance theory.*

DYADIC DISSONANCE THEORY

In this book I used a combination of well-known theories to explain how men transitioned from believing that they want monogamy, to simultaneously wanting but not wanting it; and ultimately how they rationalized cheating as a way to maintain symbiosis and longevity with their monogamous partners. The "dyad" in my theory refers to a couple, and the "dissonance" refers to the growing cognitive dissonance that monogamism places them into.

My theory showed why men desire monogamy in the first place (using hegemony theory), how they grew conflicted as sexual habituation set in (using cognitive dissonance theory), and ultimately how cheating makes sense as a tool in navigating this dissonance (rational choice theory). The basis of my theory is that our cultural affinity for monogamy and stigma of any other form of sexual/romantic coupling places men into a Catch-22. Here, if they stick by the rules of monogamy, they are destined to a life of anger and contempt at not being permitted to have what they so desperately desire. Yet if they cheat, they suffer from anxiety and guilt—and ultimately they could lose their romantic partners if they are caught. Whereas sexually open relationships solve this Catch-22, we are nonetheless prevented from even entertaining the idea of being in one because of the hegemony that monogamy maintains, *monogamism*.

MONOGAMISM

I desired to highlight the hegemonic mechanisms associated with the cultural ideal of monogamy, describing the process of subordination and stratification through the cultural stigmatization of nonmonogamies as an effect of monogamism. As with other forms of hegemonic oppression, I showed that my participants desired to be associated with the privileged sexual paradigm (Rubin, 1984) and consequently extol the virtues of monogamy, even if they did not themselves adhere to its basic principles. And, as with other types of hegemonic oppression, I showed that monogamism necessarily meant that the institution of monogamy itself went largely unexamined. Instead, all critical discourse regarded the "immorality" of nonmonogamies. So, even though I showed that monogamy, as a social institution, failed most of the men I studied, it nonetheless retained its privileged social position as the only acceptable form of romantic coupling. Here I suggested that monogamy came into sharp contrast with sexual social scripts for single men that emphasize recreational sex with "hookups" and/or "friends with benefits" (Mongeau, Williams, Shaw, Knight & Ramirez, 2009).

I suggested that the construction of monogamy as the only acceptable sexual script (monogamism) is so strong that the influence occurs at the cultural (cultural narratives), interpersonal (one's engagement with these scripts), and psychological (adjudicating psychological desires for sex with others versus monogamy) levels. Monogamy's hegemony is so powerful that my participants saw no other viable alternatives. This was even the case for gay men, despite their gay culture's previous experience in breaking free from the interpersonal and psychic scripts of heterosexuality. Thus, my research suggests that this lesson—of standing against social norms—is not as easily adopted when it comes to challenging monogamy. Although gay men are more open to the idea of nonmonogamies, very few young gay men are able to break the social, interpersonal, and psychic script of monogamy. And if horny gay men can't do this without social condemnation, what chance have heterosexuals got?

Because of the strength of the monogamous grip on these men (gay and straight), I suggested that cheating presented itself as a rational response to the irrational situation that monogamy presents. Cheating seems to be the best way to rectify the dissonance created by wanting two contradicting things, *the monogamy gap*.

THE MONOGAMY GAP

I described the monogamy gap as a transitional space in a couple's relationship. Upon first entering a dyadic relationship, men experienced fantastic and frequent sex, and this made it easy to fall into the practice and valuing of monogamy without criticism. However, as a relationship progressed throughout the stages from romance to performing, sex became less frequent and less enjoyable. Men grew desensitized to their sex, and efforts to spice it up only lasted so long.

But just because men started to develop sexual desires for others, it did not mean that they desired a sexually open relationship. These men so continue to subscribe to the value of monogamy, and the immorality of open relationships, that they either thought that they must no longer love their partners because they desired sex with others, or they suffered in silence.

The monogamy gap emerged at different times in their relationship for different men, but on average it seemed fairly predictable that it would almost always have emerged within 2 years of constant monogamy. I also suggested that the pornication of society, the frequent and easier access to sex before being in a monogamous relationship, and the rich sexual marketplace these men belonged to brought about desensitization to sex with their partner sooner. Not wanting an open relationship, but desperately wanting sex with someone else, these men got drunk, placed themselves into a situation where they could be tempted, and found a way to temporarily rectify the dissonance of the monogamy gap: *cheating*.

CHEATING

Under current social conditions, I suggested that cheating occurs for most men as a result of weighing the opportunity for recreational sex against the cost of breaking up (or other emotional hardship) if their cheating is discovered or divulged. Participants in this research suggested that they cheated because they wanted or needed recreational sex, not because they desired an emotional affair. This desire is then helped by the sheer availability of potential sexual partners to cheat with in a rich sexual marketplace.

I argued that these data call for a more complex view of cheating than monogamism offers. The cultural ascriptions of character weakness and personality disorder that many attribute to those who cheat (Vaughan, 2003) largely fail to critique the structural power relations between social morality, natural (or naturalized) sexual desires, and sexual recreation (Haritaworn, Lin & Christian, 2006)—something that comes with a more sociological approach to the construction of sexual and gendered identities and behaviors.

Instead of describing participants who cheated as lacking character, love, or morality—social scripts that hold monogamy as a test of personal character and romantic fortitude (Smith, 1991)—my interviews suggest that cheating for these men emerged from a culture that offers no socially acceptable alternatives to the sexual habituation and frustration that occur with relatively long-term monogamy for young, virile men (Glass & Wright, 1985; Treas & Giesen, 2000). The dominant cultural, political, religious, and media messages that contribute to a sex-negative and monogamist culture demonize all but a select few "charmed" sexual practices and sexual identities (Califia, 2000; Rubin, 1984), so that the monogamous mantra of "cheating as the product of failed love or psychological disease" constrains other possibilities from social or personal consideration.

In light of the near-total social control that monogamism has over the practice of those who choose to enter into romantic relationships in this culture, I suggested that cheating becomes the *rational* answer to the monogamy gap. Cheating provided men with the best chance to have their desires for extradyadic sex met, while also maintaining their relationship status. Cheating permitted them to manage their social identities in a way that honesty with their partners would not. These men were quite clear that honesty would most likely result in their losing the relationship. Thus, covert cheating occurred for these men as a result of the infeasibility of monogamy to sustain a sexually charged and varied sexual relationship alongside the cost of monogamism.

I am not suggesting that the only reason men cheat is because they need a variety of sexual partners. I think that this was the case for the men in my study, because these are very young men, just at the beginning of their sexual lives. However, it is also possible that middle-aged couples cheat because they are unhappy yet feel stuck in their relationships. But one cannot, for example, know whether they are unhappy because they are sexually bored or whether they are unhappy with the emotional intimacy. Accordingly, we need further research to investigate why middle-aged men cheat, and particularly why they have affairs. We also need research into studying the emotional and relationship costs associated with men who are prevented by their partners from receiving extradyadic sex. Clearly, we need to apply the dyadic dissonance theory to women as well.

What is perhaps even more fascinating than the influences that drive men to cheat, however, is how they process their cheating afterward. Men feel a host of negative emotions: guilt, fear, and anxiety, yet most cheat again. In fact, the more they cheated, the less guilt they felt about their cheating.

It is also illuminating to see that even for men who cheated a dozen times, they still identified as monogamous. Monogamy therefore became more about an idea, an illusion, than a reality. Part of this is because dominant social scripts say that one should be monogamous if one loves his partner, and these men do love their partners. In fact, one might view their cheating as odd proof that they do.

CHEATING OUT OF LOVE

It would be hard to argue that three-quarters of those I studied did not actually love (or at least be in romance about) their partners. Common sense would suggest that if they did not, they would break up with their partners. After all, these are

young men without significant financial or familial reasons to stay with their partners. Instead, I maintained that for most of these men, cheating ironically served
as a symbolic representation that they actually did love their partners. I showed
that their cheating was a way to maintain their emotional monogamy, while having
their physical desires met: that it was the best way to rectify (even if temporarily)
the monogamy gap, with as little risk to losing their partner as possible.

If, after all, these men did not love their partners, it is obvious that they are
socially, legally, and morally free to have left them. It seems obvious that if they
did not love them they would have left them anyhow. If they did not love them,
they wouldn't have felt extreme sadness, sometimes even despair, and occasionally
a longing for their partner even years after breaking up.

I suggested that given that both gay and heterosexual sex is easy to obtain in
today's university hookup culture (Bogle, 2008), staying with one's partners reflects
a legitimate emotional attachment. These facts, even these unanticipated consequences, categorically dispute the commonly held mantra that "all" men who
cheat on their partners do not love their partners—exposing cheating to be a
much more complicated bio-psycho-social phenomena that we, as a society, have
failed to grasp: that because of monogamism, we have not wanted to even entertain. It is for these reasons that I suggest that people who break up with a partner,
simply because they cheated, are placing too much emphasis on the wrong variable of importance in a relationship. Through this perspective, breaking up with a
partner over cheating is a socially constructed antithesis to long term emotional
relationship stability.

I showed that cheating for these men is based upon an opportunity/cost analysis
to provide cheaters with the recreational sex they want with the monogamy (or at
least the presentation of monogamy) that they are culturally compelled to maintain. Cheating is a safer strategy for acquiring recreational sex than requesting permission from their partners, but cheating also has an added, selfish, advantage.

Although almost all of the cheating men I talked with said that while they (in
some capacity) desired the ability to have sex with other women, few were willing to
permit their partners to do the same. Thus, cheating results not only because men
fear losing their partners (should they ask for extradyadic sex), but it remains a way
for men to have their cake and eat it, too. Men continue to desire to restrict their
partners' sexual lives, while justifying their own sexual transgressions. Most men
said that they would rather keep a relationship monogamous, and continue to cheat,
than to have honesty about their desires for sex if it meant that their partners would
also have access to extradyadic sex. Accordingly, a strong double standard exists.

This double standard also existed among the gay men I talked with, and
although I have not interviewed women to find out what their perspectives of
sexual ownership are, I suspect that some women would prefer to have extradyadic sex without permitting their partners the same luxury. Monogamy, therefore,
is perhaps more about ownership and self-interest than it is any romanticized
notion of desiring to sacrifice for one's love. Monogamy—as an institution—is a
structured system of hypocrisy. Declaring to one's partner that he or she is monogamous can only be taken as a declaration of intent.

The implication here is that if your partner cheats, it may mean that he's not happy in bed—and there may be nothing you can do about that—but he likely does love you. Now, matters might be different for men who stand to lose a great deal of financial status should they divorce; or for men who will lose their children. It is possible that men with significant financial interests have fallen out of love, and it is possible that family men might exist in a failed relationship for the sake of the children, but for those in my research (those who do not have financial interdependence or children), it is irrational to assume that cheating represents a lack of love or respect. Assuming that cheating results from a lack of love is a victimization model that causes a great deal of pain. Too many families have broken up because a couple has falsely made cheating a litmus test of romantic love. Still, this does not mean that cheating is the best solution to the monogamy gap. Cheating has its problems as well.

CHEATING AS A BAND-AID

Cheating on a partner has multiple consequences. Not only does one risk hurting their partners and their relationships, but they simultaneously subject themselves to guilt, shame, anxiety, and confusion—all for the manner in which they rectify their dissonance. Monogamists therefore go about living between the oppressive layers of sexual want and emotional contentment. Those espousing the value and righteousness of monogamy while simultaneously cheating not only promote their own cognitive dissonance, but they contribute to the stigma of those who are capable of outthinking social oppression.

I therefore view cheating as a temporary solution to the stress related to the gap between the competing and incompatible desires of wanting new, exciting, and thrilling sexual stimuli, while simultaneously being socially constructed to desire monogamy, all the while fearing telling one's partner they desire otherwise. Supporting this thesis, the longer men were coupled, the more likely they were to cheat.

This is not a matter of men having just one cheating episode to quash their desires, however. The more the men in my study cheated, the less guilt they felt about it. This permitted them to cheat more. The more they cheated, the more meticulous they grew in their methods, the more cautious they were about using condoms, and the less guilt they felt after each cheating episode. Thus, as odd as it might sound, for a cheater's emotional health it might make more sense to cheat multiple times instead of just once.

WHY SOME MEN DON'T CHEAT

One thing that I was not able to tease out well enough with my 120 interviews is why some men do not cheat. It is obvious that those who lack sexual capital are geographically removed from rich sexual marketplaces, or who lack the ability to pay for sexual services are less likely to cheat. But why is it that some men, with high sexual capital who exist in rich sexual marketplaces, do not cheat? My interviews, nor the volumes of secondary research that I drew upon, do not answer this question.

For researchers interested, I believe a fruitful place to examine for why most men in this research cheat and others do not might come from Bowlby's (1969) attachment theory. This could be done by correlating one's attachment type (a diagnostic test) with cheating behaviors. It is possible that securely attached individuals could be more comfortable in an open relationship and/or cheating as they are secure enough with themselves not to view others as a threat to their relationship. Whereas non-securely attached individuals might view their partner's consensual extradyadic sex as threatening their relationship, or that they fear their partner prefers the other person. Conversely, it might be that men with attachment avoidance are more likely to cheat as a way of distancing themselves from intimacy with their partners.

There is very limited existing research on the relationship between attachment and cheating (Allen & Baucom, 2004; Bogaert & Sadava, 2002; Cooper, Pioli, Levitt, Talley, Micheas & Collins, 2006) and it is a very complicated field to assess. There is some (minimally significant) evidence (Allen & Baucom, 2004; Cooper et al., 2006) showing that undergraduate men with attachment avoidance cheat more, although Bogaert and Sadava (2002) reported no significant relationship between attachment avoidance and a past-year infidelity factor.

In the most recent research on this (Beaulieu-Pelletiera, Philippeb, Lecoursa & Couturea, 2011), researchers controlled for strength of sexual desire and sexual satisfaction in one's relationship, concluding that attachment avoidance plays a role in extradyadic sex independently of one's sexual desire and sexual satisfaction. These researchers suggest that men might use extradyadic sex to reduce their discomfort with the desire for intimacy and engagement of their partner (Mikulincer & Shaver, 2007; Stephan & Bachman, 1999). They suggest that individuals characterized by attachment avoidance who feel pressure of their partner to grow emotionally closer can become irritated and that they might use cheating as a way to distance themselves with their partner as a mean to lower their irritation (Baumeister, Vohs, DeWall & Zhang, 2007) I certainly found men cheating after being irritated with their partners in my research.

Overall, the literature on attachment styles and cheating is very much in its infancy and I would be cautious about drawing many conclusions from it. I should also highlight that this casting of minorities (in this case, those who do not cheat) as being psychologically disordered or even empowered poses political considerations. I would be concerned that this research be framed in order to avoid producing stigma against those who are monogamous and those who are not. Although monogamism makes it unlikely that those who do not cheat are stigmatized, my intent with this book is to suggest that we need various relationship category types available, without hierarchy or hegemony. This includes monogamy, polyamory, celibacy, and sexually open relationships.

OPEN RELATIONSHIPS

My research highlights that the failure to analyze monogamy critically has certain, measurable costs for couples who identify as monogamous, but nonetheless are not. This is because, when cheating is discovered or divulged to one's partner, it is described as leading to unnecessary grief, pain, and often breakup (Pittman, 1989; Ritchie & Barker, 2006; Vaughn, 2003). Divorce exists among over half of all married couples today, and most of this results from the consequences that couples are expected to bring when they find out a partner has cheated (Amato, 1996, 2003; Amato & Rogers, 1997; McLanahan & Casper, 1995). But I do not want readers to think that they can prevent their men from cheating and save their relationships by sexing themselves up, or spicing up their sex life in other ways. You cannot. Or at least, this technique has limited viability. The need for sex with others is simply too great for too many men (and may be for women as well).

To enhance a relationship in a culture of mass cheating, we need to be honest about our desires and facilitate them as best as possible. One would be far better off to at least encourage the use of pornography as a way of providing your partner with the opportunity to have symbolic sex with someone else than to stigmatize him for doing this. One would be better off talking about declining sexual interests, rather than pretending that these issues do not exist.

One might also find that open sexual relationships are more conducive to emotional stability than monogamous relationships. This is because nonmonogamous forms of coupling can somewhat remove cheating as a source of relationships stress (Ahmed, 2004), while simultaneously challenging jealousy social scripts that may lead to relationship trouble. Open relationships are based in honest communication, and they help avoid attaching anger toward a partner who is sometimes viewed as the obstacle in preventing one from having sex.

Open relationships have other advantages, too. They might even help erode at violence against women (Barnett, Martinez, & Bluestein, 1995; Hansen, 1985; Robinson, 1997). Several academic investigations show that nonmonogamous people construct alternatives to the conventional understandings of and reactions to jealousy (de Visser & McDonald, 2007; Mint, 2010; Ritchie & Barker, 2006). In other words, because monogamy embeds men within an ownership script in patriarchal cultures (Aune & Comstock, 1997; Barnett et al., 1995), it is worth considering that the structure of monogamy may be more likely to contribute to violence against women than the structure of open sexual relationships.

Of course, monogamist perspectives will make these advantages difficult for readers to grasp. Monogamists will be stuck in the framework of "What about jealousy?" For those readers, I ask them to think, to question, which is more important? Which, I ask, is more honorable? A corrupt monogamy? Or an open and honest relationship? Which, I ask, is more conducive to an emotionally healthy relationship, expecting your partner to be honest about sexual desires for others and a lack of desire for you, or pretending he does not desire others and does desire you? Of course, for open sexual relationships to work, one needs to view his or her partner engaging in extradyadic sex the same way one views his or her own extradyadic sexual activities.

Thus, this research also suggests that more investigation is needed of those who are in open sexual relationships, particularly how young men can talk to their partners about open relationships without losing their partners for the mere suggestion. There also exists a great need for research that examines perhaps how those in open sexual relationships might have more sexual joy in their lives, less feelings of jealousy, and how it might serve as a bonding mechanism when choosing others to engage with for threesomes or group sex. In other words, we need to reverse the monogamist project and examine the ways in which open sexual relationships might in some ways be superior to monogamous ones, so that we have more informed choices to make.

There is some hope. If my English students are representative of youth more broadly, open relationships might be increasingly popular with youth. When I first began asking my students to indicate whether they thought they might like to be in an open relationship 5 years ago, only a few hands went into the air. But I've noticed a steady increase in those desiring such. In 2010 I asked my 80 students how many thought they might like one, and 20 raised their hands (12 women and 8 men).

FINAL THOUGHTS

The mere suggestion that men may cheat *because* they love their partners may close off critical inquiry, even among intellectuals. But it is important to remember that, consistent with research on men in other cultures (Ho, 2006), my participants do not publicly identify as nonmonogamous, even when they are cheating. This highlights the resiliency of monogamy's dominance over all other forms of relationship coupling (Leap & Boellstorff, 2004). Accordingly, I suggest that the reality of monogamy has failed these men (and consequently their partners), but the illusion of monogamy persists. However, my cheating participants tragically fail to examine cheating and breakup in this light; instead, they fall upon their own swords of monogamous morality. They do so because monogamy remains as synonymous with "morality" as heterosexuality is with "family values," even if both are built upon unexamined assumptions.

When one is within the monogamy bubble, he or she is convinced that monogamy is the only way to do things; he or she can't see the outside world clearly. The monogamy bubble represents the boundaries of the emotional/relationship universe. However, once one breaks free from the bubble, they look around to others in their monogamy bubbles and see them as ridiculous.

But it should be noted that I am not politically concerned with making nonmonogamies gain cultural hegemony. My research indicates the need for the cultural recognition of varying relationship models without a presumption of the superiority or morality of monogamy. I desire multiple sexual social scripts and multiple models of relationships to coexist as equally viable and moral.

Yet this possibility is currently nullified by the hegemonic control monogamy maintains.

If we had more cultural discourse about the value of open relationships in society, as well as other forms of nonmonogamies, we might better empower individuals to have honest conversations about their sexual and romantic feelings. We might find (as I suspect) that monogamy might be a sensible way to grow a relationship, before couples open up sexually.

In final analysis, a relationship might be like growing a tree in a green house. It is a safe thing to do until the tree is strong enough to stand the winds of nature. But leave it in the greenhouse too long, and it might just crack its confining ceiling. Of course, people aren't trees; we have the advantage of being able to communicate with our partner's about issues of emotional safety and/or feelings of sexual incarceration through discussion. Hopefully this research will help our society better have those discussions.

REFERENCES

Adam, B. (2006). Relationship innovation in male couples. *Sexualities, 9*(1), 5–26.

Adam, B., Sears, A., & Schellenberg, G. (2000). Accounting for unsafe sex. *Journal of Sex Research, 37*, 259–271.

Adams, A., & Anderson, E. (forthcoming). Homosexuality and sport: Exploring the influence of coming out to the teammates of a small, Midwestern Catholic college soccer team. *Sport, Education and Society.*

Ahmed, S. (2004). *The cultural politics of emotion.* Edinburgh, Scotland: Edinburgh University Press.

Alexander, R. D. (1980). *Darwinism and human affairs.* London: Pitman Publishing.

Allen, E. S., Atkins, D. C., Baucom, D. H., Snyder, D. K., Gordon, K. C., & Glass, S. P. (2005). Intrapersonal, interpersonal, and contextual factors in engaging in and responding to extramarital involvement. *Clinical Psychology: Science and Practice, 12*, 101–130.

Amato, P. R. (1996). Explaining the intergenerational transmission of divorce. *Journal of Marriage and the Family, 58*, 628–640.

Amato, P. R. (2003). People's reasons for divorcing: Gender, social class, the life course, and adjustment. *Journal of Family issues, 24*, 602–626.

Amato, P. R., & Rogers, S. J. (1997). A longitudinal study of marital problems and subsequent divorce. *Journal of Marriage and the Family, 59*, 612–624.

Anderlini-D'Onofrio, S. (2004). *Plural loves: Designs for bi and poly living.* Binghamton, NY: Harrington Park Press.

Anderson, E. (2000). *Trailblazing: The true story of America's first openly gay track coach.* Hollywood, CA: Alyson Press.

Anderson, E. (2002). Contesting hegemonic masculinity in a homophobic environment. *Gender and Society, 16*(6), 860–877.

Anderson, E. (2005a). *In the game: Gay athletes and the cult of masculinity.* Albany, NY: State University of New York Press.

Anderson, E. (2005b). Orthodox & inclusive masculinity: Competing masculinities among heterosexual men in a feminized terrain. *Sociological Perspectives, 48*(3), 337–355.

Anderson, E. (2008a). "Being masculine is not about who you sleep with...": Heterosexual athletes contesting masculinity and the one-time rule of homosexuality. *Sex Roles: A Journal of Research, 58*(1–2), 104–115.

Anderson, E. (2008b). Inclusive masculinity in a fraternal setting. *Men and Masculinities.* *10*(5), 604–620.

Anderson, E. (2009). *Inclusive masculinity: The changing nature of masculinities.* New York: Routledge.

Anderson, E. (2010a). *Sport, theory and social problems: A critical introduction.* London and New York: Routledge.

Anderson, E. (2010b). "'At least with cheating there is an attempt at monogamy'": Cheating and monogamism among undergraduate heterosexual men. *Journal of Social and Personal Relationships, 27*(7), 851–872.

Anderson, E., Adams, A., & Rivers, I. (2010). "You wouldn't believe what straight men are doing with each other": Kissing, cuddling and loving. *Archives of Sexual Behavior.*

Anderson, E., & McGuire, R. (2010). Inclusive masculinity and the gendered politics of men's rugby. *The Journal of Gender Studies, 19*(3), 249–261.

Anderson, K. (2006). How well does paternity confidence match actual paternity? *Current Anthropology, 47*, 513–520.

Aronson, E. (1969). A theory of cognitive dissonance: A current perspective. In L. Berkowitz (Ed.), *Advances in experimental social psychology* (pp. 1–34). New York: Academic Press.

Asch, S. (1946). Forming impressions of personality. *Journal of Abnormal and Social Psychology, 41*, 258–290.

Atkins, D. C., Baucom, D. H., & Jacobson, N. S. (2001). Understanding infidelity: Correlates in a national random sample. *Journal of Family Psychology, 15*, 735–749.

Atkinson, T. (1974). *Amazon odyssey.* New York: Links Books.

Attwood, F. (2010). *Porn.com: Making sense of online pornography.* New York: Peter Lang.

Atwater, L. (1982). *The extramarital connection: Sex, intimacy and identity.* New York: Irvington.

Aune, K. S., & Comstock, J. (1997). Effect of relationship length on the experience, expression, and perceived appropriateness of jealousy. *Journal of Social Psychology, 137*(1), 23–31.

Bagemihl, B. (1999). *Biological exuberance: Animal homosexuality and natural diversity.* New York: St. Martin's Press.

Baker, W. E. (1984). The social structure of a national securities market. *American Journal of Sociology, 89*(4), 775–811.

Banfield, S., & McCabe, M. P. (2001). Extra relationship involvement among women: Are they different from men? *Archives of Sexual Behavior, 30*, 119–142.

Barash, D., & Lipton, J. E. (2001). *The myth of monogamy: Fidelity and infidelity in animals and people.* New York: Henry Holt & Company.

Barash, D., & Lipton, J. E. (2009). *Strange bedfellows: The surprising connection between sex, evolution and monogamy.* New York: Bellevue Literary Press.

Barker, M. (2007). Heteronormativity and the exclusion of bisexuality in psychology. In V. Clarke & E. Peel (Eds.), *Out in psychology: Lesbian, gay, bisexual, trans, and queer perspectives* (pp. 86–118). Chichester, England: Wiley.

Barker, M., & Langdridge, D. (2010a). Whatever happened to non-monogamies? Critical reflections on recent research and theory. *Sexualities, 13*(6), 748–772.

Barker, M., & Langdridge, D. (Eds.). (2010b). *Understanding non-monogamies.* New York: Routledge.

Barnett, O. W., Martinez, T. E., & Bluestein, B. W. (1995). Jealousy and romantic attachment in martially violent and nonviolent men. *Journal of Interpersonal Violence, 10*(4), 473–486.

Barrios, B. A., Corbitt, L. C., Estes J. P., & Topping, J. S. (1976). Effect of a social stigma on interpersonal distance. *Psychological Record, 26*(3), 343–348.

Battles, J. (2009, October 4). Monogamous women at risk of more STIs. *The Sunday Times.* Retrieved from: http://www.timesonline.co.uk/tol/news/world/ireland/article6860374.ece

Baumeister, R. F., & Bratslavsky, E. (1999). Passion, intimacy, and time: Passionate love as a function of change in intimacy. *Personality and Social Psychology Review, 3,* 49–67.

Bearman, P., & Brückner, H. (2001). Promising the future: Virginity pledges and first intercourse. *American Journal of Sociology, 106,* 859–912.

Bellis, M. A., Hughes, K., Hughes, S. & Ashton, J. R. (2005). Measuring paternal discrepancy and its public health consequences. *Journal of Epidemiological Community Health, 59,* 749–754.

Bem, D. J. (1967). Self-perception: An alternative interpretation of cognitive dissonance phenomena. *Psychological Review, 74,* 183–200.

Benson, P. J. (2008). *The polyamory handbook.* Bloomington, IN: Author House.

Bereczkei, T., Gyuris, P., & Weisfeld, G. E. (2004). Sexual imprinting in human mate choice. *Proceedings of the Royal Society Biological Sciences, 271*(1544): 1129–1134.

Berkowitz, B., & Yager-Berkowitz, S. (2007). *He's just not up for it anymore.* New York: Harper Collins.

Bersani, L. (2009). *Is the rectum a grave?: And other essays.* Chicago, IL: University of Chicago Press.

Betzig, L. (1989). Causes of conjugal dissolution: A cross cultural study. *Current Anthropology, 30,* 654–676.

Blake, S., & Lowen, L. (2010). Beyond monogamy: Lessons from long-term male couples in non-monogamous relationships. Retrieved May 2011, from, http://thecouplesstudy.com/wp-content/uploads/BeyondMonogamy_1_01.pdf

Blanchard, R., & Bogaert, A. F. (1996). Biodemographic comparisons of homosexual and heterosexual men in the Kinsey interview data. *Archives of Sexual Behavior, 25*(6), 551–579.

Blasband, D., & Peplau, L. (1985). Sexual exclusivity versus openness in gay couples. *Archives of Sexual Behavior, 14*(5), 395–412.

Blum, D. (1997). *Sex on the brain: The biological differences between men and women.* New York: Vintage.

Blumstein, P., & Schwartz, P. (1983). *American couples: Money-work-sex.* New York: William Morrow & Co.

Bogaert, A. F., & Hershberger, S. (1999). The relation between sexual orientation and penile size. *Archives of Sexual Behavior, 28*(3), 213–221.

Bogle, K. A. (2008). *Hooking up: Sex, dating, and relationships on campus.* New York: New York University Press.

Bonello, C. (2009). Gay monogamy and extradyadic sex: A critical review of the theoretical and empirical literature. *Counselling Psychology Review, 24*(3-4), 51–65.

Booth, A., Shelley, G., Mazur, A., Tharp, G., & Kittok, R. (1989). Testosterone, and winning and losing in human competition. *Hormones and Behavior, 23*(4), 556–571.

Bowlby, J. (1969/1982). *Attachment and loss: Vol. 1. Attachment* (2nd ed.). New York: Basic Books.

Bowlby, J. (1979). *The making and breaking of affectional bonds.* London: Tavistock.

Brewster, P. W. H., Mullin, C. R., Dobrin, R. A., & Steeves, J. K. E. (2010). Sex differences in face processing are mediated by handedness and sexual orientation. *Laterality: Asymmetries of Body, Brain and Cognition, 16*(2), 188–200.

Brown, B. B. (1999). "'You're going out with who?'" Peer group influences on adolescent romantic relationships. In W. Furman, B. Brown, & C. Feiring (Eds.), *The Development of Romantic Relationships in Adolescence* (pp. 291–329) Cambridge, England: Cambridge University Press.

Brown, B. B., Feiring, C., & Furman, W. (1999). Missing the love boat: why researchers have shied away from adolescent romance. In W. Furman, B. Brown, & C. Feiring (Eds.), *The Development of Romantic Relationships in Adolescence* (pp. 1–18). Cambridge, England: Cambridge University Press.

Brown. E. M. (1991). *Patterns of infidelity and their treatment.* New York: Brunner-Mazel.

Buntin, J., Lechtman, Z., & Laumann, E. (2004). Violence and sexuality: Examining Intimate partner violence and forced sexual activity. In E. Laumann, S. Ellingson, J. Mahay, A. Paik, & Y. Youm (Eds.), *The Sexual Organization of the City,* (pp. 259–276). Chicago, IL: University of Chicago Press.

Burdette, A. M., Ellison, C. G., Sherkat, D. E., & Gore, K. A. (2007). Are there religious variations in marital infidelity? *Journal of Family Issues, 28,* 1553–1581.

Buss, D. M. (1995). Evolutionary psychology: A new paradigm for psychological science. *Psychological Inquiry, 6,* 1–30.

Buss, D. M., Larsen, R. J., Westen, D., & Semmelroth, J. (1992). Sex differences in jealousy: Evolution, physiology, and psychology. *Psychological Science, 3,* 251–255.

Buunk, B. (1980). Extramarital sex in the Netherlands: Motivation in social and marital context. *Alternative Lifestyles, 3,* 11–39.

Califia, P. (2000). *Public sex* (2nd ed.). San Francisco, CA: Cleis Press.

Call, V., Sprecher, S., & Schwartz, P. (1995). The incidence and frequency of marital sex in a national sample. *Journal of Marriage and the Family, 57,* 639–652.

Caldwell, J. C., Orubuloye, I.O., & Caldwell, P. (1991). The destabilization of the traditional Yoruba sexual system. *Population and Development Review, 17*(2), 229–262.

Cancian, F. (1987). *Love in America.* Cambridge, England: Cambridge University Press

Carter, S. C. (1998). Neuroendocrine perspectives on social attachment and love. *Psychoneuroendocrinology, 23*(8), 779–818.

Charney, I. W. (1992). *Existential/dialectical marital therapy: Breaking the secret code of marital therapy.* New York: Brunner Mazel.

Cherlin, A. J. (2004). The deinstitutionalization of American marriage. *Journal of Marriage and Family, 74,* 102–127.

Cheung, M. W. L., Wong, P. W. C., Liu, K., Yip, P. S. F., Fan, S. Y. S., & Lam, T. H. (2008). A study of sexual satisfaction and frequency of sex among Hong Kong Chinese Couples. *Journal of Sex Research, 45*(2), 129–139.

Choi, K-H., Catania, J. A., & Dolcini, M. M. (1994). Extramarital sex and HIV risk behavior among American adults: Results from the national AIDS behavioral survey. *American Journal of Public Health, 84,* 2003–2007.

Christopher, F. S., & Cate, R. M. (1985). Premarital sexual pathways and relationship development. *Journal of Social and Personal Relationships, 2,* 271–288.

Civic, D. (1999). The association between characteristics of dating relationships and condom use among heterosexual young adults. *AIDS Education Prevention, 11,* 343–352.

Coan, J. A., Schaefer, H. S., & Davidson, R. J. (2006). Lending a hand: Social regulation of the neural response to threat. *Psychological Science, 17*(12), 1032–1039.

Cochran, S., & Mays, V. (1987). Acquired Immunodeficiency syndrome and black Americans: Special psychosocial issues. *Public Health Reports, 102,* 224–231.

Coleman, J. S. (1988). Social capital in the creation of human capital. *American Journal of Sociology, 94,* 95–120.

Connell, R. W. (1987). *Gender and power.* Cambridge, England: Polity Press.

Connell, R. W. (1992). A very straight gay: Masculinity, homosexual experience, and the dynamics of gender. *American Sociological Review, 57,* 735–751.

Connolly, J., & Goldberg, A. (1999). Romantic relationships in adolescence. The role of friends and peers in their emergence and development. In W. Furman, B. Brown, & C. Feiring (Eds.), *The Development of Romantic Relationships in Adolescence* (pp. 266–290). Cambridge, England: Cambridge University Press.

Crouter, A. C., & Booth, A. (2006). *Romance and sex in adolescence and emerging adulthood: Risks and opportunities.* Mahwah, NJ: Lawrence Erlbaum and Associates.

Crowe, M., & Ridley, J. (2000). *Therapy with couples: A behavioural-systems approach to couple relationship and sexual problems.* Oxford, England: Blackwell.

Cunningham, M. R. (1986). Measuring the physical in physical attractiveness: Quasi experiments on the sociobiology of female facial beauty. *Journal of Personality and Social Psychology, 50*(5), 925–935.

Cunningham, M. R., Barbee, A. P., & Pike, C. L. (1990). What do women want? Facial metric assessment of multiple motives in the perception of male physical attractiveness. *Journal of Personality and Social Psychology, 59,* 61–72.

Daly, M., & Wilson, M. (1983). Sex, evolution, and behavior (2nd ed.). Belmont, CA: Wadsworth.

Daly, M., Wilson, M., & Weghorst, S. (1982). Male sexual jealousy. *Ethology and Sociobiology, 3,* 11–27.

Demaris, A. (2009). Distal and proximal influences on the risk of extramarital sex: A prospective study of longer duration marriages. *Journal of Sex Research, 46*(6), 597–607.

Deleuze, G., & Guattari, F. (1999). *A thousand plateaus: Capitalism & schizophrenia* (Brian Massumi, Trans.). London: The Athlone Press.

Denizet-Lewis, B. (2003, August 3). Double lives on the down low. *New York Times Magazine,* p. 28.

DeSteno, D., & Bartlett, M. (2002). Sex differences in jealousy: Evolution mechanism or artifact of measurement. *Journal of Personality and Social Psychology, 83,* 1103–1116.

DeSteno, D. A., & Salovey, P. (1996). Evolutionary origins of sex differences in jealousy? Questioning the "fitness" of the model. *Psychological Science, 7,* 367–372.

de Visser, R., & McDonald, D. (2007). Swings and roundabouts: Management of jealousy in heterosexual "swinging" couples. *British Journal of Social Psychology, 46*(2), 459–476.

de Visser R., & Smith, A. (1999). Predictors of heterosexual condom use: Characteristics of the sexual encounter are more important than characteristics of individual. *Psychology, Health and Medicine, 4,* 265–279.

de Visser, R., & Smith, A. (2001). Relationship between sexual partners influences rates and correlates of condom use. *AIDS Education Prevention, 13*(5), 413–428.

DeVries, C., & Glasper, E. R. (2005) Social structure influences effects of pair-housing on wound healing. *Brain, Behavior, and Immunity, 19*(1), 61–68.

Dines, G. (2010). *Pornland: How porn has hijacked our sexuality.* Boston, MA: Beacon Press.

Dion, K. K., Berschied, E., & Walster, E. (1972). What is beautiful is good. *Journal of Personality and Social Psychology, 24*, 285–290.

Downey, G., Freitas, A., Michaelis, B., & Khouri, H. (1998). The self-fulfilling prophecy in close relationships: Do rejection-sensitive women get rejected by their partners? *Journal of Personality and Social Psychology, 75*, 545–560.

Drigotas, S., & Barta, W. (2001). The cheating heart: Scientific explorations of infidelity. *Current Directions in Psychological Science, 10*, 177–180.

Duncombe, J., Harrison, K., Allan, G., & Marsden, D. (Eds.). (2004). *The state of affairs: Explorations in infidelity and commitment.* Mahwah, NJ: Erlbaum.

Duncombe, J., & Marsden, D. (1999). Love and intimacy: The gender division of emotion and "emotion work": A neglected aspect of sociological discussion of heterosexual relationships. In G.

Easton, D., & Hardy, J. W. (2009). *The ethical slut: A practical guide to polyamory, open relationships & other adventures* (2nd ed.). Berkeley, CA: Celestial Arts.

Edwards, J. N. (1973). Extramarital involvement: Fact and theory. *Journal of Sex Research, 9*, 210–224.

Eigenberg, H. M. (2000). Correctional officers and their perceptions of homosexuality, rape, and prostitution in male prisoners. *The Prison Journal, 80*(4), 415–433.

Eisenthal, Y., Dror, G., & Ruppin, E. (2005). Facial attractiveness: Beauty and the machine. *Neural Computation, 18*, 119–142.

Ellis, K., O'Dair, B., & Tallmer, A. (1990). Feminism and pornography. *Feminist Review, 36*, 15–18.

Engels, F. (1884). *Origin of the family, private property and the state.* New York: International Publishers Company.

England, P., Fitzgibbons Shafer, E., & Fogarty, A. C. K. (2008). Hooking up and forming romantic relationships on today's college campuses. In M. Kimmel & A. Aronson (Eds.), *The gendered society reader* (pp. 531–547). New York: Oxford University Press.

Erikson, E. H. (1963). *Childhood and society.* New York: Norton.

Faurie, C., Pontier, D., & Raymond, M. (2004). Student athletes claim to have more sexual partners than other students. *Evolution and Human Behavior, 25*, 1–8.

Fein, E., & Schneider, S. (2007). *All the rules: Time-tested secrets for capturing the heart of Mr. Right.* Clayton, VIC: Warner Books.

Feingold, A. (1992). Good-looking people are not what we think. *Psychological Bulletin, 111*, 304–341.

Feldman, S., & Cauffman, E. (1999). Your cheatin' heart: Attitudes, behaviors, and correlates of sexual betrayal in late adolescents. *Journal of Research on Adolescence, 9*, 227–252.

Festinger, L. (1957). *A theory of cognitive dissonance.* Stanford, CA: Stanford University Press.

Fielder, R. L., & Carey, M. P. (2010). Predictors and consequences of sexual "hookups" among college students: A short-term prospective study. *Archives of Sexual Behavior, 39*(5), 1105–1119.

Filene, P. G. (1975). *Him/her/self: Sex roles in modern America*. San Diego, CA: Harcourt Brace Jovanovich.

Filiault, S. M., & Drummond, M. J. (2008). Athletes and body image: Interviews with gay sportsmen. *Qualitative Research in Psychology, 5*(4), 311–333.

Finn, M., & Malson, H. (2008). Speaking of home truth: (Re)productions of dyadic commitment in non-monogamous relationships. *British Journal of Social Psychology, 47*(3), 519–533.

Fischer, C. S. (1982). What do we mean by "friend": An inductive study. *Social Networks, 3*, 287–306.

Fisher, H. (2004). *Why we love: The nature and chemistry of romantic love*. New York: Henry Holt.

Foucault, M. (1980). *The history of sexuality. 1: An introduction*. New York: Vintage Books.

Foucault, M. (1990). *The history of sexuality* (3 Vols.). New York: Vintage.

Forste, R., & Tanfer, K. (1996). Sexual exclusivity among dating, cohabiting, and married women. *Journal of Marriage and the Family, 58*, 33–47.

Fraley, R. C., & Davis, K. E. (1997). Attachment formation and transfer in young adults' close friendships and romantic relationships. *Personal Relationships, 4*, 131–144.

Frank, K., & DeLamater, J. (2010). Deconstructing monogamy: Boundaries, identities, and fluidities across relationships. In M. Barker & D. Langdridge, (Eds.), *Understanding non monogamies* (pp. 9–22). New York: Routledge.

Freire, P. (1972). *Pedagogy of the oppressed*. Middlesex, England: Penguin.

Freud, S. (1949). *Three essays on the theory of sexuality*. London: Imago Publishing Company.

Frijda, N. H. (1986). *The emotions*. Cambridge, England: Cambridge University Press.

Gangestad S. W., & Simpson, J. A. (2000). The evolution of human mating: Trade-offs and strategic pluralism. *Behavioral and Brain Sciences, 23*, 573–644.

Geary, D. C. (1998). *Male, female: The evolution of human sex differences*. Washington, DC: American Psychological Association.

Gerressu, M., Mercer, C. H., Grahamm, C. A., Wellings, K., & Johnson, A. M. (2008). Prevalence of masturbation and associated factors in a British National Probability Survey. *Archives of Sexual Behavior, 37*, 266–278.

Giddens, A. (1976). *Functionalism: après la lutte. Social Research, 43*, 325–366.

Giddens, A. (1992). *The transformation of intimacy*. Cambridge, England: Polity.

Glass, S., & Wright, T. (1985). The relationship of extramarital sex, length of marriage, and sex differences on marital satisfaction and romanticism: Athanasiou's data reanalyzed. *Journal of Marriage and the Family, 39*, 691–704.

Goffman, E. (1959). *The presentation of self in everyday life*. New York: Doubleday.

Goldmeier, D., & Richardson, D. (2005). Romantic love and sexually transmitted infection acquisition: Hypothesis and review. *International Journal of STD and AIDS, 16*, 585–587.

Gombrich, E. H. (1984). *The sense of order: A study in the psychology of decorative art*. London, England: Phaidon.

Goodall, J. (1990). *Through a window: My thirty years with the chimpanzees of Gombe*. New York: Soko Publications.

Gottman, J. M. (1993). A theory of marital dissolution and stability. *Journal of Family Psychology, 7*, 57–75.

Gough, B., & Edwards, G. (1998). The beer talking: Four lads, a carry out, and the reproduction of masculinity. *Sociological Review, 46*(3), 409–435.

Graham, K., & Wells, S. (2003). Somebody's gonna get their head kicked in tonight: Aggression among young males in bars- A question of values? *British Journal of Criminology, 43,* 546–566.

Gramsci, A. (1971). *Selections from prison notebooks.* London: New Left Books.

Gray, J. (2002). *Men are from Mars and women are from Venus.* London: Thorsons.

Gray, M., & Steinberg, L. (1999). Adolescent romance and the parent–child relationship: A contextual perspective. In W. Furman, B. Brown, & C. Feiring (Eds.), *The Development of Romantic Relationships in Adolescence* (pp. 235–265). Cambridge, England: Cambridge University Press

Greeley, A. M. (1991). *Faithful attraction.* New York: A Tom Doherty Associates Book.

Greenberg, M., & Littlewood, R. (1995). Post adoption incest and phenotypic matching: Experience, personal meanings and biosocial implications. *British Journal of Medical Psychology, 68,* 29–44.

Guo, K., Meints, K., Hall, C., Hall, S., & Mills, D. (2009). Left gaze bias in humans, rhesus monkeys and domestic dogs. *Animal Cognition, 12*(3), 1435–1496.

Ha, T., Overbeek, G., & Engels, R. (2010). Effects of attractiveness and social status on dating desire in heterosexual adolescents: An experimental study. *Archives of Sexual Behavior, 39*(5), 1063–1071.

Halperin, D. T. (1999) Heterosexual anal intercourse: Prevalence, cultural factors, and HIV infection and other health risks, part I. *AIDS Patient Care and STDs, 13,* 717–730.

Halpern, C. T., Udry, J. R., Campbell, B., & Suchindran, C. (1993). Testosterone and pubertal development as predictors of sexual activity: A panel analysis of adolescent males. *Psychosomatic Medicine, 55,* 436–447.

Hansen, G. L. (1985). Perceived threats and marital jealousy. *Social Psychology Quarterly, 48,* 262–268.

Hansen, G. L. (1987). Extradyadic relations during courtship. *Journal of Sex Research, 23,* 382–390.

Hammer, J., Fisher, J., Fitzgerald, P., & Fisher, W. (1996). When two heads aren't better than one: AIDS risk behavior in college-age couples. *Journal of Applied Social Psychology, 26,* 375–397.

Haritaworn, J., Lin, C.-J., & Christian K. (2006). Poly/logue: A critical introduction to Polyamory. *Sexualities, 9*(5), 515–529.

Harris, C. (2002). Sexual and romantic jealousy in heterosexual and homosexual adults. *Psychological Science, 13*(1), 7–12.

Harris, C. (2003). A review of sex differences in sexual jealousy, including self-report data, psychophysiological responses, interpersonal violence, and morbid jealousy. *Personality and Social Psychology Review, 7*(2), 102–128.

Harris, C. R., & Christenfeld, N. (1996). Gender, jealousy, and reason. *Psychological Science, 7,* 364–366.

Harry, J. (1984). *Gay couples.* New York: Praeger.

Hart, S., & Carrington, H. A. (2002). Jealousy in six-month-old infants. *Infancy, 3,* 395–402.

Hart, S., Carrington, H. A., Tronick, E. Z., & Carroll, S. (2004). When infants lose exclusive maternal attention: Is it jealousy? *Infancy, 6*(1), 57–78.

Hart, S., Field, T., del Valle, C., & Letourneau, M. (1998). Infants protest their mothers' attending to an infant-size doll. *Social Development, 7,* 54–61.

Hatfield, E., Pillemer, J. T., O'Brien, M. U., Sprecher, S., & Le, Y. L. (2008). The endurance of love: Passionate and companionate love in newlywed and long-term marriages. *Interpersona: An International Journal on Personal Relationships*, *2*, 35–64.

Hazan, C., & Zeifman, D. (1999). Pair-bonds as attachments: Evaluating the evidence. In J. Cassidy & P. R. Shaver (Eds.), *Handbook of attachment: Theory, research, and clinical applications* (pp. 336–354). New York: Guilford.

Heaphy, B., Donovan, C., & Weeks, J. (2004). A different affair? Openness and non monogamy in same-sex relationships. In J. Duncombe, K. Harrison, G. Allan, & D. Marsden (Eds.), *The state of affairs: Explorations in infidelity and commitment* (pp. 167–186). Mahwah, NJ: Erlbaum.

Heaton, J. P. W. (2003). Prolactin: An integral player in hormonal politics. *Contemporary Urology*, *15*, 17–25.

Henrich, N., & Henrich, J. (2007). *Why humans cooperate: A cultural and evolutionary explanation*. Oxford, England: Oxford University Press.

Henry, G. (1942). *Sex variants: A study of homosexual patterns*. New York: Paul B. Hoeber.

Herek, G. M. (1994). Assessing heterosexuals' attitudes toward lesbian and gay men: A review of empirical research with the ATLG scale. In B. Greene & G. M. Herek (Eds.), *Lesbian and gay psychology: Theory, research, and clinical applications* (pp. 206–228). Thousand Oaks, CA: Sage.

Herz, R. S., & Cahill, E. D. (1997). Differential use of sensory information in sexual behavior as a function of gender. *Human Nature*, *8*, 275–286.

Hill, C. T., Rubin, Z., & Peplau, L. A. (1976). Breakups before marriage: The end of 103 affairs. *Journal of Social Issues*, *32*, 147–168.

Hirschfeld, M. (1914). *Die Homosexualitat ded Mannes und des Weibes*. Berlin, Germany: Lewis Marcus.

Hite, S. (1991). *The Hite Report on Love, Passion and Emotional Violence*. London: Optima.

Hite, S (1993). *Women as revolutionary agents of change: The Hite reports 1972–1993*. London: Bloomsbury.

Ho, P. S. Y. (2006). The (charmed) circle game: Reflections on sexual hierarchy through multiple sexual relationships. *Sexualities*, *9*(5), 547–564.

Hoff, C. C., Beougher, S. C., Chakravarty, D., Darbes, L. A., & Neilands, T. B. (2010). Relationship characteristics and motivations behind agreements among gay male couples: Differences by agreement type and couple serostatus. *AIDS Care*, *22*(7), 827–835.

Holstege, G., Georgiadis, J. R., Paans, A. M. J., Meiners, L. C., van der Graaf, F., & Reinders, S. (2003). Brain activation during human male ejaculation. *The Journal of Neuroscience*, *23*(27), 9185–9193.

Homans, G. C. (1950). *The human group*. New York: Harcourt Brace Jovanovich.

Huesmann, L. (1980). Toward a predictive model of romantic behavior. In K. Pope (Ed.), *On love and aging* (pp. 152–171). San Francisco, CA: Jossey-Bass.

Hughes, G., Catchpole, M., & Rogers, P.A, (2000). Comparison of risk factors for four sexually transmitted infections: Results from a study of attenders at three genitourinary medicine clinics in England. *Sex Transmitted Infections*, *76*, 262–267.

Humbad, M. N., Donnellan, M. B., Iacono, W. G., & Burt, S. A. (2010). Is spousal similarity for personality a matter of convergence or selection? *Personality and Individual Differences*, *49*(7), 827–830.

Huston, T. L., & Burgess, R. L. (1979). Social exchange in developing relationships: An overview. In R. L. Burgess & T. L. Huston (Eds.), *Social exchange in developing relationships* (pp. 3–28). New York: Academic Press.

Hyrum, J. (1885). *The history and philosophy of marriage; or, polygamy and monogamy compared.* Salt Lake City, UT: Joseph Hyrum Parry.

Jackson, S., & Scott, S. (2004). Whatever happened to feminist critiques of monogamy? In H. Graham, A. Kaloski, A. Neilson, & E. Robertson (Eds.), *The feminist seventies* (pp. 87–106). York, England: Raw Nerve Books.

Jamieson, L. (2004). Intimacy, negotiated non-monogamy and the limits of the couple. In The state of affairs: explorations in infidelity and commitment By Jean Duncombe. (pp. 13–30). Routledge: New york

Johnson, M. P. (1999). Personal, moral, and structural commitment to relationships: Experiences of choice and constraint. In J. M. Adams & W. H. Jones (Eds.), *Handbook on interpersonal commitment and relationship stability* (pp. 73–87). New York: Kluwer Academic/Plenum.

Johnson, J. M. (2002). In depth interviewing. In J. F. Gubrium & J. A. Holstein (Eds.), *Handbook of Interview research: Context & Method* (pp. 103–119). Thousand Oaks, CA: Sage.

Kanazawa, S., & Still, M. (1999). Why monogamy? *Social Forces, 78,* 25–50.

King, J. L. (2004). *On the down low: A journey into the lives of "straight" Black men who sleep with men.* New York: Broadway Books.

Kinsey, A., Pomeroy, W. & Martin, C. (1948). *Sexual Behavior in the Human Male.* W.B. Saunders Company: Philadelphia.

Klein, F. (1993). *The bisexual option* (2nd ed.). Binghamton, NY: The Haworth Press.

Klesse, C. (2005). Bisexual women, nonmonogamy and differentialist anti-promiscuity discourses. *Sexualities, 8,* 445–464.

Klesse, C. (2006). Polyamory and its "others": Contesting the terms of nonmonogamy. *Sexualities, 9,* 565–583.

Knapp, M. (1984). *Interpersonal communication and human relationships.* Boston, MA: Allyn and Bacon.

Kong, T. K., Mahoney, D., & Plummer, K. (2002). Queering the interview. In J. F. Gubrium & J. A. Holstein (Eds.), *Handbook of interview research: Context and method* (pp. 239–258). Thousand Oaks, CA: Sage.

Kontula, O. (2010). *Between sexual desire and reality: The evolution of sex in Finland.* Helsinki, Finland: Vaestoliitto Publications (Publications of the Population Research Institute).

Kontula, O., & Haavio-Mannila (2004). Renaissance of romanticism in the era of increasing individualism. In J. Duncombe, K. Harrison, G. Allan, & D. Marsden (Eds.), *The state of affairs: explorations in infidelity and commitment* (pp. 33–47). Mahwah, NJ: Lawrence Erlbaum Associates.

Korobov, N., & Bamberg, M. (2004). Positioning a "mature" self in interactive practices: How adolescent males negotiate "physical attraction" in group talk. *British Journal of Developmental Psychology, 22,* 471–492.

Krahe, B., Scheinberger-Olwig, R., & Kolpin, S. (2000). Ambiguous communication of sexual intentions as a risk marker of sexual aggression. *Sex Roles, 42,* 313–337.

Langlois, J. H., Roggman, L. A., Casey, R. J., Ritter, J. M., Rieser-Danner, L. A., & Jenkins, V. Y. (1987). Infant preferences for attractive faces: Rudiments of a stereotype? *Developmental Psychology, 23,* 363–369.

LaSala, M. C. (2001). Monogamous or not: Understanding and counseling gay male couples. *Families in Society, 82*, 605–611.

LaSala, M. (2004a). Extradyadic sex and gay male couples: Comparing monogamous and nonmonogamous relationships. *Families in Society, 85*, 405–412.

LaSala, M. (2004b). Monogamy of the heart: A qualitative study of extradyadic sex among gay male couples. *Journal of Gay and Lesbian Social Services, 17*(3), 1–24.

Laumann, E. (1973). *Bonds of pluralism: The form and substance of urban social networks.* New York: Wiley.

Laumann, E., Ellingson, S., Mahay, J., Paik, A., & Youm, Y. (2004). *The sexual organization of the city.* Chicago, IL: University of Chicago Press.

Laumann, E., Gagnon, J. H., Michael, R. T., & Michaels, S. (1994). *The social organization of sexuality: Sexual practices in the United States.* Chicago, IL: University of Chicago Press.

Laursen, B. (1993). The perceived impact of conflict on adolescent relationships. *Merrill-Palmer Quarterly, 39*, 535–550.

Lawson, A. (1988). *Adultery: An analysis of love and betrayal.* New York: Basic Books.

Lazarus, R. S., & Lazarus, B. N. (1994). *Passion and reason: Making sense of our emotions.* New York: Oxford University Press.

Leap, W. L., & Boellstorff, T. (2004). *Speaking in queer tongues: Globalisation and gay language.* Champagne, IL: University of Illinois Press.

Lehmiller, J. L. (2009). Secret romantic relationships: Consequences for personal and relational well-being. *Personality and Social Psychology Bulletin, 35*, 1452–1466.

Leichliter, J. S., Chandra, A., Liddon, N., Fenton, K. A., & Aral, S. (2007). Prevalence and correlates of heterosexual anal and oral sex in adolescents and adults in the United States. *Journal of Infectious Disease, 196*, 1852–1859.

Leigh, B. C., Temple, M. T., & Trocki, K. F. (1993). The sexual behavior of U.S. adults: Results from a national survey. *American Journal of Public Health, 83*, 1400–1408.

Lewis, R. A. (1973). Social reaction and the formation of dyads: An interactionist approach to mate selection. *Sociometry, 36*, 409–418.

Little, A. C., Burt, D. M., Penton-Voakm, I. S., & Perrett, D. I. (2001). Self-perceived attractiveness influences human female preferences for sexual dimorphism and symmetry in male faces. *Proceedings of the Royal Society of London B: Biological Sciences, 268*(1462), 39–44.

Little, A. C., & Jones, B. C. (2006). Attraction independent of detection suggests special mechanisms for symmetry preferences in human face perception. *Proceedings of the Royal Society of London B: Biological Sciences, 273*(1605): 3093–3099.

Lloyd, S. A., Cate, R. M., & Henton, J. M. (1984). Predicting pre-marital relationship stability: A methodological refinement. *Journal of Marriage and the Family, 46*, 71–76.

Loftus, J. (2001). America's liberalization in attitudes toward homosexuality, 1973 to 1998. *American Sociological Review, 66*, 762–782.

Luo, S., Cartun, M. A., & Snider, A. G. (2010). Assessing extradyadic behavior: A review, a new measure, and two new models. *Personality and Individual Differences, 49*, 155–163. [epub ahead of print].

Mahoney, C. A., Thombs, D. L., & Ford, O. J. (1995). Health belief model and self-efficacy models: Their utility in explaining college student condom use. *AIDS Education Prevention, 7*(1), 32–49.

Maillu, D. G. (1988). *Our kind of polygamy.* Nairobi: Heinemann Kenya.

Martikainen, P., & Valkonen, T. (1996). Mortality after the death of a spouse: Rates and causes of death in a large Finnish cohort. *American Journal of Public Health, 86*(8), 1087–1093.

Mathes, E. W. (1991). A cognitive theory of jealousy. In P. Salovey (Ed.), *The psychology of jealousy and envy* (pp. 52–78). New York: Guilford.

Matik, W. O. (2002). *Redefining our relationships: Guidelines for responsible open relationships.* Oakland, CA: Defiant Times Press.

Maykovich, M. K. (1976). Attitudes versus behavior in extramarital sexual relations. *Journal of Marriage and the Family, 38*, 693–699.

McCormack, M. (2010). The declining significance of homohysteria for male students in three sixth forms in the south of England. *British Educational Research Journal,* iFirst, 1–17.

McCormack, M. (2011). *Gay friendly high schools: Masculinities, sexualities and education.* New York: Oxford University Press.

McCormack, M., & Anderson, E. (2010). "It's just not acceptable anymore": The erosion of homophobia and the softening of masculinity in an English state school. *Sociology, 44*(5), 843–859.

McLanahan, S. S., & Casper, L. (1995). Growing diversity and Inequality in the American family. In R. Farley (Ed.), *State of the union: America in the 1990's* (pp. 1–45). New York: Sage.

McNair, B. (2002). *Striptease culture: The democratization of desire.* London: Routledge.

McWhirter, D. P., & Mattison, A. M. (1984). *The male couple: How relationships develop.* Englewood Cliffs, NJ: Prentice-Hall.

Mead, M. (1931). Jealousy primitive and civilized. In S. D. Schmalhauser & V. F. Calverton (Eds.), Woman's coming of age (pp. 35–48). New York: Liveright.

Meirer, A., & Allen, G. (2008). Intimate relationship development during the transition to adulthood: differences by social class. *New Directions for Child and Adolescent Development, 119*, 25–39.

Messner, M. (1992). *Power at play: Sports and the problem of masculinity.* Boston, MA: Beacon Press.

Meston, M. M., & Tierney, A. (2008). Ethnic, gender and acculturation influences on sexual behaviors. *Archives of Sexual Behavior, 39*(1), 179–189.

Mint, P. (2010). The power mechanisms of jealousy. In M. Barker & D. Langdridge (Eds.), *Understanding non-monogamies* (pp. 201–206). New York: Routledge.

Mohr, J. J., Israel, T., & Sedlacek, W. E. (2001). Counselors' attitudes regarding bisexuality as predictors of counselors' clinical responses: An analogue study of a female bisexual client. *Journal of Counselling Psychology, 48*(2), 212–222.

Moi, T. (1982). Jealousy and sexual difference. In K. Lebacqz & D. Sinacore-Guinn (Eds.), *Femisit Revie, 11*, (pp. 53–68). London: Virago.

Mongeau, P. A., Williams, J., Shaw, C., Knight, K., & Ramirez, A. (2009). Definitions and diversity of friends with benefits relationships: A two-wave, cross-region, study. Unpublished DataMontgomery, M. J. (2005). Psychosocial intimacy and identity: From early adolescence to emerging adulthood. *Journal of Adolescent Research, 20*, 346–374.

Mosher, W. D., Chandra, A., & Jones, J. (2005). Sexual behavior and selected health measures: Men and women 15–44 years of age, United States, 2002. *Advance Data from Vital and Health Statistics, 362*. Retrieved June 2009, from http://www.cdc.gov/nchs/data/ad/ad362.pdf

Muehlenhard, C., & Rodgers, C. S. (1998). Token resistance to sex: New perspectives on an old stereotype. *Psychology of Women Quarterly, 22*, 443–463.

Mullen, P. E., & Martin, J. (1994). Jealousy: A community study. *British Journal of Psychiatry, 164*, 35–43.

Munson, M., & Stelboum, J. P. (1999). *The lesbian polyamory reader: Open relationships, non-monogamy, and casual sex.* New York: Haworth Press.

Mutchler, M. (2000). Young gay men's stories in the States: Social scripts, sex, and safety in the time of AIDS. *Sexualities, 3*, 31–54.

Møller, A. P., & Alatalo, R. V. (1999). Good genes effects in sexual selection. *Proceedings of the Royal Society of London B: Biological Sciences, 266*, 85–91.

Møller, A. P., & Thornhill, R. (1998). Bilateral symmetry and sexual selection: A meta-analysis. *The American Naturalist, 151*, 174–192.

Nardi, P. (1999). *Gay men's friendships: Invincible communities.* Chicago, IL: University of Chicago Press.

Neuman, M. G. (2008). *The truth about cheating.* San Francisco, CA: Wiley.

Newmann, S., Sarin, P., Kumarasamy, N., Amalraj, E., Rogers, M., Madhivanan, P., … Soloman, S. (2000). Marriage, monogamy and HIV: A profile of HIV-infected women in South India. *International Journal of STD and AIDS, 11*(3), 250–253.

Nichols, M. (1990). Lesbian relationships: Implications for the study of sexuality and gender. In D. P. McWhirther, S. A. Sanders, & J. M. Reinsich (Eds), *Homosexuality/heterosexuality: The Kinsey scale and current research* (pp. 350–364). New York: Oxford University Press.

Ochs, R. (1996). Biphobia: It goes more than two ways. In B. A. Firestein (Ed.), *Bisexuality: The psychology and politics of an invisible minority* (pp. 217–239). Thousand Oaks, CA: Sage.

Owen, J. J., Rhoades, G. K., Stanley, M. S., & Fincham, F. D. (2010). "'Hooking up'" among college students: Demographic and psychosocial correlates. *Archives of Sexual Behavior, 39*, 653–663.

Paik, A., Laumann, E., & Van Haitsma, M. (2004). Commitment, jealousy and the quality of life. In E. Laumann, S. Ellingson, J. Mahay, A. Paik, & Y. Youm (Eds.), *The sexual organization of the city.* Chicago, IL: University of Chicago Press.

Park, R. E. (1929). The city as a social laboratory. In R. H. Turner (Ed.), *Robert E. Park on social control and collective behavior* (pp. 3–18). Chicago, IL: University of Chicago Press.

Parks, M. R., Stan, C. M., & Eggert, L. L. (1983). Romantic involvement and social network involvement. *Social Psychology Quarterly, 46*, 116–131.

Parrott, W. G. (1991). The emotional experiences of envy and jealousy. In P. Salovey (Ed.), *The psychology of jealousy and envy* (pp. 3–30). New York: Guilford.

Penton-Voak, I. S., Little, A. C., Jones, B. C., Burt, D. M., & Perrett, D. I. (2003). Measures of human female condition predict preferences for sexually dimorphic characteristics in men's faces. *Journal of Comparative Psychology, 117*, 264–271.

Peplau, L., & Cochran, S. (1988). Value orientations in the intimate relationships of gay men. *Journal of Homosexuality, 6*(3), 1–19.

Peplau, L., Cochran, S., & Mays, V. (1997). A national survey of the intimate relationships of African American lesbian and gay men. In B. Greene (Ed.), *Ethnic and cultural diversity among lesbians and gay men* (pp. 11–35). Thousand Oaks, CA: Sage.

Peralta, R. L. (2007). College alcohol use and the embodiment of hegemonic masculinity among European American men. *Sex Roles, 56*, 741–756.

Perrett, D. I. (1999). Symmetry, sexual dimorphism in facial proportions, and male facial attractiveness. *Proceedings of the Royal Society of London, 268*(1476), 1617–1623.

Perrett, D. I., Burt, D. M., Penton-Voak, I. S., Lee, K. J., Rowland, D. A., & Edwards, R. (1999). Symmetry and human facial attractiveness. *Evolution and Human Behavior, 20*(5), 295–307.

Phillips, S. (2010). There were three in the bed: Discursive desire and the sex lives of swingers. In M. Barker & D. Langdridge (Eds.), *Understanding non-monogamies* (pp. 82–86). New York: Routledge.

Pieper, M., & Bauer, R. (2005). Call for papers: International conference on polyamory and mono-normativity. University of Hamburg, November 5th/6th 2005. Retrieved from http://www.wiso.uni-hamburg.de/index.php?id=3495 on 31/08/08

Pinker, S. *The Better Angels of our Nature: Why violence has declined.* New York: Penguin.

Pittman, E. (1989). *Private lives: Infidelity and the betrayal of intimacy.* New York: W. W. Norton.

Pivnick, A. (1993). HIV infection and the meaning of condoms. *Culture, Medicine and Psychiatry, 17,* 431–453.

Popenoe, D. (1993). American family decline, 1960–1990: A review and appraisal. *Journal of Marriage and the Family, 55,* 527–542.

Popkins, N. C. (1998). Natural characteristics that influence environment: How physical appearance affects personality. Retrieved October 2001, from Northwestern University, Personality Research Web site: http://www.personalityresearch.org/papers/popkins2.html

Ponterotto, J. G. (2005). Qualitative research in counseling psychology: A primer on research paradigms and philosophy of science. *Journal of Counseling Psychology, 52,* 126–136.

Prince A., & Bernard, A. L. (1998). Sexual behaviors and safer sex practices of college students on a commuter campus. *Journal of American College Health, 47*(1), 11–21.

Rainwater, L. (1966). Some aspects of lower-class sexual behavior. *Journal of Social Issues, 22,* 96–108.

Raley, R. K., Crissy, S., & Muller, C. (2007). Of sex and romance: Late adolescent relationships and young adult union formation. *Journal of Marriage and the Family, 69,* 1210–1226.

Ravenscroft, T. (2004). *Polyamory: Roadmaps for the clueless & hopeful.* Santa Fe, NM: Crossquarter Publishing Group.

Reiss, I. L., & Miller, B. C. (1979). Heterosexual permissiveness: A theoretical analysis. In W. R. Burr, R. Hill, F. I. Nye, & I. L. Reiss (Eds.), *Contemporary theories about the family* (Vol. 1, pp. 57–100). New York: Free Press.

Remez, L. (2000). Oral sex among adolescents: Is it sex or is it abstinence? *Family Planning Perspectives, 32,* 298–304.

Rensch, B. (1963). Vesuche uber menschliche Auslosermerkmale beider Geschlecter. *Zeitschrift fur Morphologische Anthropologie, 53,* 139–164.

Rhodes, G., Proffitt, F., Grady, J., & Sumich, A. (1998). Facial symmetry and the perception of beauty. *Psychonomic Bulletin and Review, 5*(4), 659–669.

Rhodes, G., Yoshikawa, S., Clarkm A., Lee, K., McKay, R., & Akamatsu, S. (2001). Attractiveness of facial averageness and symmetry in non-Western populations: in search of biologically based standards of beauty. *Perception, 30*(5), 611–625.

Richards, C. (2010). Trans and non-monogamy. In M. Barker & D. Langdridge, (Eds.), *Understanding non-monogamies* (pp. 121–133). New York: Routledge.

Rimmele, U., Hediger, K., Heinrichs, M., & Klaver, P. (2009). Oxytocin makes a face in memory familiar. *The Journal of Neuroscience, 29*(1), 38–42.

Ringer, J. (2001). Constitution nonmonogamies. In M. Bernstein & R. Reimann (Eds.), *Queer families, queer politics: Challenging culture and the state* (pp. 137–155). New York: Columbia University Press.

Ritchie, A., & Barker, M. (2006). "There aren't words for what we do or how we feel so we have to make them up": Constructing polyamorous languages in a culture of compulsory monogamy. *Sexualities, 9*(5), 584–601.

Robinson, M. (2010). *Cupid's poisoned arrow: From habit to harmony in sexual relationships.* Berkeley, CA: North Atlantic Books.

Robinson, S. L. (1996). Trust and breach of the psychological contract. *Administrative Science Quarterly, 41*, 574–99.

Robinson, V. (1997). My baby just cares for me: Feminism, heterosexuality and non-monogamy. *Journal of Gender Studies, 6*, 143–147.

Rosa, B. (1994). Anti-monogamy: A radical challenge to compulsory heterosexuality. In G. Griffin, M. Hester, S. Rai, & S. Roseneil (Eds), *Stirring it: Challenges for feminism* (pp. 107–120). London: Taylor and Francis.

Roscoe, B., Cavanaugh, L. E., & Kennedy, D. R. (1988). Dating infidelity: Behaviors, reasons and consequences. *Adolescence, 23*, 35–43.

Rose, S. (1996). Lesbian and gay love social scripts. In E. D. Rothblum & L. A. Bond (Eds.), *Preventing heterosexism and homophobia* (pp. 151–173). Thousand Oaks, CA: Sage Publications.

Rotello, G. (1997) *Sexual ecology: AIDS and the destiny of gay men.* Boston, MA: Dutton.

Rotermann, S., & McKay, A. (2009). Condom use at last sexual intercourse among unmarried, not living common-law 20- to 34-year-old Canadian young adults. *The Canadian Journal of Human Sexuality, 18*(3), 75–88.

Rubin, G. (1975). The traffic in women: Notes on the 'political economy' of sex. In R. R. Reiter (Ed.), *Toward an anthropology of women* (pp. 157–210). New York and London: Monthly Review Press.

Rubin, G. (1984). Thinking sex: Notes for a radical theory of the politics of sexuality. In C. S. Vance (Ed.), *Pleasure and danger: Exploring female sexuality* (pp. 275–296). Boston, MA: Routledge.

Rubin, G. (1993). Misguided, dangerous and wrong: An analysis of anti-pornography politics. In A. Assiter & A. Carol (Eds.), *Bad girls and dirty pictures: The challenge to reclaim feminism.* London: Pluto Press.

Rusbult, C. E. (1980). Commitment and satisfaction in romantic associations: A test of the investment model. *Journal of Experimental Social Psychology, 16*, 172–186.

Ryan, C., & Jethá, C. (2010). *Sex at dawn: The prehistoric origins of modern sexuality.* New York: Harper Collins.

Safilios-Rothschild, C. (1977). *Love, sex, and sex roles.* Englewood Cliffs, NJ: Prentice Hall.

Salovey, P., & Rothman, A. (1991). Envy and jealousy: Self and society. In P. Salovey (Ed.), *The psychology of jealousy and envy* (pp. 271–286). New York: Guilford.

Sanday Reeves, P. (1990). *Fraternity gang rape: Sex, brotherhood and privilege on campus* (2nd ed.). New York: New York University Press.

Schoen, R., & Weinick, R. (1993). Partner choice in marriage and cohabitation. *Journal of Marriage and the Family, 55*, 408–414.

Schwartz, P., & Rutter, V. (2000). *The gender of sexuality*. Walnut Creek, CA: AltaMira Press.

Schwartz, P., & Young, L. (2009). Sexual satisfaction in committed relationships. *Sexuality Research and Social Policy, 6*(1), 1–17.

Segal, L. (1994). *Straight sex: Rethinking the politics of pleasure*. Berkeley, CA: University of California Press.

Seutter, R., & Rovers, M. (2004). Emotionally absent fathers: Furthering the understanding of homosexuality. *Journal of Psychology and Theology, 32*(1), 43–49.

Sharma, V. P. (1991). *The causes, outcomes, and solutions when jealousy gets out of hand*. Cleveland, OH: Mind Publications.

Shelton, M. (2008). *Boy crazy: Why monogamy is so hard for gay men and what you can do about it*. Hollywood, CA: Alyson Books.

Shiely, F., Horgan, M., & Hayes, K. (2009). Increased sexually transmitted infection incidence in a low risk population: Identifying the risk factors. *European Journal of Public Health*, (Advanced release), 1–6.

Shotland, R. L., & Hunter, B. A. (1995). Women's "token resistance" and compliant sexual behaviors are related to uncertain sexual intentions and rape. *Personality and Social Psychology Bulletin, 21*, 226–236.

Simon, R. W., & Barrett, A. E. (2010). Nonmarital romantic relationships and mental health in early adulthood: Does the association differ for women and men? *Journal of Health and Social Behavior, 51*(2), 168–182.

Simpson, J. A. (1987). The dissolution of romantic relationships: Factors involved in relationship stability and emotional distress. *Journal of Personality and Social Psychology, 53*, 683–692.

Slater, A., Von der Schulenberg, C., Brown, E., Badenoch, M., Butterworth, G., Parsons, S., & Samuels, C., (1998). Newborn infants prefer attractive faces. *Infant Behavior and Development, 21*, 345–354.

Smith, D. (1993). The standard North American family. *Journal of Family Issues, 14*, 50–65.

Smith, T. (1991). Adult sexual behavior in 1989: Numbers of partners, frequency of intercourse and risk of AIDS. *Family Planning Perspectives, 23*, 102–107.

Smith, T. (1998). *American sexual behavior: Trends, socio-demographic differences, and risk behavior*. GSS Topical Report No. 25. Chicago, IL: NORC.

Sobo, E. (1995). *Choosing unsafe sex*. Philadelphia: University of Pennsylvania Press.

South, S. L., & Lloyd, K. M. (1995). Spousal alternatives and marital dissolution. *American Sociological Review, 60*, 21–35.

South, S. J., Trent, K., & Shen, Y. (2001). Changing partners: Toward a macrostructural opportunity theory of marital dissolution. *Journal of Marriage and Family, 63*, 743–754.

Spencer, C. (1995). *Homosexuality in history*. New York: Harcourt Brace.

Spradley, J. P. (1970). *You owe yourself a drunk: An ethnography of urban nomads*. Boston, MA: Little & Brown.

Sprecher, S., Hatfield, E., Cortese, A., Potapova, E., & Levitskaya, A. (1994). Token resistance to sexual intercourse and consent to unwanted sexual intercourse: College students' dating experiences in three countries. *Journal of Sex Research, 31*, 125–132.

Strauss, N. (2005). *The game: Penetrating the secret society of pickup artists*. New York: Regan Books.

Stepp, L. S. (2007). *Unhooked: How young men pursue sex, delay love, and lose at both.* New York: Riverhead Books.

Sternberg, R. J. (1986). A triangular theory of love. *Psychological Review, 93*(2), 119–135.

Subotnik, R. (2007). Cyber-infidelity. In P. R. Peluso (Ed.), *Infidelity: A practitioners guide to working with couples in crisis* (pp. 169–190). New York: Routledge.

Suleman, M. A., Wango, E., Sapolsky, R., Odongo, H., & Hau, J. (2004). Physiologic manifestations of stress from capture and restraint of free-ranging male African green monkeys (cercopithecus aethiops. *Journal of Zoo and Wildlife Medicine, 35*(1), 20–24.

Symons, D. (1979). *The evolution of human sexuality.* New York: Oxford University Press.

Synnott, A. (1989). Truth and goodness, mirrors and masks–Part I: A sociology of beauty and the face. *The British Journal of Sociology, 40*(4), 607–636.

Tafoya, M. A., & Spitzberg, B. H. (2007). The dark side of infidelity: Its nature, prevalence, and communicative functions. In B. H. Spitzberg & W. R. Cupach (Eds.), *The dark side of interpersonal communication* (2nd ed., pp. 201–242). Mahwah, NJ: Erlbaum.

Tanenbaum, L. (1999). *Slut.* New York: Seven Stories Press.

Taormino, T. (2008). *Opening up: A guide to creating and sustaining open relationships.* San Francisco, CA: Cleis Press.

Tennov, D. (1979). *Love and Limerence.* Baltimore, MD: Scarborough House.

Thornhill, R., & Gangestad, S. W. (1998). Facial attractiveness. *Trends in Cognitive Sciences, 3*(12), 452–460.

Thornhill, R., & Gangestad, S. W. (1999). The scent of symmetry: A human sex pheromone that signals fitness? *Evolution and Human Behavior, 20*(3), 175–201.

Treas, J., & Giesen, D., (2000). Sexual infidelity among married and cohabitating Americans. *Journal of Marriage and the Family, 62*, 48–60.

Trussler, T., Perchal, P., & Barker, A. (2000). "Between what is said and what is done": Cultural constructs and young gay men's HIV vulnerability. *Psychology, Health and Medicine, 5*(3), 295–306.

Tuckman, B. (1965). Developmental sequence in small groups. *Psychological Bulletin, 63*, 384–399.

Turner, R. H. (1970). *Family interaction.* New York: Wiley.

Udry, J. R. (1988). Biological predispositions and social control in adolescent sexual behavior. *American Sociological Review, 53*, 709–722.

Umberson, D., Meichu, D., Chen, J. S., House, K. H., & Slaten, E. (1996). The effect of social relationships on psychological well-being: Are men and women really so different? *American Sociological Review, 61*, 837–857.

Unni, J. (2010). Adolescent attitudes and relevance to family life education programs. *Indian Pediatrics, 47*(2), 176–179.

Vail-Smith, K., Whetstone, M. L., & Knox, D. (2010). The illusion of safety in "monogamous" undergraduate relationships. *American Journal of Health Behaviors, 34*(1), 12–20.

Vangelisti, A. L., & Gerstenberger, M. (2004). Communication and marital infidelity. In J. Duncombe, K. Harrison, G. Allan, & D. Marsden (Eds.), *The state of affairs: Explorations in infidelity and commitment* (pp. 59–78). Mahwah, NJ: Erlbaum.

Vaughn, D. (1986). *Uncoupling.* Oxford, England: Oxford University Press.

Vaughan, P. (2003). *The monogamy myth: A personal handbook for recovering from affairs.* New York: New Market Press.

Vaillant, M. (2009). *Les Hommes, L'amour, la Fidélité.* Paris, France: Albin Michel.

Vanneman, R. D., & Pettigrew, T. (1972). Race and relative deprivation in the urban United States, *Race, 13,* 461–486.

Waite, L., & Gallagher, M. (2001). *The case for marriage: Why married people are happier, healthier, and better off financially.* Broadway, NY: Broadway Publishers.

Walster, E., Walster, G. W., & Berscheid, E. (1978). Equity: Theory and research. Boston, MA: Allyn & Bacon.

Wellings, K., Field, J., Johnson, A., & Wadsworth, J. (1994). *Sexual behavior in Britain.* London: Penguin Books.

Weiderman, M., & Hurd, C. (1999). Extradyadic involvement during dating. *Journal of Social and Personal Relationships, 2,* 265–274.

Wenger, G. C. (2002). Interviewing older people. In J. F. Gubrium & J. A. Holstein (Eds.), *Handbook of interview research: Context and method* (pp. 259–276). Thousand Oaks, CA: Sage.

West, C. (1996). *Lesbian polyfidelity.* San Francisco, CA: Booklegger Publishing.

Weston, K. (1991). *Families we choose.* New York: Columbia University Press.

Whisman, M. A., & Snyder, D. K. (2007). Sexual infidelity in a national survey of American women: Differences in prevalence and correlates as a function of method of assessment. *Journal of Family Psychology, 21,* 147–154.

White, G., & Mullen, P. E. (1989). Jealousy: Theory, research, and clinical strategies. New York: Guilford.

White, J. W., & Kowalski, R. M. (1998). Male violence toward women: An integrated perspective. In R. G. Geen & E. Donnerstein (Eds.), *Human aggression: Theories, research and implications for social policy* (pp. 203–228). San Diego, CA: Academic.

Wiederman, M. W., & Hurd, C. (1999). Extradyadic involvement during dating. *Journal of Social and Personal Relationships, 16,* 265–274.

Wight, D. (1992). Impediments to safer heterosexual sex: A review of research with young people. *AIDS Care, 4,* 11–23.

Wilkinson, E. (2010). What's queer about non-monogamy now? In M. Barker & D. Langdridge, (Eds.), *Understanding non-monogamies* (pp. 243–254). New York: Routledge.

Willetts, M., Sprecher, S., & Beck, F. D. (2004). Overview of sexual practices and attitudes within relational contexts. In J. Harvey, A. Wenzel, & S. Sprecher (Eds.), *The handbook of sexuality in close relationships* (pp. 57–86). Mahwah, NJ: Erlbaum.

Willey, A. (2006). "Christian nations," "polygamic races" and women's rights: Toward a genealogy of non/monogamy and whiteness. *Sexualities, 9,* 530–546.

Williams, K. (2003). Has the future of marriage arrived? A contemporary examination of gender, marriage, and psychological well-being." *Journal of Health and Social Behavior, 44,* 470–487.

Wolf, N. (1997). *Promiscuities.* London: Chatto & Windus.

Wood, W., & Eagly, A. H. (2002). A cross-cultural analysis of the behavior of women and men: Implications for the origins of sex differences. *Psychological Bulletin, 129,* 699–727.

Worden, W. (2009). *Grief counseling and grief therapy* (4th ed.). New York: Springer.

Worth, H., Reid, A., & McMillan, H. (2002). Somewhere over the rainbow: Love, trust and monogamy in gay relationships. *Journal of Sociology, 38*(3), 237–253.

Wosick-Correa, K. (2010). Agreements, rules, and agentic fidelity in polyamorous relationships. *Psychology & Sexuality, 1*(1) 44–61.

Zak, P. (2010). *Psychology Today Blog*. Retrieved June 2010, from, http://www.psychology today.com/blog/the-moral-molecule/200810/handshake-or-hug-why-we-touch